Access Denied

Access Denied
Freedom of Information in the Information Age

Edited by
Charles N. Davis and Sigman L. Splichal

IOWA STATE UNIVERSITY PRESS • Ames

Charles N. Davis, PhD, is an assistant professor in the News-Editorial Department at the University of Missouri School of Journalism. Dr. Davis teaches courses in the principles of American journalism, reporting and media law.

Sigman L. Splichal, PhD, is an assistant professor and a member of the graduate faculty in the School of Communication/Journalism at the University of Miami, Coral Gables, Florida.

© 2000 Iowa State University Press
All rights reserved

Iowa State University Press
2121 South State Avenue, Ames, Iowa 50014

Orders: 1-800-862-6657
Office: 1-515-292-0140
Fax: 515-292-3348
Web site: ww.isupress.edu

Authorization to photocopy items for internal or personal use, or the internal or personal use of specific clients, is granted by Iowa State University Press, provided that the base fee of $.10 per copy is paid directly to the Copyright Clearance Center, 222 Rosewood Drive, Danvers, MA 01923. For those organizations that have been granted a photocopy license by CCC, a separate system of payments has been arranged. The fee code for users of the Transactional Reporting Service is 0-8138-2567-9/2000 $.10.

♾Printed on acid-free paper in the United States of America

First edition, 2000

International Standard Book Number: 0-8138-2567-9

Library of Congress Cataloging-in-Publication Data
Access denied: freedom of information in the information age / edited by Charles N. Davis and Sigman L. Splichal.—1st ed.
     p. cm.
   Includes bibliographical references and index.
   ISBN 0-8138-2567-9 (alk. paper)
     1. Freedom of information—United States. 2. Government information—United States. 3. Electronic records—Access control—United States. 4. Data protection—Law and legislation—United States. 5. Disclosure of information—Law and legislation—United States. 6. Privacy, Right of—United States. I. Davis, Charles N. II. Splichal, Sigman L.

KF4774.A927 2000
342.73′0853—dc21
                                                              00-040728

The last digit is the print number: 9 8 7 6 5 4 3 2 1

More than 45 years ago Harold Cross, commissioned by the American Society of Newspaper Editors, helped ignite a revolution when he eloquently argued for improved public access to government meetings and records.

Cross said that "freedom of information" provided the foundation for our representative government and the freedoms guaranteed by the First Amendment. He said the business of government is the "public's business" and the "people have a right to know" what their officials are doing. Cross, contending that the citizens of a self-governing society "must have a *legal* right to examine and investigate the conduct of its affairs,"[1] became the first to comprehensively discuss the law governing access to government records and meetings in the 50 states.

Cross joined Rep. John Moss of California to help provide the spark that eventually led to the adoption of the federal Freedom of Information Act in 1966. Soon thereafter, many states adopted modern acts requiring government officials to open decision making and to disclose records. Since the 1960s, some state laws have been adjusted to meet new technological demands, including the widespread use of computers to create and store records. Enforcement of those laws has increased somewhat over the years in some states but has remained appallingly lax in most—perhaps all—of the states. Unfortunately, executive branch officials and legislators also often find a way to add the exceptions to the law.

The fight for access takes place daily on many fronts. State access laws long have been championed by the Reporters Committee for

Freedom of the Press and such nationally based organizations as the Society of Professional Journalists and the American Association of Newspaper Editors. Moreover, in the last few decades, citizens and journalists in several states have established independent organizations dedicated to fighting for open meetings and open records. In the mid-1980s, under the leadership of Nancy Monson of the Texas Freedom of Information Foundation and others, the state groups united to form the National Freedom of Information Coalition. The NFOIC sponsored an e-mail discussion list and an FOI resource page on the web, solicited grants to support the individual state groups, and supported the development of new groups.

It was at one NFOIC meeting that the idea for this book was first hatched. Not since 1953 has a book been published—other than practical guides for lawyers and journalists—that focused on the access laws of the 50 states. Clearly such a book was way overdue. Herb Strentz, a Drake University journalism professor and access advocate, conceptualized the book and urged editors Davis and Splichal to take on the project.

Credit for this book goes not only to the editors, the authors and the NFOIC, but also to Marion Brechner and the late Joseph L. Brechner, former Florida broadcast station owners and devotees of freedom of information. Joseph Brechner gave more than $1 million to the University of Florida to endow the Joseph L. Brechner Eminent Scholar of Freedom of Information and to fund the activities of the Brechner Center for Freedom of Information. Joseph Brechner and Ralph Lowenstein, then dean of the College of Journalism and Communications at the University of Florida, encouraged and inspired teaching and research in freedom of information.

Later, Joe's widow, Marion Brechner, provided additional funding to the center, including an endowment for the Marion Brechner Citizen Access Project, a comprehensive 50-state study of public records and open meetings. The Brechners also helped fund Sigman Splichal and Charles Davis while they were pursuing their doctoral studies at the University of Florida, both ultimately writing dissertations about freedom of information. In fact, they also partially funded the doctoral studies of contributors Martin Halstuk, Michele Bush and Paul Gates. Contributor Matthew Bunker also worked as a fellow in the Brechner Center, and like the others, edited the center's publication *The Brechner Report,* which reviews monthly developments in media law in the state of Florida. In addition, yet another contributor to the book, Sandra Chance, is director of the Brechner Center.

So I salute the many dedicated people who made this book possible, including the Iowa State University Press. I also challenge the book's readers to make this only the beginning of their personal reading, research and advocacy on behalf of the cause of freedom of information. Many states need FOI organizations. Those organizations that do exist need help. All states need improved FOI laws. And we all need to know much more about those laws and how they work. We cannot afford to wait another 45 years before the third book on this topic is written.

— Bill F. Chamberlin
Joseph L. Brechner Eminent Scholar
of Mass Communication
College of Journalism and Communication
University of Florida, Gainesville

Note:

[1] Harold L. Cross, *The People's Right to Know; Legal Access to Public Records and Proceedings* xiii (Columbia University Press, 1953).

This book is dedicated to all who fight daily for the public's right to know, to the countless volunteers who spend countless hours educating the public and public officials about access law. Without your tireless efforts, the issues discussed in this book would fall on deaf ears.

The editors would also like to thank the book's contributors, whose research on freedom of information issues in the past provided the impetus for this collection. Thanks also to our families—you know who you are!—for patiently minding children, pets and bills while we toiled. Our debt to you all is immeasurable.

Matthew D. Bunker is Reese Phifer Professor of Journalism at the College of Communication at the University of Alabama in Tuscaloosa.

Michele Bush is a doctoral student in the College of Journalism and Communications at the University of Florida.

Bill F. Chamberlin is the Joseph L. Brechner Eminent Scholar of Mass Communication in the College of Journalism and Communication at the University of Florida in Gainesville. He was a founding director of the Brechner Center for Freedom of Information and is currently director of the Marion Brechner Citizen Access Project. He is an affiliate professor in the College of Law at the University of Florida.

Sandra F. Chance, Esq., is Director of the Brechner Center for Freedom of Information and an associate professor in the College of Journalism and Communication at the University of Florida in Gainesville.

Charles N. Davis is an assistant professor of journalism in the Editorial Sequence at the University of Missouri School of Journalism.

Paul D. Driscoll is a professor of broadcasting in the School of Communication at the University of Miami in Coral Gables, Fla.

Wallace Eberhard is a retired professor of journalism in the Henry W. Grady School of Journalism and Mass Communication at the University of Georgia in Athens.

Bruce Garrison is a professor of journalism in the School of Communication at the University of Miami in Coral Gables, Fla.

Paul H. Gates, Jr. is an assistant professor of journalism at Appalachian State University in Boone, N.C.

Martin E. Halstuk is an assistant professor in the Hank Greenspun School of Communication at the University of Nevada in Las Vegas.

Kathleen Richardson is an Iowa FOI Council graduate assistant at Drake University.

Susan Dente Ross is an assistant professor and head of the Journalism Sequence in the Edward R. Murrow School of Journalism and Communication at Washington State University in Pullman.

Michael B. Salwen is a professor of journalism in the School of Communication at the University of Miami in Coral Gables, Fla.

Sigman L. Splichal is an associate professor of journalism in the School of Communication at the University of Miami in Coral Gables, Fla.

Herb Strentz is a professor of journalism and mass communication at Drake University in Des Moines, Iowa, and is the executive secretary of the Iowa Freedom of Information Council.

Access Denied

The Right to Know

Sigman L. Splichal

Access law in the United States is a story of battles won and lost, of lawmakers prescient and near-sighted, of public scrutiny and public apathy. Its roots, however, lie in the bedrock principles of democratic self-governance espoused by the country's leading libertarian thinkers. Freedom of information found no formal statutory support beyond common-law declarations until the 1960s, but its origins can be traced to John Locke, James Madison, Thomas Jefferson and John Stuart Mill, among others. This chapter traces these origins from pre-colonial America to the present, providing a historical backdrop for the access battles of today. Review of the open government movement at the federal and state levels demonstrates convincingly that while the issues may change, the arguments over openness and secrecy never cease.

When the Founding Fathers gathered in Philadelphia more than 200 years ago to sort out differences endangering the tenuous union, they met in private. With an agenda that included potentially divisive issues, the Founders apparently believed secrecy more accommodating to the needs of the infant nation than the rigors of public debate. Self-preservation seemed paramount.[1]

Yet this seemingly inauspicious beginning for a policy of public access to the government's business belies the sentiments expressed in numerous writings by those instrumental in the American Revolution and by those who steadied the nation as it took its first unsure steps. A recurring theme was that the government served the people, that it existed only with the knowledge and consent of those governed. As James Madison, the dominant force behind the Bill of Rights, noted, "If we aver to the nature of Republic Government, we shall find that the censorial power is in the people over government, and not in the Government over people."[2] From writings such as Madison's evolved a theory of democratic self-governance by an informed electorate, with a free and vigorous press as a fundamental instrument in that process.

This collection of topical essays explores the modern condition of the principle that government business—be it local, state or national—is the people's business and that therefore the people have a fundamental right of access to that process and to information and records related to it. This chapter serves as a launching point for the book, tracing the philosophical principles that gave rise to the values of free expression and a free press that influenced the Founding Fathers, and discussing how those values helped mold the new nation. The chapter also traces the growth of values supporting access to government information that is integral to the contemporary concept of a self-governing society. In addition, it looks at how the courts have viewed a right of access from a constitutional perspective and at how access has been incorporated into positive law through the legislative process.

Toward a Theory of Self-Governance

The free speech and free press clauses of the First Amendment to the U.S. Constitution and the concept of a well-informed, self-governing society grew from seeds planted more than a century before by English social and political philosophers. They wrote of the importance within a society of the freedom to write and speak without government interference. These seeds put down roots before and during the American Revolution and flourished in the words of the Founding Fathers, even if their actions sometimes seemed inconsistent with these words.[3]

Libertarian Underpinnings

By most accounts, the genesis of libertarian thought was the English poet John Milton's essay *Aeropagitica* in 1644, with its frequently quoted passage: "Give me liberty to know, to utter, and to argue freely according to conscience, above all liberties."[4] In *Aeropagitica*, Milton railed against the government, which had suppressed his earlier writings calling for changes in the divorce laws. Milton argued that government licensing of printers impeded the free flow of information and ideas, a process essential to the betterment of life and society. Milton said that people were capable of judging ideas and information for what they were worth, that in the process of sorting the good from the bad, truth would prevail. Said Milton, "And though all the winds of doctrine were let loose to play upon the earth, so Truth be in the field. . . . Let her and Falsehood grapple; who ever knew Truth put to the worse, in a free and open encounter?"⁵

Rivaling Milton as a philosopher influential on the libertarian sentiments of the Founding Fathers' generation was John Locke, who maintained that governments have a duty to protect certain fundamental rights of citizens, such as life, liberty and property. Compared to Milton, Locke held a radically different concept of the role of truth in public discourse. While Milton focused on the tyranny and futility of suppression and in the belief that truth ultimately would triumph, Locke viewed truth as essentially unknowable.⁶ He said people should be skeptical of their own opinions because they never could know for certain whether they were correct. Because knowledge was so frail and truth unknowable, Locke argued, it would be best to put all ideas before the public. Said Locke: "We should do well to commiserate our mutual ignorance, and endeavor to remove it in all the gentle and fair ways of information, and not instantly treat others ill or obstinate and perverse because they will not renounce their own and receive our opinions, or at least those we would force upon them, when it is more probable that we are no less obstinate in not embracing some of theirs. For where is the man that has uncontested evidence of the truth of all that he holds, or of the falsehoods of all he condemns; or can say, that he examined to the bottom all of his own and other men's opinions?"⁷

Locke also argued that individuals enter society freely and as a matter of choice. Consequently, the government may exercise control over individuals only with their consent. All power to make laws resides with the citizenry, and only through the delegation of that power to the state may the state act.⁸

Later essays by Englishmen John Trenchard and Thomas Gordon, writing under the pseudonym "Cato," also were a significant force behind the propagation of libertarian thought in colonial America. The essays were reprinted widely in the colonial press and were popular reading. Said Cato: "That men ought to speak well of their Governors, is true, while their Governors deserve to be well spoken of; but to do public Mischief, without hearing of it, is only the Prerogative of Felicity and Tyranny; A free People will be shewing that they are so, by the freedom of speech."⁹

Building on the Revolutionary Experience

The words of Milton, Locke and Cato resonated through the colonists' revolutionary rhetoric as they became increasingly alienated under British rule. Locke's notion of the fundamental rights of individuals rings out in the Declaration of Independence, and the values of life, liberty and property pervade the Bill of Rights. The belief that free speech and a free press served as an essential check on the powers of government also found eloquent expression in the writings of those who helped shape the new democracy.

Thomas Paine's *Common Sense,* published on the eve of the American Revolution, helped draw waffling patriots into the revolutionary fold, expounding on the benefits of a representative democracy and the need for a full public accounting of government actions. Paine later wrote: "In the representative system, the reason for everything must publicly appear. Every man is a proprietor in government, and considers it a necessary part of his business to understand. It concerns his interest because it affects his property. He examines the costs, and compares it with the advantages; and above all, he does not adopt the slavish custom of following what in other governments are called leaders."[10]

James Madison, the major proponent of the Bill of Rights, amplified the virtue of an informed society. Although writing about the role of information in the context of education, his premise suggests a parallel lesson for democratic society in general. He cautioned, "A popular government without popular information or the means of acquiring it, is but a prologue to a farce or a tragedy, or perhaps both."[11]

Thomas Jefferson, writing in 1823, years after the tumult of the Revolution and the stressful period immediately following, cast himself "into the ranks of the most advanced libertarians . . . [with] his final testament on freedom of the press—a reflex of the best Enlightenment theory."[12] Drawing on his own experience and observations, and on the collective wisdom of the libertarian philosophers, Jefferson described the press as a conveyor of information about the workings of government and as a stabilizing force in the rough-and-tumble of democratic society: "This formidable censor of the public functionaries, by arraigning them at the tribunal of public opinion, produces reform peaceably, which must otherwise be done by revolution. It is also the best instrument for enlightening the mind of man, and improving him as a rational, moral being."[13]

Interestingly, although Jefferson saw a free and vigorous press as a cornerstone of democracy, he did not view the press as free from "liability for personal injuries." And at one point, not long after the expiration of the controversial Sedition Act in 1801, he suggested that the states should keep an unruly "Tory" press in check. Writing to Gov. Thomas McKean of Pennsylvania, Jefferson opined that state restraints on the press might have a "wholesome effect in restoring the integrity of the presses . . . [and would] place the whole band more on their guard."[14]

During the century that followed the American Revolution, when free speech and free press rhetoric flourished and strengthened the values underlying the First Amendment, another influential political philosopher added to the theory that truth must have its day. John Stuart Mill acknowledged the value of free expression advanced by earlier libertarian philosophers but discounted the argument that truth, given an opportunity, would always prevail. Mill, an ardent critic of American slavery, noted that truth frequently was suppressed, and that its only chance to succeed lay in the right of free expression.[15] Mill also wrote about the concepts underlying a democratic society. Of the role of the individual in representative government, he suggested that government derives its authority from the governed; no democratic government would succeed without citizens willing to abide by certain rules and to do what was necessary to preserve it.[16] The foundation for such a society, Mill argued, was the existence of powerful ideas and the ability of the majority to persuade others of their correctness.[17]

Legal Theory in the 20th Century

The principles of the early libertarians and the words of the Founding Fathers and others laid the foundation for 20th-century legal theory and social philosophy supporting the role of a free and vigorous press in American society and its need for public information. Woodrow Wilson, in the first year of his presidency in 1913, eloquently expressed the sentiments of the nation's founders that government prospered only with the knowledge and consent of the people: "Whenever any public business is transacted, wherever plans affecting the public are laid or enterprises touching the public welfare, comfort or convenience go forward, wherever political programs are formulated, or candidates agreed on, over that place a voice must speak, with the divine prerogative of a people's will, the words: 'Let there be light.'"[18]

The 20th-century concept of free expression was brought into focus in the second decade of the new century, as it faced a severe test at a time when fears of social revolution dominated the legal and political establishments. In 1919, amid the post-World War I social and political tumult in the United States over the Bolshevik revolution in Russia, U.S. Supreme Court Justice Oliver Wendell Holmes carried Milton's notion of free speech into 20th-century discourse through the American free enterprise metaphor of the marketplace. The occasion was the Supreme Court's opinion in *Abrams v. United States,* which upheld criminal convictions under the newly enacted Espionage Act.[19] The defendants were convicted of distributing materials critical of the United States' war effort that encouraged "disaffection, sedition, riots, and even revolution."[20] The offending pamphlets, tossed from windows to passers-by, criticized the United States' decision to send troops to aid the czar during the revolution. In a dissenting opinion, Holmes took up the libertarian standard of free expression to reject the majority reasoning upholding the convictions based on words, not deeds. He argued for "free trade in ideas," even those we "loathe and believe to be fraught with death." Holmes said that the "best test of truth is the power of the thought to get itself accepted in the competition of the market."[21] Holmes' notion of "the free trade in ideas" was often quoted by legal and political scholars when free speech was in question, and the importance of a free press in the marketplace of ideas became a rallying cry in the First Amendment lexicon.

In 1927, Justice Louis Brandeis, a dominant judicial force behind the idea of a fundamental right of privacy, argued with equal force for unfettered free expression limited only by the need "to protect the state" from "clear and imminent danger."[22] In a concurring opinion in *Whitney v. California,* Justice Brandeis denounced a California syndicalism law as a threat to the fundamental principles of an informed, self-governing democracy on which the nation was founded. He noted:

> Those who won our independence believed that the final end of the state was to make men free to develop their faculties, and that in its government the deliberative forces should prevail over the arbitrary. They valued liberty as both an end and as a means. . . . They believed that freedom to think as you will and to speak as you think are indispensable to the discovery and spread of political truth . . . that public discussion is a political duty; and that this should be a fundamental principle of the American government. . . . Believing in the power of reason as applied through public discussion, they eschewed silence coerced by law—the argument of force in its worst form. Recognizing the occasional tyrannies of governing majorities, they amended the Constitution so that free speech and assembly would be guaranteed. [23]

The majority of the Court soon amplified this theme. In the 1931 case *Stromberg v. California,* the Court said that the First Amendment ensured "the opportunity for free political discussions to the end that government may be responsive to the will of the people and that changes may be obtained by lawful means."[24] Alexander Meiklejohn best articulated the role of a free press in the process of democratic self-governance. Writing some 300 years after John Locke, Meiklejohn rejected the idea that freedom of speech derived solely from the natural law or rules of reason espoused by the Enlightenment philosophers. Rather, the venerable scholar anchored his theory of free expression in the very nature of a self-governing democracy. Meiklejohn reasoned that the "principle of free speech springs from the necessity of the program of self-government. . . . It is a deduction from the basic American agreement that public issues shall be decided by universal suffrage."[25] He said the First Amendment's protections for the practice of self-government are to ensure that the public retains control over government in the process of self-governance. He would have afforded absolute protection for expression about issues of self-governance because, he said, citizens need to gather and share information and opinions about their government to participate intelligently in the democratic process.[26]

Abraham Maslow's theory established an ascending hierarchy of individuals' essential needs in society. At the bottom were basic physical needs, such as food and shelter; at the top were the psychological needs of individuals to realize their full potential—or to be self-actualized.[27] Legal scholar Thomas Emerson couched Locke's principles of natural rights in the modern theory of self-actualization. Emerson saw free speech and expression as essential to the attainment of these higher needs. To Emerson, free expression was the embodiment of "the widely accepted premise of Western thought that the proper end of man is the realization of his own character and potentialities as a human being."[28]

Legal scholar Vincent Blasi offered another rationale for a strong, free press in American society. Echoing the sentiments of Paine and Jefferson that a free press as a "formidable censor of public functionaries" was essential to a democracy, he contended that a strong, free press is the most effective—if not the only effective—check on the potential abuse of power by government. Blasi accepted both Locke's argument for free expression based on fundamental rights and Meiklejohn's theory of self-governance. But he also cast the press—particularly the large, influential press—in another essential role as the only viable check on the equally powerful government. [29]

Blasi's arguments reflect those espoused by former Supreme Court Justice Potter Stewart, who saw in the First Amendment a "structural provision" giving the press rights separate and distinct from those of free speech. In a 1970 address at Yale Law School titled "Or of the Press," Stewart rejected the view that the press should be only a neutral forum in the "marketplace of ideas." The press was not merely a vehicle for the balanced discussion of diverse ideas, he said. "Instead, the free press meant organized, expert scrutiny of government."[30] Implicit in both Meiklejohn's First Amendment theory of self-governance and Blasi's theory of the press as a fundamental check on government excess is the need for public and media access to the information government uses in decision-making.

While freedom of the press and the implied importance of access to information have found solid support in the American experience, the legal parameters of press freedoms and a right of access have been shaped by legislatures and the courts. This development occurred at three levels. The first is the common law, where the notion of access to public information evolved through the daily application of laws and customs to resolve disputes and issues. The second is constitutional law. Constitutional analysis was triggered when the press asserted First Amendment rights to keep the public informed about the business of government. The third is statutory law, or positive laws enacted by legislatures recognizing varying degrees of a right of access.

A Common Law Right of Access

A legal concept of public access to government information developed within the common law. This concept initially was based on the personal interests of individuals in specific information, not on the premise that the public had a general right to inspect public records. Usually, access under the common law involved records sought during litigation. A Kentucky court summed up the general status of common law access: "There is no common law right in all persons to inspect public documents or records; and that right, if it exists, depends entirely on the statutory grant. But . . . every person is entitled [to inspect public records] . . . provided he has an interest therein which is such as would enable him to maintain or defend any action for which the document or record sought can furnish evidence of necessary information."[31]

Other courts, however, have expanded the kinds of interest that would warrant access to public information. In 1903, for example, the state of Tennessee recognized a general taxpayers' interest in records concerning the financial condition of city government.[32] In some jurisdictions, courts have abandoned entirely interest tests for access to public records.[33] Despite the willingness of some jurisdictions to recognize a broad-based public right under the common law, the most effective tools for access continue to be statutory. The statutory dimensions of public access will be discussed in a later section of this chapter.

Access and the Constitution

Acknowledging the important role of the press as a primary source of information in a self-governing society, the Supreme Court has recognized the constitutional right of the press to publish information it gathers about public issues. [34] But the Court has not articulated a First Amendment right of the press to obtain information that the government gathers, creates or possesses outside the limited area of court proceedings. One jurist has likened the press without a right to gather and publish news to a "river without water." [35]

Before 1925, the First Amendment had functioned only as a limitation on actions of the federal government. But in that year, the Supreme Court first applied the First Amendment to actions of a state in a case that upheld a conviction based on the distribution of revolutionary literature. In *Gitlow v. New York*, the Court said that First Amendment rights protected from abridgment by Congress were "among the fundamental personal rights and liberties protected by the due process clause of the Fourteenth Amendment from impairment by the states." [36] This selective application of certain parts of the Bill of Rights to the states through the Fourteenth Amendment is known as incorporation. [37]

Since *Gitlow*, numerous cases have applied the First Amendment to affirm the roles of free speech and a free press in American society. For example, in 1931, the Supreme Court issued a landmark opinion in *Near v. Minnesota* that held prior restraints against the press were impermissible in all but the most extreme of circumstances. [38] More important to the development of a theory of access, however, are cases in which the Supreme Court has addressed the rights of individuals to receive information and the rights of the public and the press to have access to government proceedings and information held by the government.

A right of the public to know about the workings of government, as such, is not stated in the U.S. Constitution. But the framers of the Constitution did include provisions for making government accountable to the people. The Constitution, in general terms, requires the legislative and executive branches of government to report regularly about their activities. Both chambers of Congress must keep and publish a "journal of its proceedings,"[39] but may decide for themselves what might "require secrecy" and be withheld.[40] Congress also is required to "publish from time to time . . . a regular Statement and Account of the Receipts and Expenditures of all public Money."[41] Similarly, the president is required to report to Congress "Information of the State of the Union."[42] While these requirements for government accountability seem limited by modern access standards, they nonetheless reflected the fundamental principle that government should not function in secret or withhold information without good cause. Indeed, the fact the Constitution gives Congress the authority to determine what might "require secrecy" presupposes secrecy is the exception rather than the rule. The limited expression of openness in the Constitution perhaps reflected the realities of communications during the nation's formative years. The movement of information, even urgent information, was measured in terms of weeks and sometimes months. In times of war, battles were sometimes fought before word of an armistice could reach the battlefield.

The Right to Receive Information

The Supreme Court has never recognized a constitutional right of access to government information, or a right to gather information, on a par with the right to publish without prior government interference. The press may publish what it gathers, but government has no affirmative duty to facilitate the news gathering process. The Court, however, has been more receptive to the rights of the public to receive information.

The Supreme Court has specifically recognized the rights of individuals to receive information in several cases. Perhaps the first is *Grosjean v. American Press Co.*, a 1936 case involving a challenge to a state tax that affected only large-circulation publication. A unanimous Court struck down the tax as a violation of the First Amendment. The Court said a free press is a vital source of information and that "informed public opinion is the most potent of all restraints upon misgovernment."[43] The Court said First Amendment freedoms went "to the heart of the natural right of the members of an organized society, united in their common good, to impart and acquire information about their common interests."[44] The Court concluded that the Louisiana tax would "limit the circulation of information to which the public is entitled by virtue of constitutional guarantees."[45]

In 1969, the Supreme Court again recognized the public's right to receive information. In a broadcast regulation case involving the

Federal Communications Commission's Fairness Doctrine, *Red Lion Broadcasting Co. v. FCC,* the Court held that broadcasters, who operated under a government license, may be compelled to grant individuals the right to reply on the air to political editorials and personal attacks. The Court recognized that government-regulated broadcasters had First Amendment rights, but concluded that, on balance, the First Amendment rights of broadcast audiences to receive information were paramount. Interestingly, the court reasoned that broadcasters, by virtue of their license relationship with the government, had an affirmative duty to facilitate public access to information and ideas—a concept the Court has never imposed on government itself.[46] Neither has the Court imposed on the print media an affirmative duty to provide access to different points of view.[47]

The Court also recognized the public's First Amendment right to receive information—even commercial information—in *Virginia State Board of Pharmacy v. Virginia Citizens Consumer Council Inc.*[48] The Court struck down a state statue barring pharmacists from advertising prescription drug prices. The Court's opinion focused on the public's strong interest in access to commercial information.[49] Such information, the Court reasoned, was essential if citizens were to make thoughtful consumer choices that, in the aggregate, could affect political issues such as the allocation of resources. "To this end, the free flow of commercial information is indispensable," the opinion stated.[50]

The Court applied the First Amendment to the receipt of political information in *First National Bank v. Bellotti,* when it struck down a state law forbidding political advocacy by corporations. The Court reasoned that the public right to receive political information is not diminished by the corporate identity of the speaker. The Court said the First Amendment's role was not only to foster individual expression but also to afford "the public access to discussion, debate, and the dissemination of information and ideas.[51] The Court rejected the argument that "the relative voice of corporations" might drown out other, less powerful speakers on controversial public issues. Instead, the Court said that in a democracy the public must choose among messages, whether the speaker is weak or strong.[52]

A Right of Access to Government Information

While the Court has recognized the right of individuals to receive information from willing speakers, the question of the public's and the media's constitutional right of access to government-held information is more problematic. Some cases, however, have implied at least a limited right of access to government functions and records. In *Branzburg v. Hayes,* the Court acknowledged that "without some protection for seeking out the news, freedom of the press could be eviscerated."[53] But on a 5-4 vote, the Court rejected a special privilege for news reporters not to have to testify before grand juries. In *Branzburg,* three journalists argued that if they were forced to reveal names of confidential sources, to whom they had pledged confidentiality, news organizations would lose their credibility. Too, sources would cease to come forward, and society might be deprived of important information, they said. Justice Powell, who joined the majority opinion as the key fifth vote, stated in a concurring opinion that any claim of press privilege should be weighed on a case-by-case basis, thus recognizing at least the possibility that in some circumstances the press might warrant special consideration.[54] Powell's reasoning, when combined with the rationale of the dissenting justices, led many appellate courts during the 1980s to recognize a limited First Amendment news gathering right for journalists with respect to protecting confidential sources, at least in cases not involving grand juries.[55]

In a pair of cases dealing with access to prisoners and prisons, the Court has said the press had no greater right of access to government than any other members of the public. In *Pell v. Procunier*[56] and *Saxbe v. Washington Post Co.,*[57] cases heard jointly, the Court upheld federal regulations restricting press interviews with prisoners. Important to the Court's analysis, however, was that access to prisons was traditionally restricted and therefore the media were not being singled out. Writing for the majority, Justice Stewart said the press is free to gather what it can and to publish what it knows. But, Stewart said, "This autonomy cuts both ways. The press is free to do battle against secrecy and deception in government. But the press cannot expect from the Constitution any guarantee that it will succeed. There is no constitutional right to have access to particular government information, or to require openness from the bureaucracy."[58]

In *Pell and Saxbe,* Justice Douglas, writing for the three dissenters, argued that the press should have a right of access greater than the public generally. He said the press, as a vehicle for the transmission of ideas and information, held a "preferred position in our constitutional scheme," and that the public's "right to know is crucial to the governing powers of the people."[59]

While the Supreme Court has said the public and media have no right of access to prisons, it has held that the First Amendment requires criminal trials to be open. In *Richmond Newspapers v. Virginia,* the Court said criminal trials "must be open to the public" unless there is an overriding competing interest, even when a defendant wants the trial closed.60 In a plurality opinion, Chief Justice Burger engaged in a historical as well as a First Amendment analysis. He noted that trials in England and in this country had historically been public affairs. The chief justice cited English customs dating to before the Norman Conquest that gave rise to the jury system. When cases were brought before courts, freemen of the community were required to attend and render a judgment. In reasoning that could apply equally to access to all forms of government proceedings, he noted, "This is no quirk of history, rather, it has long been recognized as an indispensable attribute of the Anglo-American trial. . . . It gave assurances that the proceedings were conducted fairly to all concerned, and it discouraged perjury, the misconduct of participants, and decisions based on secret bias or partiality."61

He also noted the therapeutic value of open proceedings and the importance of such openness in ensuring confidence in the process of government. "People sensed from experience and observation that, especially in the administration of criminal justice, the means used to achieve justice must have the support derived from public acceptance of both the process and the results," Burger wrote.62 The chief justice echoed Thomas Jefferson's notion that exposing government actions in the "tribunal of public opinion" diffused emotions and led to peaceable reforms. He observed that openness provided an "outlet for community concern, hostility, and emotion," and that without knowledge that the system was working "natural human reactions of outrage and protest are frustrated and may manifest themselves in some form of vengeful 'self-help,' as indeed they did regularly in the activities of vigilante 'committees' on the frontiers.63 He pointed out that people do not demand infallibility from their institutions, but that "it is difficult for them to accept what they are prohibited from observing."64

After outlining the need for openness in government—at least in court proceedings—the chief justice turned his attention directly to the special role of the press as a representative of the people. He noted that while the First Amendment right to assemble in public places and to attend trials covers the public generally, the press acts as a stand-in for the public; therefore, without press access, public access is diminished. "It is not crucial whether we describe this right to attend criminal trials to hear, see, and communicate observations concerning them as a 'right of access,' or a 'right to gather information,' for we have recognized that 'without some protection for seeking out the news, freedom of the press would be eviscerated.' The explicit, guaranteed rights to speak and publish concerning what takes place at a trial would lose much meaning if access to observe the trial could, as it were here, be foreclosed arbitrarily."[65]

Chief Justice Burger also made quick work of the argument that there was no right of public access to court proceedings because no such right was spelled out in the Constitution. He pointed out that during the debate over whether the Constitution should have a Bill of Rights, it was made clear that just because the Constitution did not grant a particular right, this did not mean no such right existed. In words that could bolster an argument for an implicit First Amendment right of access to government information modeled along the lines of the reasoning supporting a constitutional right of privacy, he noted:

> Notwithstanding the appropriate caution against reading into the Constitution rights not explicitly defined, the Court has acknowledged that certain unarticulated rights are implicit in enumerated guarantees. For example, rights of association and of privacy, the right to be presumed innocent and the right to be judged by a standard of proof beyond a reasonable doubt in a criminal trial, as well as the right to travel, appear nowhere in the Constitution or Bill of Rights. Yet these important but unarticulated rights have nonetheless been found to share constitutional protection in common with explicit guarantees. Your Fundamental rights, even though not expressly guaranteed, have been recognized by the Court as indispensable to the enjoyment of rights specifically defined.[66]

Justice William Brennan, author of the Court's landmark 1964 libel opinion in *New York Times v. Sullivan,* concurred with the result in *Richmond,* but focused on the "structural role" the media play in the American system of self-government. Alluding to Alexander Meiklejohn's theory of democratic self-governance, Justice Brennan reasoned that the First Amendment was meant to do more than protect free communication for its own sake. Rather, he said, "Implicit in this structural role is not only 'the principle that debate on public issues should be uninhibited, robust and wide-open,' but the antecedent assumption that valuable public debate—as well as other civic behavior—must be informed. The structural model links the First Amendment to that process of communication necessary for a democracy to survive, and thus entails solicitude not only for communication itself, but for the indispensable conditions of meaningful communication."[67]

For communication to be meaningful in a self-governing society, Justice Brennan concluded, public and press access to government information are essential. In words that anticipated his approach to the access/privacy conflict that would arise over the government's growing use of computers, he said, "Our decisions must therefore be understood as holding only that any privilege of access to governmental information is subject to a degree of restraint dictated by the *nature of the information and countervailing interests in security and confidentiality*"[68] (emphasis added).

In a separate concurring opinion, Justice Stevens termed *Richmond* "a watershed case," and suggested that "for the first time the court unequivocally holds that an arbitrary interference with access to important information is an abridgment of the freedom of speech and of the press."[69] In the wake of *Richmond,* some legal scholars shared Justice Stevens' position, suggesting that the opinion cast the First Amendment as a sword with which to "secure information from a reluctant government."[70] While increased access has occurred in other trial-related areas,[71] such pronouncements proved that *Richmond* was indeed "a watershed case," signaling a significant shift in access doctrine.[72]

Statutory Access to Government Information

If the Supreme Court has been reluctant to recognize a First Amendment right of access to government information beyond the courts, Congress has been willing to enact legislation opening federal regulatory agencies to public scrutiny. But statutory recognition of a public right of access to government information is a relatively new phenomenon that developed in the two decades following World War II.

In 1946, Congress enacted the Administrative Procedures Act,[73] which recognized the public character of government records gathered and kept by federal executive agencies. But the act's inexact language, which allowed agencies to determine what information "requiring secrecy in the public interest" should be exempt from disclosure, provided a loophole that led to widespread arbitrary withholding. The act, in effect, became more of a withholding statute than a disclosing one. During this post-World War II period, proponents of access to government information were given a boost when the government issued the Hoover Study Report, which led to passage of the Federal Records Act of 1950.[74]

As the 1950s unfolded, press organizations and other advocates of open government began a push to open up federal executive agencies, which had increased the level of secrecy as the Cold War and the threat of communism took hold. In one effort to promote access, the American Society of Newspaper Editors commissioned a report on the customs, laws and legislation dealing with access to government information. The result was *The People's Right to Know* by media lawyer Harold Cross.[75] Cross began his seminal study with this statement: "Public business is the public's business. The people have a *right to know*. Freedom of information is their just heritage. Without that citizens of a democracy have but changed their kings. . . . Citizens of a self-governing society must have the legal right to examine and investigate the conduct of affairs, subject only to those limitations imposed by the most urgent public necessity."[76]

Cross concluded that the solution to the problem of access to government information lay with the legislative process: "Congress is the primary source of relief. . . . The time is ripe for an end to ineffectual sputtering about executive refusals of access to official records and for Congress to begin exercising its function to regulate freedom of information for itself, the public and the press."[77]

Despite Cross' call on Congress for relief, the "ineffectual sputtering" continued. Shifting political fortunes, however, soon provided an important nudge. In 1955, President Dwight Eisenhower was elected to a second term. But while the Republican won the White House, the majority in the House of Representatives swung to the Democrats, and along with majority-party status came committee chairmanships. Congress had become increasingly concerned about its inability to pry information from Republican-controlled executive agencies. Various committees, now under Democratic leadership, provided forums for a public access debate.[78]

In 1955, California Congressman John Moss began hearings on the access issue that continued for some 10 years. The work of the Moss Committee, along with that of other access advocates such as Cross and Ralph Nader,[79] culminated in 1966 with passage of the federal Freedom of Information Act. When President Lyndon Johnson signed the legislation, he observed that "a democracy works best when the people have all the information that the security of the nation permits."[80] The purpose of the act, according to the Senate report on the legislation, was to close loopholes in the Administrative Procedures Act and to foster "a general philosophy of full agency disclosure."[81] The Supreme Court later put its imprimatur on this goal in an FOIA-related opinion. "The basic purpose of the FOIA is to ensure an informed citizenry, vital to the functioning of a democratic society, needed to check against corruption and to hold the governors accountable to the governed," the Court stated.[82]

Under the FOIA, all agency records must be disclosed unless specifically exempted. The act places the burden on the agency to justify withholding. While the FOIA's purpose is "full agency disclosure," it also contained nine exemptions that recognized competing social values.[83] Several of these exemptions discussed specifically attempt to balance the public's right to know with the privacy interests of individuals on whom the government keeps information.

In addition to access to records, Congress also passed "Government in Sunshine" legislation requiring some 50 federal agencies, boards and commissions to open most of their meetings to the public.[84]

State Access to Government Records

Legislative recognition of a public right of access to information is not limited to the federal government. Before 1940, only 12 states had substantial public access statutes. By 1992, all 50 states and the District of Columbia recognized the public right of access to government records.[85] Perhaps the preamble to the Indiana Open Records Law best sums up the thrust of most state access legislation: "A fundamental philosophy of the American constitutional form of representative government is that government is the servant of the people and not their master. Accordingly, it is the public policy of that state that all persons are entitled to full and complete information regarding the affairs of government and the official acts of those who represent them as public officials and employees."[86]

Beyond the high-minded language of the preambles, however, access laws vary widely from state to state. The state statutes vary in the degree of openness allowed and the definition of public records. Some provide access to a narrow range of records, such as records required to be kept by state law; others take a sweeping view of access, opening all records pertaining to any aspect of state business. Shaped by the political landscape peculiar to its legislature, state access law is a crazy quilt of definitions, exemptions and judicial interpretations. The case-based, state-by-state nature of access law means that each issue is treated differently from state to state, sometimes from court to court. To discuss more than a handful of access issues at the state level would fill a multivolume treatise. The technological revolution offers a rare opportunity to observe the state of access law at perhaps the most critical moment since its inception. The computer has the potential to be the greatest gateway to governmental information in history. Yet the computer's meteoric rise has spawned new concerns about privacy, about the ease with which records can be collated and created. At the end of the day, however, it is but a machine, a tool to be mastered and understood. Nothing about the computer weakens the philosophical lineage of access law, but as the following chapters demonstrate, the Information Age poses new challenges to age-old issues of access—and secrecy.

Notes

[1]Alan F. Weston, *Privacy and Freedom* (1967).

[2]4 Annals of Congress 934 (1794).

[3]For example, the constitutional convention excluded the public (see supra note 1), and Thomas Jefferson suggested in a letter to the governor of Pennsylvania soon after the expiration of the Sedition Act that the states should act to control the "Tory" press (see Leonard Levy, *Emergence of a Free Press* 341 (1985). See Nat Hentoff, *The First Freedom* 86 (1980). See generally Leonard Levy, *Jefferson and Civil Liberties: The Darker Side* (1963).

[4]As noted in Levy, *Emergence of a Free Press* 93.

[5]*The Prose Works of John Milton* 198 (Rufus W. Griswold, ed., 1856).

[6]John Locke, 4 *An Essay Concerning Human Understanding* 560–61 (1952), as noted in Levy, *Emergence of a Free Press* 97.

[7]Id.

[8]John Locke, *The Second Treatise on Government* 55–81 (T. Peardon, ed., 1952).

[9]Levy, *Emergence of a Free Press* 110. See also Emery and Emery, *The Press in America: An Interpretative History of the Mass Media* 14.

[10]Thomas Paine, *The Rights of Man* 38 (1984).

[11]Letter from James Madison to W.T. Barry (Aug. 4, 1822), pertinent portion reprinted in *The Complete Madison* 337 (Saul Padover, ed., 1953).

[12]Levy, *Jefferson and Civil Liberties* 69.

[13]*Id.*

[14]Letter from Thomas Jefferson to Gov. Thomas McKean of Pennsylvania (Feb. 19, 1803), reprinted in 9 *The Writings of Thomas Jefferson* 451–52 (Paul Leicester Ford, ed., 1892–1899). Cited in Levy, *Emergence of a Free Press* 341.

[15]See generally John Stuart Mill, *On Liberty* (1863).

[16]John Stuart Mill, *Considerations on Representative Government* 6–9 (C. Shields, ed., 1958).

[17]*Id.* 12–15.

[18]Woodrow Wilson, *The New Freedom* 86 (1913).

[19]*Abrams v. United States,* 250 U.S. 616 (1919).

[20]*Id.* at 630.

[21]*Id.* (Justice Holmes dissenting).

[22]*Whitney v. California,* 274 U.S. 357 (1927).

[23]*Id.* 375–76.

[24]*Stromberg v. California,* 274 U.S. 359, 369 (1931).

25Alexander Meiklejohn, *Free Speech and Its Relation to Self-Government* 89–94 (1948).

26*Id.*

27See generally Abraham Maslow, *Motivation and Personality* (1954), and Maslow, *Religion, Values and Peak Experience* (1970).

28Thomas Emerson, *Toward a General Theory of the First Amendment* 4–5 (1963). See also Emerson, *The Bill of Rights Today* (1973).

29Vincent Blasi, *The Checking Value in First Amendment Theory,* Am. B. Found. Res. J. 521, 538 (1977).

30Potter Stewart, *Or of the Press,* 26 Hastings L. J. 631, 633–36 (1975). See also Floyd Abrams, *The Press Is Different: Reflections on Justice Stewart and the Autonomous Press,* 7 Hofstra L. Rev. 563 (1979).

31*Fayette Co. v. Martin,* 279 Ky. 387, 396 (1939).

32*State ex rel. Wellford v. Williams,* 110 Tenn. 549 (1903). See also *Clement v. Graham,* 78 Vt. 290 (1906).

33*Burton v. Tuite,* 87 Mich. 363 (1889); *MacEwan v. Holm,* 226 Oreg. 27 (1961).

34See generally *Nebraska Press Ass'n v. Stuart,* 427 U.S. 539 (1976); *United States v. Nixon,* 418 U.S. 683 (1974).

35*In re Mack,* 368 Pa. 251, 273 (1956), cert. denied, 352 U.S. 1002 (1957).

36*Gitlow v. New York,* 268 U.S. 652 (1925).

37Through a series of opinions, the U.S. Supreme Court extended provisions of the Bill of Rights to cover actions by the states. The Court incorporated the Bill of Rights into the Fourteenth Amendment by holding that state infringements on free speech and other rights deprive individuals of due process guaranteed by the Fourteenth Amendment.

38*Near v. Minnesota,* 283 U.S. 697 (1931).

39U.S. Const, Art I, § 5, cl. 3.

40*Id.*

41*Id.,* Art. I, § 9, cl. 7.

42*Id.,* Art. III, § 3.

43*Grosjean v. American Press Co.,* 297 U.S. 233 (1936).

44*Id.* at 250.

45*Id.* at 243.

46*Red Lion Broadcasting v. FCC,* 395 U.S. 367 (1969).

47*Miami Herald v. Tornillo,* 418 U.S. 241 (1974).

48*Virginia State Board of Pharmacy v. Virginia Citizens Consumer Council,* 425 U.S. 748 (1976).

49*Id.* at 765.

50*Id.* Justice Rehnquist dissented sharply from the majority, arguing that the opinion devalued the First Amendment. He said the First Amendment should protect the "marketplace of ideas," not the commercial marketplace. Id. at 781–90.

51*First National Bank v. Bellotti,* 435 U.S. 765 (1978).

52*Id.* at 789–90.

53*Branzburg v. Hayes,* 408 U.S. 655, 681 (1972).

54*Id.* at 710 (Justice Powell concurring).

55Kent Middleton and Bill F. Chamberlin, *The Law of Public Communication* 488 (2d ed 1988).

56417 U.S. 817 (1974).

57417 U.S. 843 (1974).

58*Pell v. Procunier* at 834.

59*Id.* at 840 (Justice Douglas dissenting).

60*Richmond Newspapers v. Virginia,* 448 U.S. 555 (1980).

61*Id.* at 569.

62*Id.* at 571.

63*Id.*

64*Id.* at 572.

65*Id.* at 577.

66*Id.* at 579.

67*Id.* at 587–88.

68*Id.* at 586.

69*Id.* at 582.

70William Van Alstyne, *Interpretations of the First Amendment* 54 (1984).

71See, e.g., *Smith v. Daily Mail Publishing Co.,* 443 U.S. 97 (1979); *Globe Newspaper Co. v. Superior Court, 457 U.S. 596 (1982).*

72*Pell* at 834.

73*Administrative Procedure Act,* U.S. Code, vol. 5, § 1002 (1946).

74*Federal Records Act,* 64 U.S. Stat. 583 (1950).

75See generally Cross, *The People's Right to Know* (1953).

76*Id.* at xxx.

77*Id.* at xiv.

78See Paul E. Kostyu, "Political Pressure: The Freedom of Information Act and John E. Moss Jr.," (paper presented at the AEJMC Southeast Colloquium, Orlando, Fla., Feb. 28–March 2, 1991).

79See generally James R. Wiggins, *Freedom or Secrecy?* (1964); Ralph Nader, *Unsafe at Any Speed: The Designed-In Danger of the American Automobile* (1965).

80Quoted in Thomas Susman, *"Introduction to the Issues, Problems and Relevant Law"* in *Your Business, Your Trade Secrets and Your Government,* 34 Admin. L. Rev. 117 (1982).

81S. Rep. No. 813, 89th Cong., 1st sess. 3 (1965).

82*NLRB v. Robbins Tire & Rubber Co.,* 437 U.S. 214, 242 (1978).

83*Freedom of Information Act,* U.S. Code, vol. 5, § 552b (a).

84*Id.*

85*See Reporters Committee for Freedom of the Press, Tapping Officials' Secrets: A State Open Government Compendium (1998).*

86Ind. Code, § 5–14–3–1 (1977).

1

Public Support for Access to Government Records: A National Survey

Paul D. Driscoll, Sigman L. Splichal,
Michael B. Salwen and Bruce Garrison

The democratic principles underlying access law presume that the public will take an active interest in monitoring its government and that the majority supports a broad right of access to governmental records and meetings. In reality, little or nothing is known of the public's attitudes toward access issues. In the first study of its kind, the authors conducted a national telephone survey to measure the depth and breadth of public support for access to government information, and to explore under what circumstances the public may wish access to be curtailed. The findings of the study illustrate the public's strong support for open government as a means of keeping government activities in the sunshine, but also document the public's fear of being harmed by disclosure of personal information. Privacy and access are both important societal values, and both receive public support when thought about independently. But these values sometimes collide, clearly weakening support for access in the interest of greater privacy rights. The findings highlight the growing gulf between support for access and concerns about informational privacy, a major theme of this book.

Access to government information is a cornerstone of American public policy at both the federal and state levels. Since government derives its just power from the consent of the governed, it is crucial that information about the workings of government is accessible to citizens. A free flow of information is central to a self-governing democracy, and provides the rationale for our system of free expression outlined in the writings of First Amendment theorists such as Alexander Meiklejohn, Thomas Emerson and Vincent Blasi.[1]

The U.S. Supreme Court has not recognized an expansive First Amendment right to obtain information that the government gathers, creates or possesses. Nevertheless, access to at least some types of government information is implied by the Court's recognition of the public's right to attend trials and by a more general right to receive information.[2] Rights of public access to government records have also developed in the common law, albeit with an emphasis on the individual's need for the records rather than on the premise that the public has a general right to inspect public records.[3]

With citizens' rights of access to government records largely determined by statute, legislatures are continually revising the laws, often in attempts to restrict the availability of certain categories of records. Exemptions are often implemented at the behest of business interests or quasi-government agencies,[4] but sometimes changes in open records laws are putatively made to protect individuals' privacy interests, such as the 1994 Driver's License Protection Act.[5]

Public Attitudes Toward Access

While classical democratic political theory presupposes access to information about government, recent studies specifically ascertaining public opinion on the issue are limited. A 1998 survey of California voters' attitudes found strong support for access to a wide variety of records, including some that have been traditionally closed to the public, such as disciplinary records of public employees and court records involving juveniles. In fact, 71 percent supported strengthening the state's freedom of information laws and 67 percent said they would definitely or probably support a state constitutional amendment guaranteeing access to government information at the state and local level.[6] A poll conducted by Brown University in 1997 found that 82 percent of Rhode Islanders agreed that "government records should be generally accessible to the public and that meetings of public bodies should be open to the public."[7]

Concerns about the privacy of personal information, however, may temper Americans' favorable attitudes toward access to government records. Stories of the misuses of government records appear regularly in the press. For example, a banker who sat on a state health commission accessed a list of people who had been diagnosed as having cancer and promptly called in their loans.[8] In the 1995 Equifax-Harris Mid-Decade Consumer Privacy Survey, 80 percent of respondents reported feeling they've lost control over how their personal information is circulated and used, compared with 71 percent in 1990; 47 percent said they are "very" concerned about threats to their personal privacy.[9] It is clear that the public's fear of harmful disclosure of personal information is both genuine and well founded.

The dilemma of balancing the opposing values of open access and right to privacy is illustrated in a report from a symposium on citizen privacy in Washington state: "A Washington ACLU board member and director of its privacy project opined that public records were a problem. He thought a public disclosure law was OK because it helped citizens keep watch on government. In that way, for instance, we could make sure the local assessor didn't give friends favorable assessments and tax breaks. But he didn't want ordinary folks to be able to see how much his house was worth. That would be revealing details of his private life, he said, and should be off limits."[10]

The need for public access to government records has long been championed by the nation's press. Stories based on public records often disclose glaring shortcomings in the operation of government and expose ethical lapses or criminal behavior on the part of citizens both prominent and ordinary.[11] That the press should play a dominant role in scrutinizing the operations of government and accessing government records reflects its "watchdog" role.[12]

The buying and selling of public and private records, especially those in electronic formats, is a robust and hugely profitable enterprise in the United States.[13] The purchase of government public records by marketing firms and other businesses has led some state and local governments to regard their public "information by-products" as potential gold mines for new sources of revenue. The imposition of exorbitant fees for access to public databases presents a dangerous trend for journalism. News organizations routinely depend on access to such records to facilitate investigative reporting. For example, the Texas Department of Public Safety demanded that the *Houston Chronicle* pay $75 million for computer records of motorists' arrests and the State of Illinois wanted $37.5 million from the *Belleville News-Democrat* for driver's license records for a story on voter fraud.[14]

The Survey

Subject to the pressures of the legislative arena, the final scope of access to records laws relies on continuing public support for the proposition that the public has a right to know about government. To what extent do members of the public support this general principle? In what instances might people be willing to forego access to government records for a perceived greater good? It was with these questions in mind that a national telephone survey was undertaken to examine public attitudes about access to government records generally and to measure support for access to specific types of government records. The questionnaire was designed to explore two research questions:

1. What kinds of government records does the public think should be available?
2. What are the general attitudes of the public about the availability of government records?

Method

A representative nationwide sample of 403 adults (age 18 and older) in the United States was contacted by telephone from Nov. 5 to 15, 1998. The callers were trained graduate students. The sample was selected from the most recent *Select Phone CD-ROM*, a national telephone directories database.[15] In a repeated process, one of seven CD-ROM disks was randomly selected, then a name with a corresponding telephone number was randomly selected. If the cursor fell on a nonresidential listing, the next residential listing down was selected. The last digit of the selected number was randomly changed to include unlisted numbers. After three attempts to reach each number, the response rate (excluding nonworking numbers, faxes and ineligibles) was 61 percent.

The main parts of the questionnaire measured first, attitudes toward making a series of specific types of government records available (questions 2-10), to which respondents replied "available to anyone," "available in some instances," or "never available" and second, attitudes toward a series of statements about access to government records (questions 11-20), measured on a 5-point scale from strongly agree to strongly disagree.[16] Other questions asked whether there was a government worker in the household (question 21), political orientation (question 22), age (question 23), level of education (question 24), race (question 25) and Hispanic ethnicity. Callers coded respondents as male or female.

An attempt was made to construct a "support for access" scale using the items measuring people's attitudes toward making specific types of government records available (questions 2-10). The coefficient alpha was determined to be too low (Cronbach's alpha = .64) for the scale to be reliable.

Results

The sample was 53 percent female and 47 percent male. The distribution by race was 85.4 percent white, 9.1 percent black, 1.3 percent Asian and 3.0 percent other (1.3 percent didn't know or refused to answer). The mean age of respondents was 44; the median age was 41. One-quarter of the sample was age 28 or younger; one-quarter was age 57 or older. The distribution of highest educational level was: 5.3 percent had less than a high school degree; 20.5 percent had a high school degree; 28.1 percent had some college or voctional-technical training; 30.4 percent had a college degree; 3.5 percent had completed some graduate work; and 12.2 percent held a graduate degree. A plurality of respondents (44.3 percent) characterized their political orientation as middle-of-the-road, 29.3 percent said they were conservative and 19.5 percent said they were liberal (7 percent didn't know or refused to answer). 11.5 percent reported that they or members of their family were government employees.

Public support for access to government documents varies considerably depending on the nature of the record. As shown in Table 1.1, a majority of respondents thought only three of the eight records asked about should always be available to anyone: records from product liability lawsuits (62.8 percent), records of donations to political campaigns (53.1 percent) and driving records (52.1 percent). Interestingly, settlement records from product liability lawsuits, which garnered the greatest amount of support for unconditional access, are routinely sealed by courts.

A majority of respondents thought two types of government records should never be made available—property records reflecting prices paid for homes (54.3 percent) and the names of people who had served on juries (67.2 percent). In a culture that generally eschews public discussion of an individual's salary and economic worth, it is understandable that people would view disclosure of such information as an invasion of privacy. Ironically, property records are one of the most requested public documents. Many newspapers routinely identify the buyer, seller and the price paid for a property when it changes hands.

Table 1.1. **Public support for access to specified government records***

Percentage of respondents who think the following records should be made available . . . (n = 403)	Always	In Some Instances	Never	Don't Know/ Refused
Records of product liability lawsuits	62.8	21.6	13.2	2.5
Names of people who donate to political campaigns	53.1	20.6	22.8	3.5
Driving records	52.1	34.5	12.2	1.2
People's criminal records	46.7	43.7	7.9	1.7
Names of juveniles charged with crimes	33.1	42.0	22.4	2.5
Adoption records	29.8	43.9	22.6	3.7
Property records showing amount people paid for their home	24.3	20.3	54.3	1.0`
Names of people who served on juries	14.1	16.4	67.2	2.2

*Totals may not sum to 100 percent due to rounding error.

The strongest consensus for blocking access to a public record was for disclosure of jurors' names. Absent a compelling reason, such as protecting jurors' safety, the names of people who serve on juries are ordinarily a matter of public record. The strong sentiment against disclosure is somewhat puzzling. If it were simply a matter of protecting privacy, one would expect the same response to emerge with attitudes about disclosure of driving records. Perhaps this attitude reflects worries about being contacted by meddlesome neighbors, disgruntled litigants or the media.

Table 1.2 reports the attitudes of the American public toward access to government records overall, and toward specific groups seeking government information. A large majority (80.8 percent) believes that making government records publicly available keeps the government honest. Notwithstanding the recognition of this checking function, 51.8 percent of respondents feel that this beneficial policy of openness also threatens personal privacy. Where government records specifically name an individual, there is strong support (86.3 percent) for granting access rights to the person named in the record.

Attitudes toward access vary depending on who is seeking the information. There is solid agreement (84.6 percent) that people working for law enforcement agencies need to have access to government records to do their jobs. But support for access begins to dwindle when respondents consider other entities: 49.3 percent think journalists need access to do their job; 46.7 percent agree that banks considering making a loan need access; and only 20.7 percent agree that

Table 1.2 **Attitudes toward access to government records***

Percentage who think . . . (n = 403)	Strongly Agree	Some-what Agree	Middle	Some-what Disagree	Strongly Disagree	Don't Know/ Refused
Making government records publicly available keeps the government honest	48.0	32.8	2.7	5.2	10.9	0.2
Making government records publicly available represents a threat to people's privacy	20.3	31.5	5.2	15.6	24.6	2.7
People should have a right to receive copies of government records that specifically mention them by name	71.1	15.2	1.7	3.5	7.2	1.2
Journalists conducting news stories need to have access to government records to do their jobs	19.2	30.1	4.7	15.2	27.9	3.0
Banks considering offering people loans need to have access to government records to do their jobs	19.5	27.2	4.5	14.2	31.7	3.0
Credit card companies considering offering someone a credit card need to have access to government records to do their jobs	9.5	11.2	3.5	15.2	58.2	2.5
Law enforcement agencies investigating crimes need to have access to government records to do their jobs	55.7	28.9	4.2	4.7	4.0	2.5
Businesses that request government agencies supply them with public records should pay the agencies for the costs of retrieving the records	47.6	22.7	3.7	6.7	16.0	3.2

(continued)

Table 1.2   Attitudes toward access to government records*(*continued*)

Percentage who think . . . (n = 403)	Strongly Agree	Some-what Agree	Middle	Some-what Disagree	Strongly Disagree	Don't Know/ Refused
Private citizens who request government agencies supply them with public records should pay the agencies for the costs of retrieving the records	30.1	22.9	4.7	10.7	29.4	2.2

*Total may not sum to 100 percent due to rounding error.

credit card companies need access to do their jobs. It may be that people's attitudes about access are determined by the perceived credibility and motives of the requester. The public holds substantially different attitudes about access for banks and credit card companies, but both provide similar financial services for consumers and are often part of the same company. Perhaps the ubiquity of direct-mail solicitations for credit cards leads consumers to feel their privacy has been invaded.

When it comes to paying the cost of retrieving government records, a majority of the public agrees that the requester should pay. There is a substantial difference, however, between the amount of agreement when the requester is a business (70.3 percent) and when it is a private citizen seeking a record (53 percent). Interestingly, 29.4 percent of respondents strongly disagree with the idea that private citizens should ever have to pay for government records, while only 16 percent strongly disagree that businesses should ever have to pay.

To explore the data further, difference analyses were conducted on three of the attitude statements: whether making government records available keeps government honest; whether access to government records represents a threat to people's privacy; and whether journalists need access to public records to do their jobs. As shown in Table 1.3 and Table 1.4, attitudes about whether making government records available keeps government honest did not vary at the $p < .05$ level on any demographic or psychographic variable included in the study. Nor were differences found between groups on whether access to government records represents a threat to people's privacy, as shown in Table 1.5 and Table 1.6. Analyses of differences in attitudes about whether journalists need access to government records (Table 1.7 and Table 1.8) revealed only one statistically significant result: men were more likely than women to feel that journalists need access to government records to do their jobs. Overall, public attitudes toward access to government records appear remarkably homogeneous

Table 1.3 **T-Tests for differences in attitudes on whether making government records available keeps government honest**

		(n=)	Mean	s.d.	t - value	Sig.	
Gender	Male	187	1.88	1.27	−1.09	0.28	nsd
	Female	210	2.02	1.3			
Respondent or someone in house works for government	Yes	46	3.69	1.5	−1.75	0.08	nsd
	No	350	4.05	1.28			
Hispanic	Yes	36	3.86	1.22	−0.81	0.42	nsd
	No	353	4.05	1.31			
Race	White	336	4.08	1.26	1.21	0.23	nsd
	Black	36	3.81	1.47			

Note: Higher mean indicates greater agreement that access increases honesty

Table 1.4 **ANOVAS for differences in attitudes on whether making government records available keeps government honest**

		(n=)	Mean	s.d.			
Political orientation	Liberal	77	4.25	1.13			
	MOR	177	3.92	1.31			
	Conservative	177	4.03	1.34			
		SS	df	Mean Sq.	F	Sig.	
	Between	5.9	2	2.96	1.77	0.17	nsd
	Within	616	368	1.67			
	Total	622	370				
		(n=)	Mean	s.d.			
Age	18-30	118	3.96	1.28			
	31-50	145	3.95	1.21			
	51+	129	2.86	1.46			
		SS	df	Mean Sq.	F	Sig.	
	Between	2	2	1	0.58	0.56	nsd
	Within	674	389	1.73			
	Total	676	391				
		(n=)	Mean	s.d.			
Education	High school degree or <	102	3.84	1.5			
	College/vocational training	230	4.07	1.27			
	College Degree	62	4.1	1.1			
		SS	df	Mean Sq.	F	Sig.	
	Between	4.11	2	2.06	1.2	0.3	nsd
	Within	670	391	1.71			
	Total	674	393				

Note: Higher mean indicates greater agreement that access increases honesty

Table 1.5 **T-Tests for differences in attitudes on whether access to government records represents a threat to people's privacy**

		(n=)	Mean	s.d.	t - value	Sig.	
Gender	Male	182	3.01	1.53	1.01	0.31	nsd
	Female	206	2.85	1.52			
Respondent or someone in house works for government	Yes	44	2.77	1.57	−0.65	0.51	nsd
	No	343	2.93	1.53			
Hispanic	Yes	36	2.69	1.45	−0.96	0.34	nsd
	No	344	2.95	1.54			
Race	White	330	2.91	1.52	−0.11	0.92	nsd
	Black	34	2.94	1.61			

Note: Lower mean indicates greater threat to privacy

Table 1.6 **ANOVAS for differences in attitudes on whether access to government records represents a threat to people's privacy**

		(n=)	Mean	s.d.			
Political orientation	Liberal	76	2.72	1.49			
	MOR	173	2.91	1.49			
	Conservative	113	2.95	1.56			
		SS	df	Mean Sq.	F	Sig.	
	Between	2.6	2	1.27	0.56	0.57	nsd
	Within	823	359	2.29			
	Total	825	361				
		(n=)	Mean	s.d.			
Age	18-30	118	2.86	1.46			
	31-50	143	2.9	1.48			
	51+	123	3.02	1.65			
		SS	df	Mean Sq.	F	Sig.	
	Between	1.5	2	0.77	0.33	0.72	nsd
	Within	894	381	2.35			
	Total	896	383				
		(n=)	Mean	s.d.			
Education	High school degree or <	96	2.95	1.61			
	College/vocational training	227	2.89	1.51			
	College Degree +	62	2.9	1.45			
		SS	df	Mean Sq.	F	Sig.	
	Between	0.23	2	0.11	0.05	0.95	nsd
	Within	892	382	2.34			
	Total	893	384				

Note: Lower means indicates greater threat to privacy

Table 1.7   T-Tests for differences in attitudes on whether journalists need access to public records

		(n=)	Mean	s.d.	t - value	Sig.	
Gender	Male	183	3.18	1.54	2.34	0.02	p<.05
	Female	203	2.81	1.55			
Respondent or someone in house works for government	Yes	45	2.87	1.48	−0.47	0.64	nsd
	No	342	2.98	1.56			
Hispanic	Yes	35	3.37	1.43	1.52	0.13	nsd
	No	345	2.95	1.57			
Race	White	327	3.01	1.54	0.65	0.512	nsd
	Black	36	2.83	1.63			

Note: Higher mean indicates greater need for access

Table 1.8   ANOVAS for differences in attitudes on whether journalists need access to public records

		(n=)	Mean	s.d.			
Political orientation	Liberal	76	3.17	1.5			
	MOR	172	2.99	1.55			
	Conservative	116	2.72	1.53			
		SS	df	Mean Sq.	F	Sig.	
	Between	10.4	2	5.2	1.56	0.11	nsd
	Within	847	361	2.35			
	Total	858	363				
		(n=)	Mean	s.d.			
Age	18-30	116	3.03	1.42			
	31-50	142	3.05	1.56			
	51+	125	2.86	1.66			
		SS	df	Mean Sq.	F	Sig.	
	Between	2.6	2	1.3	0.54	0.58	nsd
	Within	920	380	2.42			
	Total	923	382				
		(n=)	Mean	s.d.			
Education	High school degree or <	98	3.02	1.61			
	College/vocational training	225	2.92	1.56			
	College Degree +	62	3.08	1.44			
		SS	df	Mean Sq.	F	Sig.	
	Between	1.47	2	0.73	0.3	0.74	nsd
	Within	920	382	2.41			
	Total	922	384				

Note: Higher mean indicates greater need for access

across conventional demographic and psychographic categories. Even comparison by political orientation showed no significant differences, suggesting that access to government records is not an issue that breaks down along liberal-conservative lines.

Conclusions

The survey results show substantial public support for access to an array of government information. There is also overwhelming recognition that access to government information helps keep government honest. But, despite its liberal attitudes toward openness, it appears that the American public is deeply concerned about the threat to individual privacy that may result from making certain government records publicly available. The public is prickly about which government records should be available, and it is disposed to condition access based on who is requesting the records.

The weakest support for public access in this study was found for the disclosure of jurors' names. Public identification of jurors is commonplace, but recent judicial trends and even legislative initiatives suggest a possible shift toward more privacy or even outright secrecy.[17] Such public sentiment may be understandable against the backdrop of the O.J. Simpson case, the Oklahoma Bombing case and other high-profile trials. Nevertheless, the ability to identify jurors serving in routine cases is crucial to the fundamental openness of the judicial system.

From the perspective of access proponents, the most troubling aspect of the survey results was the tepid support for the role of the press in the access to information equation. The news media have long played the dominant role as government watchdog, recognition that pre-dates the American Revolution. The news media—an amalgam of institutions from the elite newspapers and television networks to the supermarket tabloids—have come under intense scrutiny and criticism in recent years. But regardless of the public's perception of press credibility, the news media need to do a better job of informing the public about the importance of access to government documents and the role of the press in that process.

Finally, the results suggest that public attitudes toward access to government documents are complex phenomena. While public opinion regarding access seems exceptionally homogenous across demographic and psychographic variables, various motives may underlie the preference for disclosure in some cases and restrictions in others. Additional research is needed to uncover the various factors that shape public attitudes toward access.

Notes

1Alexander Meiklejohn. *Free Speech and Its Relation to Self-Government* (Kennikat Press, 1948); Thomas I. Emerson, *The System of Freedom of Expression.* (Vintage Books, 1970); Vincent Blasi, *The Checking Value in First Amendment Theory,* Am. B. Found. Res. J. 521 (1977).

2*Richmond Newspapers v. Virginia,* 448 U.S. 555 (1980); *Grosjean v. American Press Co.,* 297 U.S. 233 (1936); *Red Lion Broadcasting Co. v. FCC,* 395 U.S. 367 (1969); *Branzburg v. Hayes,* 408 U.S. 665 (1972).

3See, e.g., *Fayette Co. v. Martin,* 279 Ky. 387, 396, S.W. 2d 838, 843 (1939); *State ex rel. Wellford v. Williams,* 110 Tenn. 549, 74 S.W. 948 (1903); *Clement v. Graham,* 78 Vt. 290 (1906). In some jurisdictions, courts have abandoned interest tests for access to public records. See *Burton v. Tuite,* 78 Mich. 363 (1889); *MacEwan v. Holm,* 226 Oreg. 27 (1961).

4For example, Florida lawmakers added 1/ exemptions to Florida's Public Records Law in its 1997–98 legislative session. These included exemptions for private corporations running public hospitals and the names, addresses and telephone numbers of animal owners contained in rabies vaccination certificates. The rabies exemption was pushed by the state's Veterinary Association to protect client lists from direct marketers who sold pet care products cheaper than the local veterinarians. See Sandra F. Chance, *Chicken Soup Laws Undermine the Public Trust,* 22 The Brechner Report 4 (April, 1998); *Florida Legislature Enacts Several Exemptions to Access Laws,* 22 The Brechner Report 7 (July, 1998).

5The Driver's License Protection Act of 1994 prohibited states from releasing certain information contained in Department of Motor Vehicle records. While the press and the public were not given access, an exemption was made for private detectives, tow truck drivers, researchers, insurance companies and other entities.

6The survey was commissioned by the Coalition for Open Government and conducted by the Santa Monica-based research firm of Fairbank, Maslin, Maullin & Associates, in September 1998. Survey sponsors included a number of press and First Amendment interest groups. See Bettina Boxall, *California and the West, Government Secrecy Seen as a Problem, Poll: Majority of Voters Back Release of More Information, Many Support Strengthening Public Access Laws,* Los Angeles Times A3 (Oct. 25, 1998). Survey results are available at http://spj.org/foia/foi_poll/index.htm. Site visited on Nov.17, 1998.

7Chris Iven, *Public Shuns Forum on Open Records Proposals: ACCESS/RI Wants to Expand the State's Freedom of Information Laws so Mistakes or Corruption Can't Be Hidden,* Providence Journal–Bulletin 1D (Feb. 13, 1997).

8Ed Bartlett, *RMS Need to Safeguard Computerized Patient Records to Protect Hospitals,* 15 Hospital Risk Management 129–33 (1993). Cited by Ross Anderson, *NHS-wide Networking and Patient Confidentiality: Britain Seems Headed for a Poor Solution. National Health Services,* 310 (1996) British Medical Journal 5 (1995).

9Lynn Jones, *Results of the Second Equifax–Harris Privacy Survey.* Available at http://www.mediacentral.com/Magazines/Direct/Archive/11019501.htm. Site visited on Oct. 18, 1998.

10David Zeeck, *Privacy, Public Access Is Delicate Balance,* News Tribune (Tacoma, Wash.) B6 (Dec.7, 1997).

11Michael R. Fancher, *In the Electronic Age, Personal Rights and Public Access Collide,* Seattle Times A23 (Dec.7, 1997). News organizations are often rewarded specifically for addressing access issues. For example, the Brechner Center for Freedom of Information at the University of Florida annually bestows an award for coverage of access issues.

12Blasi, *Checking Value in First Amendment Theory,* 521, 538. See Herbert J. Altschull, *Agent of Power: The Media and Public Policy* (Longman, 2d ed 1995); Douglass Carter, *The Fourth Branch of Government* (Houghton Mifflin, 1953).

[13]Victoria Lemieux, *Selling Information: What Records Managers Should Know,* 30 (1) Records Management Quarterly 3 (January 1996).

[14]Iver Peterson, *Public Information, Business Rates: State Agencies Turn Data Base Records into Cash Cows,* New York Times D1 (July 14, 1997). The *Houston Chronicle* ultimately received the requested records at no charge, after the intervention of a state legislator. See also Bruce Garrison, *Computer-Assisted Reporting* (LEA, 2d ed 1998).

[15]*Select Phone* CD-ROM (ProCD, 1998.)

[16]A middle category (e.g., "neither agree nor disagree") was not given as part of the response set. However, the questionnaire accommodated a middle response category if the respondent voluntarily gave such a response.

[17]The state of Texas, for example, recently passed controversial legislation that shifted the presumption from openness to secrecy. Wendy Benjaminson, *Shroud of Secrecy Increasingly Veils Trials in Texas,* Houston Chronicle A1 (March 13, 1994).

2

Access to Electronic Records in the States: How Many Are Computer-Friendly?

Michele Bush and Bill F. Chamberlin

Access to government information is threatened on a number of fronts as courts and legislatures struggle to balance conflicting social interests. Many of these conflicts are as old as the process of government record keeping itself. Laws and customs defining levels of access to information and records have never been static, but the parameters of access had remained somewhat stable over time. The advent of the computer as a major fixture in government information gathering and record keeping, however, has raised a range of novel legal and public policy issues that are shifting the access balance. The following chapter discusses these issues and their implications for public access to government information in the computer age.

Computers are revolutionizing how governments gather, store and analyze information. New technology also affords numerous opportunities to enhance public access to a vast array of information held by governments. Computers make it possible for governments to provide members of the public far more information faster and in more useful forms than ever before.[1] Information and records can be stored on servers—which function as huge electronic file cabinets—that allow anyone to freely access the contents at their convenience. Data, from single records to large databases, can easily be transferred from servers to computer disks and taken to homes and offices for study and analysis.

Unfortunately, relatively few governments have shown an interest in taking full advantage of computer technology to enhance public access. During the last decade, as governments have stored more and more information in computers, public access has not been a priority. In fact, often access has been made *more difficult* by officials unable or unwilling to advance the public's right to know about the workings of their public officials and institutions. The indifference of one public employee in Schuykill County, Pa., is indicative: "We don't have a policy for releasing computer data, so our policy right now is not to release any."[2]

Public access to government records allows citizens to monitor government activity and participate more effectively in the process of self-government. Yet, although the Founders of the nation believed public knowledge about the government was essential to the nation's well-being,[3] few provisions for this were made in the Constitution or early statutes.[4] Explicit governmental recognition of a public right to examine and copy public records in most states took more than 160 years. By the early 1950s, only a minority of states had enacted public records statutes.[5]

The Freedom of Information Act, enacted in 1966, provides access to federal agencies' records, except those specifically exempted from disclosure.[6] Each state has adopted legislation determining which state, county and municipal records are open to public inspection.[7] Not only do individual state statutes differ widely, so do interpretations of those laws in state courts. Similarly, state legislatures and courts have reacted differently to the challenge of ensuring access to government records as those records were being transformed from paper documents in ubiquitous file cabinets to a series of 1s and 0s on computer hard drives, tapes and disks.[8]

The advent of the Information Age made obsolete access laws written in the 1950s, 1960s and 1970s, when most public documents were produced by sliding a sheet of paper into a typewriter. Many of these laws incorporated definitions of public records that did not contemplate records being stored in electronic form.[9] More importantly, none of the statutes envisioned the novel access issues raised by computerizing government records.

This chapter discusses access issues arising from the computerization of public records and examines state responses based on a series of pro-access criteria gleaned from the relevant literature in the 1990s. The researchers examined each state's access statutes, case law and attorney general opinions. Access laws in each state were measured against 10 criteria. The authors examined whether state laws

1. Consider electronic records by definition to be public records;
2. Grant access to the same records whether on paper or in computer form;
3. Require that computer hardware and software be user-friendly;
4. Consider software to be a public record;
5. Include fee structures for electronic records;
6. Require agencies to remove confidential information from electronic records so the non-confidential information in those records can be released;
7. Require records custodians to customize searches for requesters;
8. Allow requesters to choose the format for the records they are seeking;
9. Require agencies to index their computerized records;
10. At least encourage agencies to enhance the public's ability to access public records by providing remote access and public-access terminals.

The first six criteria were selected because they are important in ensuring that existing levels of access under state laws, based on the concept of *paper* records, are not eroded in the computer age. The last four criteria were selected because of their importance in providing meaningful access to electronic records.[10] Electronic records are potentially more useful to requesters than paper records because they can be analyzed efficiently using sophisticated programs and other techniques, but only if public officials are willing to meet the needs of requesters.

The 10 categories were developed by reading the observations and recommendations of scholars, interest group representatives and public officials during the development of computerized records in the 1990s.[11] Also considered were provisions already built into some state laws and the federal Electronic Freedom of Information Act Amendments of 1996.[12]

State-by-State Analysis of Electronic Access

Fewer than a third of state access laws declare that public records include not only paper records but also records stored electronically. Statutory recognition of computerized records, however, does not necessarily guarantee effective public access to them.

1. Public Records Defined

In theory, the best way to ensure that computer records are fully accessible is to include electronic government information in the definition of public records. However, only 14 states specifically define public records to include all kinds of electronically stored data. Those states are Florida,[13] Georgia,[14] Hawaii,[15] Illinois,[16] Maine,[17] Maryland,[18] Michigan,[19] Missouri,[20] New York,[21] North Carolina,[22] Texas,[23] Vermont,[24] Virginia[25] and Wisconsin.[26]

Half the states do not specifically acknowledge electronically stored data in the definitions of public records, but use general language that could include such data. Of those states, 21 describe public records to include information "regardless of physical forms or characteristics."[27] Three states use similarly general language, defining public records as information recorded by "any method,"[28] "any medium"[29] or by any "other material."[30] In at least one state with generalized language, Ohio, courts have said state statutes protect access to electronic records.[31]

Twelve states—Alabama,[32] Alaska,[33] Arizona,[34] Arkansas,[35] Colorado,[36] Montana,[37] Nevada,[38]New Hampshire,[39] New Jersey,[40] North Dakota,[41] Pennsylvania[42] and South Dakota[43]—have no language in their public records statutes discussing electronically stored data, and no language that might be considered general enough to include such data. In fact, the New Jersey Supreme Court ruled in 1995 that the state's "right to know" law did not require agencies to provide public records on computer tapes. In *Higg-A-Rella, Inc. v. County of Essex*, the court acknowledged that state law was narrow and had been strictly construed. The court said New Jersey's definition of a public record as one "required by law to be made, maintained or kept on file" did not mandate that computer tapes be made or maintained.[44]

On the other hand, the New Hampshire Supreme Court held that a computer tape was a public record under that state's "right to know" law. In *Menge v. City of Manchester*,[45] an economics professor at Dartmouth College sought access to a computerized database of real estate tax assessments for the city of Manchester to conduct a tax study. Only the real estate tax assessment records in paper form, which consisted of 35,000 field record cards, were considered public records. To resolve the case, the New Hampshire Supreme Court, noting that the state public records law did not define public records, relied on related statutes and its own intent "to provide the utmost information." In particular, the court cited statutes that referred to public records in such terms as "records . . . and documents of every kind" and documents "and other material, regardless of physical form or characteristics, made or received pursuant to law or in connection with the transaction of official business."[46]

2. Equal Access for Computerized Records

Computerizing public records makes it easier to retrieve, search, divide and assemble them. However, some state laws suggest that public officials wonder whether records that had been available on paper should be equally available when those same records are drawn together in a computer. Although most states exempt the same records whether they are kept on paper or in a computer, there are a few exceptions. For example, Alabama limited access to electronic records of the Alabama Criminal Justice Information Center on a "right to know" or "need to know"[47] basis. The records contained within the center's database are public in paper form at the originating agencies, but not when compiled in a database.[48]

Mississippi is the only state with a specific exemption for e-mail.[49] Hawaii grants records custodians the discretion to decide on a case-by-case basis whether electronic mail should be disclosed.[50] Electronic mail did not exist before computers. Although e-mail has a paper equivalent, regular mail and e-mail are not always treated the same by state law. Very few states directly address the issue of e-mail access in their laws. Only four states—Arizona,[51] Colorado,[52] Florida[53] and Maryland[54]—have specifically stated that e-mail is subject to public disclosure.

A few state courts—in Michigan, New Jersey and Massachusetts—have said citizens may have a greater privacy interest in records stored in computers than in the same paper records stored in file cabinets. In 1982, a divided Michigan Supreme Court affirmed a lower court's decision blocking release of computer tapes of otherwise public documents. In *Kestenbaum v. Michigan State University*,[55] Lawrence Kestenbaum asked for a copy of a computer tape used to produce the university's paperbound student directory. Kestenbaum wanted the tape to obtain addresses for mailings in a 1978 political campaign. The court held that release of the computer tape, containing the names and addresses of university students, would constitute a "clearly unwarranted invasion of personal privacy" under Michigan's Freedom of Information Act, even though distribution of the printed directory did not. The court said that "form, not just content, affects the nature of information. Seemingly benign data in an intrusive form takes on quite different characteristics than if it were merely printed."[56] The court held it "is not seriously debated" that computer technology has led to "an ever-increasing erosion of personal privacy;" computers have led to the accumulation of more information about individuals that is "readily accessible and easily manipulated" and easily combined with other data to create "new, more comprehensive banks of information."[57]

In a 1988 decision, *Doe v. Registrar of Motor Vehicles*,[58] a Massachusetts Appeals Court reasoned that putting personal information into computer databases open to public scrutiny can be detrimental to both individual privacy interests and the public interest. In *Doe*, at least three registered drivers in Massachusetts sought to block the Massachusetts Registrar of Motor Vehicles from making their age, heights and social security numbers available to the public. The appellate court said several factors must be considered when deciding whether such access constituted "an unwarranted invasion of personal privacy" under state law. Among the issues were the impact "on the privacy of the total number of people whose data are disseminated."[59] The court also said the ability to combine data in one database with data in other databases should be considered.[60] The court remanded the case so the lower court could more closely consider the arguments of the Registrar of Motor Vehicles in favor of disclosure.

In 1995, the New Jersey Supreme Court suggested computerized records were more threatening to privacy than their paper counterparts. In *Higg-A-Rella, Inc. v. County of Essex*,[61] the court, in dicta, recognized that computerized records could be more revealing and intrusive than paper records because the former can "be rapidly retrieved, searched and reassembled in novel and unique ways, not previously imagined."[62] Although the court said the computerized tax assessment records at issue should be released under state common law, it emphasized the limited nature of its holding.[63]

Another kind of electronic record, of great interest to journalists and others concerned with government planning and policy, does not have a precise paper equivalent. Geographic Information Systems (GIS) are costly digitized computer mapping systems. GIS software allows agencies to digitize demographic, geological and land-use information so it can be superimposed in "layers" on maps. Some states are specifically limiting access to the data in GIS, even though data in GIS may be publicly available in paper form.[64]

3. New Computer Purchases Facilitating Access

Access to computerized records can be delayed or even thwarted if records are stored in computer programs that prevent the record requester from routinely reading or analyzing the information in meaningful ways. Dealings with such access problems in existing computer systems can be time-consuming and costly. Preventing future software-based access problems is much easier with a little foresight before new computer systems are installed. Access-friendly software can be built into computer systems at the design stage, making retrieving documents easier and actually reducing costs. For example, programs can be designed with data fields that segregate confidential and nonconfidential information as the data are entered. Simply including or excluding certain data fields to meet requests allows records custodians, using a few simple keystrokes, to extract nonconfidential information. Systems not designed to anticipate database segregation problems require agencies to reprogram the computer to meet requests for nonconfidential information. This "new" programming to filter out exempt information is time-consuming and costly, to either the agency or the requester.[65]

Ten states have enacted statutes that require government agencies to consider public access when planning or purchasing computer systems. Statutes in Arkansas,[66] California,[67] Florida,[68] Indiana,[69] Iowa,[70] Mississippi,[71] Missouri,[72] Nebraska,[73] North Carolina,[74] and Washington[75] direct agencies to include access to public records in any new plans or policies regarding electronically stored information. For example, North Carolina's statute specifically states that agencies cannot acquire electronic data-processing systems for public records without first determining the systems will not impede public access.[76] Similarly, California's statute requires that agencies centralize information in data centers[77] and train personnel to distribute electronically stored public information.[78] The statute also requires that agencies develop remote access networks for the public to use to obtain public information.[79] Washington's statute sets itself apart from others because it not only includes a requirement for plans to facilitate public access to government information,[80] it also specifically mentions planning for accessibility by people with disabilities.[81]

4. Software

When public records are stored in computers, requesters sometimes find it necessary to use the same computer software a public agency uses to read or copy the information. The software may have been developed by a government agency; or it may be proprietary software owned by a private business. More often than not, states do not recognize software as a public record. Agencies, therefore, can refuse to release it, effectively blocking access.

Statutes in only three states specify software as a public record: Florida,[82] Maine[83] and Mississippi.[84] In Wisconsin, the attorney general has issued an opinion stating that computer programs written by state agencies are public records.[85]

Twenty-six states have no statutes, case law or attorneys' general opinions that clarify records requesters' rights of access to computer software needed to make meaningful access to records possible.[86] Eighteen states have provisions that specifically exclude software from their public records laws. Fifteen of those states—Alaska,[87] Arkansas,[88] California,[89] Colorado,[90] Georgia,[91] Hawaii,[92] Idaho,[93] Kansas,[94] Kentucky,[95] Michigan,[96] Missouri,[97] New Mexico,[98] Oklahoma,[99] Utah[100] and Virginia[101]—have statutory exclusions. Ohio's Supreme Court has said that proprietary software is not a public record, even if the software is necessary to read public records on computer tapes.[102] Nevada's attorney general has said software is not a public record.[103] The attorney general of Texas[104] has said software "need not be released" as a public record. Two states give records custodians discretion to decide whether to release software to the public: Indiana[105] and Oregon.[106]

5. Fees

Fee schedules developed for providing paper records do not necessarily address the expenses agencies face when responding to requests for computerized records. A printer linked to a computer, rather than a copying machine, often provides the record. In addition, requesters often ask for records on computer tapes or disks rather than on paper. The cost of obtaining computerized records raises novel issues and potential barriers to access, especially when budget-strapped agencies seek computer databases as a potential source of revenue.

One prominent Florida newspaper editor has said officials in that state charge more for computerized records than allowed by law.[107] Dan Keating of *The Miami Herald* said agencies charge more for records when they are computerized, often because they consider computerized information a profit-making asset.

Most states, 33, authorize charges for electronic records based on "actual costs," whether or not the term public record is defined to include electronic records.[108] But the meaning of "actual costs" varies greatly. Depending on the state, the term may include the cost to duplicate records, the cost of materials used to make the copies and the cost of labor required. Four states include overhead expenses, including cost of the equipment and maintaining the computer systems, when determining "actual cost."[109] Some states, including Connecticut, Florida and North Carolina, allow additional charges for "extensive use" of personnel or technology resources, including computer use.[110] Florida's statute allows custodians to levy special charges when records requests would "require extensive use of information technology resources or extensive clerical or supervisory assistance by personnel of the agency involved."[111] North Carolina allows agencies to charge special service fees when records requests require "extensive use of information technology resources or extensive clerical or supervisory assistance."[112]

The New Jersey Supreme Court has held that extensive use fees might be applicable to requests for computerized public records. New Jersey's public records statute does not distinguish computerized records when it discusses fees. Agencies in New Jersey are authorized to charge a flat rate based on the number of pages copied.[113] The New Jersey Supreme Court determined in *Higg-A-Rella, Inc. v. County of Essex* that charging for copying may not be enough to compensate for the differences between paper and computerized records.[114] The court suggested a "reasonable fee" for computerized tax records might include costs of developing, operating and maintaining computer systems.[115]

Two states have caps on rates for access to computerized public records. Rhode Island charges no more than $15 per hour for search and retrieval of computerized records.[116] Tennessee allows a charge of no more the $5 for computer searches for any public record having a commercial value.[117]

Fee schedules in 13 states are less definitive. Four of those states—Minnesota,[118] Nevada,[119] New Mexico[120] and Wyoming[121]—allow records custodians to determine fees on a case-by-case basis. Nine states—Delaware,[122] Indiana,[123] Iowa,[124] Kentucky,[125] Louisiana,[126] Nebraska,[127] Oklahoma,[128] Pennsylvania[129] and South Dakota[130]—allow records custodians to determine "reasonable fees" for duplicating public records. Nebraska allows records custodians in counties with populations more than 100,000 to charge a "reasonable fee" for transmitting public record information via modems.[131] This "reasonable fee" may include costs for the amortization of computer equipment or software.[132] Alabama and Hawaii have no provisions for charging for copies of electronic public records.

6. Redaction

Most state statutes require public officials to redact, or remove, confidential information from records that otherwise can be made public under the law. The computerization of records has complicated the issue of redaction in at least three ways. First, some state agencies have argued that their computer hardware and software make it impossible for them to redact confidential information without significant computer reprogramming. Second, some state agencies have wanted to charge for even simple redactions in computerized records even though they assessed no similar charge for paper records. Third, in the case of computer records it is difficult to know when an official has redacted material. When shielding confidential information from paper records, officials usually use a pen or marker to blacken the exempt information, rendering it unreadable. When redacting information from computer records, officials can delete information from files before printing what remains without the requester knowing either the context or how much has been deleted.

Most states rely on language developed for paper records when redacting electronic records. Forty states have statutes, case law or attorney general opinions advising that when confidential and nonconfidential information are in one record, custodians must remove, or redact, the confidential information and release the remaining nonconfidential information.[133] It is, of course, impossible to know by examining only the statutes and case law whether agencies provide equal service in segregating confidential material from computer records as well as paper records.

Two states, however, directly address the issues faced when attempting to redact computerized records, including the inability to determine what records have been redacted. Michigan's statute requires that the exempt portions be removed and what remains of the record be available for public inspection.[134] Michigan's law also requires records custodians to "generally describe the material exempted."[135] Alaska's statute requires agencies to write a program to extract, delete or mask confidential information from electronic records that are otherwise available to the public.[136]

In two states, courts have held that public access to computerized records cannot be blocked because the documents contain both confidential and nonconfidential information. The Ohio Supreme Court held that the state's Registrar of Motor Vehicles must release data from motor vehicle registration records despite the registrar's contention that the requested information was commingled with confidential information.[137] In Texas, a trial court said agencies must develop extraction programs to separate confidential and non-confidential information.[138]

Six states—Alabama, Missouri, Nevada, New Hampshire, South Dakota and Tennessee—have no statutory language or case law providing for the segregation of confidential and non-confidential information.

7. Customized Records

Computers afford records requesters many opportunities not available when government documents could be obtained only in print. For example, computers can provide requesters with information that has not been compiled into a specific document. Agencies may not always use all the information in their databases, or they may not have organized it in ways most convenient for the requester. Computers make it possible to reorganize data and to compile information from several documents or databases to meet a request. When information in public records is reassembled in a new way at the initiative of a requester, government agencies usually consider the reorganization the creation of a new record.

For example, in *Seigle v. Barry*, a Florida appellate court held that a government agency was not required to search and retrieve public information in a configuration determined by the requester.[139] The requesters wanted access to particular sections of computerized records maintained by the Broward County School Board for use in collective bargaining negotiations.[140] The court said it would be "ludicrous to require public officials to provide such a service when it can be as easily obtained by paying an expert in the private sector to reclassify the information."[141]

Only nine states have statutory provisions that allow requesters to ask for customized searches of computerized public records. The nine are Colorado,[142] Minnesota,[143] Missouri,[144] Montana,[145] New Hampshire,[146] Oregon,[147] Rhode Island,[148] South Carolina[149] and Virginia.[150] For example, Oregon records custodians are required to provide customized searches as long as the agency possesses the software necessary for the search.[151] If information cannot be provided in the form requested, custodians may provide the record in the form in which it is maintained.[152]

Ten states—Alaska,[153] California,[154] Hawaii,[155] Indiana,[156] Kentucky,[157] Maryland,[158] New Mexico,[159] New York,[160] North Carolina[161] and Wisconsin[162]—have specific provisions in their public records laws stating that agencies are not required to conduct customized searches.

Courts in New Jersey and Illinois have found a limited right to customize electronic documents in response to records requests.[163] The New Jersey Supreme Court said that under state common law the Newark Board of Education should be able to selectively copy individual health records from a State Health Benefits Plan database as long as it was willing to pay for the effort.[164] Case law and attorney general opinions in six states have determined that records custodians do not have to conduct customized public records searches. Florida,[165] Georgia,[166] Louisiana,[167] Ohio[168] and New Jersey rely on case law. Arkansas has attorney general opinions establishing that customized searches are not required.[169] Alabama's attorney general has concluded that records custodians need not compile or assimilate public records information when responding to records requests.[170]

Many states have neither statutes nor case law addressing whether requesters have a right to customized searches. The 23 states silent on this issue are Arizona, Connecticut, Delaware, Idaho, Iowa, Kansas, Maine, Massachusetts, Michigan, Mississippi, Nebraska, Nevada, North Dakota, Oklahoma, Pennsylvania, South Dakota, Tennessee, Texas, Utah, Vermont, Washington, West Virginia and Wyoming.

8. Format

Computers provide requesters with another potential benefit—choice of record format. Although some requesters may prefer paper records, many computer users prefer documents on disks or tapes that can be manipulated without being rekeyed.[171] However, states do not always allow requesters to choose the format most appropriate for their needs.

Sixteen states have statutes that allow requesters to choose the format of computerized records: Colorado,[172] Connecticut,[173] Florida,[174] Indiana,[175] Kansas,[176] Massachusetts,[177] Mississippi,[178] Montana,[179] New Mexico,[180] North Carolina,[181] Oregon,[182] South Carolina,[183] Texas,[184] Utah,[185] Vermont[186] and West Virginia.[187] The attorneys general in two additional states have said requesters should be given the choice of format when agencies hold records in computerized form.[188]

Statutes in four states do not give requesters a choice of format, but language in case law does.[189] In New Hampshire, for example, the state's supreme court ordered the city of Manchester to provide a computer tape of property tax assessments for a study of the structure of the state's property taxes by a Dartmouth College economics professor.[190] The trial court had calculated that if the professor worked from the 35,000 data cards that had been transferred onto a computer tape, it would take more than 200 days at a cost of $10,000. However, the bank that put the records on tape said the cost of reproducing it was $55, including the cost of the tape itself. The bank said it would cost an additional $40 to $100 to create a computer program to block out confidential information on the tape. The New Hampshire Supreme Court said it was common sense to take advantage of the "ease and minimal costs of the tape reproduction" compared to the expense and labor involved in taking the information from the data cards.

In four other states, access to public records in any form might be inferred from the language in statutes. In Maine, the statute does not discuss directly whether the public can choose electronic records instead of paper records, but one statute says that records are available in both versions.[191]

Some states mention the availability of different formats for public records, but they do not mandate that requesters may choose. Missouri records custodians are encouraged, but not required, to provide information in the format a requesters chooses.[192] Similar language appears in public records laws in Alaska,[193] New Jersey,[194] North Dakota,[195] and Virginia.[196] Agencies in those states may, but are not required to, provide records in the requester's format choice.

Just four states—California,[197] Kentucky,[198] Maryland[199] and Oklahoma[200]—have statutes that leave the format up to the records custodian. Alabama's public records statute contains no language about format choice, but the state attorney general has concluded requesters do not have the right to designate the format in which records are dispersed.[201]

Wisconsin records requesters can ask for public records on paper if computerized versions are "not in a readily comprehensible form."[202]

Sixteen states—Arizona, Delaware, Georgia, Idaho, Iowa, Louisiana, Minnesota, Nebraska, Nevada, New York, Pennsylvania, Rhode Island, South Dakota, Tennessee, Washington and Wyoming—have no statutes, case law or attorney general opinions regarding format choice.

9. Indexing

Records requesters seldom have had the benefit of an agency's filing index when seeking paper records. Records usually were handed to them. However, requesters using computer records often need a way to know what records are available in the computer and how they are organized. Governments should have accurate documentation of records and information stored in computers. Providing access to indexes will facilitate public access to government information and ensure that records requests can be answered efficiently.[203]

Only North Carolina requires government agencies to maintain indices of electronically stored public records. In 1997, North

Carolina required every public agency to compile by 1998 an index of computer databases "that includes more information helpful to a records requester than a simple listing of contents."[204] The indexes must contain lists of data fields, descriptions of records formats available, the schedule of updates to the database, the costs for copying the database, and a description of the data fields to which public access is restricted.[205] California requires only the Secretary of State to maintain an index of that office's computerized public records.[206] In Texas, statutory language states that government agencies "may" maintain indexes for electronically stored public records.[207]

10. *Facilitating the Public's Ability to Access Documents*

States can increase opportunities for public access to records by establishing procedures that make it easier to retrieve electronic records. A few states allow records requesters to retrieve documents by electronic transfer through sites remote from the government agency storing the records. Records requesters may be able to see records by using the Internet or by directly accessing an agency computer. Even fewer states provide by statute that agencies can provide public computer terminals for accessing records.

Only four states—Arkansas,[208] California,[209] Nebraska[210] and Washington[211]—have statutory requirements for remote or online access of public records. Washington's statute is relatively progressive because it requires that a committee from each state agency establish a plan and implement policies for remote access that enhance ways to receive and transmit public information. The agency committee's must also plan and implement technologies that would allow 24-hour access to government agencies and that involves "little or no cost to access, and are capable of being used by persons without extensive technological ability."[212]

Statutes in five states—Alaska,[213] Coloroda,[214] Florida,[215] Indiana,[216] and Kentucky[217]—allow or encourage remote access, but do not require it. In these states, it is left to individual agencies to decide whether to provide remote access and to establish procedures for doing so. Alaska's statute requires agencies to provide public computer terminals when the agencies provide online access to files or databases,[218] while Colorado's statute recommends public terminals as an option for enhancing access to electronic records.[219] No state statutes prohibit the use of public terminals, and state agencies may have the power to employ them without specific statutory authority.

Conclusion

Analyses of various state electronic access provisions shows that the process of ensuring access to computerized records has several dimensions and raises important questions. Are computerized records considered public records? Are computerized records as accessible to requesters as public records on paper? And are governments taking advantage of the new technology to maximize public access and use of electronic records?

Many states have not revised their records statutes to reflect the new computer technologies. Too often, citizens do not know how laws written for paper records might apply to records now in electronic form. This failure of governments to respond to the realities of the computer age frequently acts to limit access to public information, as the example of Pennsylvania public employee ("We don't have a policy for releasing computer data, so our policy right now is not to release any.") cited earlier illustrates.

Only 14 states specifically include electronically stored information in their public records definitions, although most state statutes use ambiguous language that may be interpreted to include computerized public records.

Some states may bar access to some public records specifically because the information is computerized. For example, courts in Michigan, New Jersey and Massachusetts have said there may be greater privacy interests in records stored in computers rather than on paper. These courts reasoned that computerized public records may be more invasive because the information is more accessible and more easily manipulated.

Only 10 states require government agencies to provide for public access to information when the agencies plan or purchase computer systems. Hardware and software that ensure access to public information can be introduced when agencies plan and design computer systems. Such foresight may reduce barriers to accessing public information after the systems have been installed—barriers that are often costly to overcome after the planning/design stage.

Only three states include provisions for access to software in their public records statutes even though records requesters may need access to the software used by the state to read or obtain records that are by law open to the public. Most states may be able to refuse public access to software that is necessary for reading or copying public records.

Most states do not have specific provisions for fees they may charge to duplicate computerized public records. They rely on ambiguous language that allows records custodians to charge requesters for "actual costs" incurred during the duplication process or for "extensive use" of labor or facilities.

Only two states have addressed in their statutes how to redact confidential information that is commingled with nonconfidential information in the same public record. Forty states rely on redaction provisions enacted in response to paper records even though redacting information from computerized information raises different issues. For example, few states require records custodians to show where in an electronic record information has been redacted.

Just nine states have statutory provisions allowing requesters to ask for customized searches of public records, including asking for portions of a record, a compilation of several records, or a reorganization of the data. In fact, 10 states have provisions in their public records laws stating that agencies are not required to provide customized searches of records.

Twenty-two states have provisions recommending that records requesters be allowed to choose whether records are on paper or on a computer disk or tape. Many states have ambiguous provisions or no provisions regarding whether a requester may choose a format. Four states allow the records custodian to dictate the format.

While providing indexes of computerized information would facilitate public access, just one state requires that government agencies do so. Few states discuss in their statutes specific ways to encourage public access to computerized information. Four states require agencies to provide remote or online access to computerized public records. Two states encourage agencies to provide public computer terminals to enhance access to computerized records.

Citizen access to records should not be limited because paper records are giving way to computerized information. In fact, computers provide many opportunities to better serve members of the public seeking records. However, many officials appear concerned that computers make it easier to manipulate, sort and retrieve information.

The concern that many legislators, executive branch personnel, and citizens have for the increased potential of manipulating and disseminating computerized records can be seen in the language of several court opinions that discuss personally identifiable information. In 1977, the U.S. Supreme Court said in *Whalen v. Roe* that accumulation of large amounts of personal information in computers constitutes a threat to personal privacy.[220] The Court, in its 1989 decision *Justice Department v. Reporters Committee for Freedom of the Press*,[221] said that computerized information threatens individual privacy interests because "in today's society the computer can accumulate and store information that would otherwise surely have been forgotten."[222]

Three state courts have also suggested that data accumulated in computers constitute a threat to personal privacy. The Michigan Supreme Court said in *Kestenbaum v. Michigan State University* that "While it is true that the computer era brought untold benefits for society, it is also fraught with potential dangers to our notions of individual autonomy. Vigilance is necessary, lest the right of privacy atrophy due to lack of exercise.[223] The New Jersey Supreme Court in its 1995 decision in *Higg-A-Rella, Inc. v. County of Essex*[224] said that because computerized records can be searched and assembled in so many ways, they have the potential to be more revealing and intrusive than paper records. In 1988, the Massachusetts Court of Appeal stated in *Doe v. Registrar of Motor Vehicles*[225] that records amassed in one location are detrimental to citizens' privacy interests.

The courts should perhaps be applauded for their recognition of a potential social problem. However, the courts should not be rewriting access law. First, judges should not be legislating. Second, inhibiting access to electronic records because they are easier to search and manipulate is like forcing citizens to climb the stairs of public buildings even though elevators make them easier to get from one floor to another. Legislators also need to carefully consider efforts to deny the public the benefits of new information technology based on undocumented threats and problems. Compelling individual problems should trigger only narrow, appropriate solutions.

Until significant harm caused by access to electronic records is demonstrated, requesters should have access to the public records of their choice, in the formats of their choice, as long as an office is capable of providing them. Public information should be equally available whether stored on paper or in a computer. Advances in technology should be used to enhance access to public information, not to impede it.

Notes

[1]*See* Matthew Bunker et al., *Access to Government-Held Information in the Computer Age: Applying Legal Doctrine to Emerging Technology*, 20 Fla. St. U. L. Rev. 543, 594 (1993).

[2]Jack Kraft and David Washburn, *Public Records: Access Denied; Computer Data, Costly Hard to Get* [sic], The Morning Call (Allentown, Pa.) A1 (Feb. 19, 1995).

[3]*See*, e.g., Andrew A. Lipscomb, *The Writings of Thomas Jefferson* 33–35 (1905).

In a June 28, 1804 letter to Judge John Tyler, Thomas Jefferson extolled the value of giving the citizenry full access to the truth about their leaders: "No experiment can be more interesting than that we are now trying, and which we trust will end in establishing the fact, that man may be governed by reason and truth. Our first object should therefore be, to leave open to him all avenues to truth. . . . I hold it, therefore, certain, that to open the doors of truth, and to fortify the habit of testing everything by reason, are the most effectual manacles we can rivet on the hands of our successors to prevent their manacling the people with their own consent."

[4]Daniel N. Hoffman, *Governmental Secrecy and the Founding Fathers: A Study in Constitutional Controls* 11–39 (1981). The U.S. Supreme Court has found no constitutional right to access to government information. See, e.g., *Pell v. Procunier*, 417 U.S. 817 (1974).

[5]The 15 states that had enacted access statutes by the 1950s, according to one author, were California, 1949; Delaware, 1935; Idaho, 1941; Illinois (no enactment date reported); Kansas, 1949; Louisiana, 1940; Maryland, 1939; Massachusetts (no enactment date reported); Montana, 1947; New Jersey, 1947; North Carolina, 1943; Oregon (no enactment date reported); Tennessee, 1934; Texas, (no enactment date reported); and Utah, 1945. Harold Cross, *The People's Right to Know* 328–36 (1953).

[6]5 U.S.C. § 552 (1966).

[7]*Ala. Code* § 36–12–40, –41 (1996); *Alaska Stat.* § 09.25.100 (Michie 1993); *Ariz. Rev. Stat. Ann.* § 39–121 (West 1985); *Ark. Code Ann.* § 25–19–101 (Michie 1993); *Calif. Gov't Code* § 6250 (West 1994); *Colo. Rev. Stat.* § 24–72–201 (1996); *Conn. Gen. Stat.* § 1–15 (1993); *Del. Code Ann.* tit. 29, § 10001 (1991); *Fla. Stat.* ch. 119.011 (1997); *Ga. Code Ann.* § 50–18–70 (1996); *Hawaii Rev. Stat.* § 92F (1992); *Idaho Code* § 9–301 (1990); *Ill. Comp. Stat.* 5 /140 (West 1997); *Ind. Code* § 5–14–1 through 10 (1993); *Iowa Code* § 22.1 (1997); *Kan. Stat. Ann.* § 45–215 (1993); *Ky. Rev. Stat. Ann.* § 61.870 (Michie 1994); *La. Rev. Stat. Ann.* § 44:1 (West 1982); *Maine Rev. Stat. Ann.* tit. 1, § 401 (1993); *Md. Code Ann., State Gov't* § 10–611 (1993); *Mass. Gen. Laws Ann.* ch. 4, § 7 (West 1994); *Mich. Comp. Laws* § 15231 (1994); *Minn. Stat.* § 13.01 (1993); *Miss. Code Ann.* § 25–61–1 through 10 (1991); *Mo. Rev. Stat.* § 610.010 (1993); *Mont. Code Ann.* § 2–6–101 (1993); *Neb. Rev. Stat.* § 84–712.01 (1994); *Nev. Rev. Stat.* § 239.006 (1993); *N.H. Rev. Stat. Ann.* § 91A (1990); *N.J. Stat. Ann.* § 47:1A–1 (West 1994); *N.M. Stat. Ann.* § 14–2–1 (Michie 1994); *N.Y. Pub. Off. Law* § 84 (McKinney 1988); *N.C. Gen. Stat.* § 132 (1993); *N.D. Cent. Code* § 44–04–18 (1978); *Ohio Rev. Code Ann.* § 149.43 (Anderson 1993); *Okla. Stat.* tit. 51, § 24A (1991); *Ore. Rev. Stat.* § 192.410 (1993); *Pa. Const. Stat.* tit. 65, § 66.1 (West 1992); *R.I. Gen. Laws* § 38–2–1 (1990); *S.C. Code Ann.* § 30–4–10 (Law Co-Op. 1991); *S.D. Codified Laws* § 1–27–1 (Michie 1994); *Tenn. Code Ann.* § 10–7–503 (1996); *Texas Gov't Code Ann.* § 552.002 (West 1995); *Utah Code Ann.* § 63–2–103 (1993); *Vt. Stat. Ann.* tit. 1, § 315 (1985); *Va. Code Ann.* § 2.1–3–340 (Michie 1994); *Wash. Rev. Code* § 42.17.020 (1992); *W. Va. Code* § 29B–1–1 (1993); *Wis. Stat.* § 19.31 (1992); *Wyo. Stat. Ann.* § 16–4–201 (Michie 1982).

[8]At least 97 percent of state and local agencies used computers by 1985. See Kenneth L. Kraemer et al., *Trends in Municipal Information Systems 1975–1985*, 18 Baseline Data Report 2 (1986). All 50 states have websites and at least some computerized records. See National Newspaper Ass'n & the American Ct. and Commercial Newspapers Inc., *Government for Sale; The Electronic Access Project Report* 2 49–79 (September 1997).

The federal government, by 1994, had about 25,250 small computers (costing $10,000 to $100,000 each); 8,500 medium computers (costing 100,000 to $1 million each); and 890 large computers (costing more than $1 million each). See S. Rep. No. 104–272, at 8 (1996) (Senate report accompanying S. 1090, the Electronic Freedom of Information Improvement Act of 1995.)

[9]See *infra* text accompanying notes 13–26.

[10]Of course, the inclusion of a few of the criteria could be justified by both rationales. For example, the right of access to software protects requesters' ability to read and copy records as they could paper records. Access to software also makes access to computerized records meaningful in the sense that a requester can be given computerized records but not be able to use them without the appropriate software. Fee structures friendly to computerized access also satisfy both rationales.

[11]Jerry Berman, *The Right To Know: Public Access to Electronic Public Information*, 3 Software L.J. 491, 523–24 (1989); Matthew Bunker et al., *Access to Government-Held Information in the Computer Age: Applying Legal Doctrine to Emerging Technology*, 20 Fla. St. U. L. Rev. 543 (1993); Daniel F. Hunter, *Electronic Mail and Michigan's Public Disclosure Laws: The Argument for Public Access to Governmental Electronic Mail*, 28 U. Mich. J.L. Reform 977 (1995); Elliot Jaspin and Mark Sabelman, *News Media Access to Computer Records: Updating Information Laws in the Electronic Age*, 36 St. Louis U. L .J. 349 (1991); Henry H. Perritt Jr., *Law and the Information Superhighway* 498–99 (1996); Barbara A. Petersen and Charlie Roberts, *Access to Electronic Public Records*, 22 Fla. St. U. L. Rev. 443 (1994); Joint Legis. Info. Tech. Resource Comm., *Electronic Records Access: Problems and Issues* 34 (1994); Sandra Sanders, *Note: Arizona's Public Records Laws and the Technology Age: Applying "Paper" Laws to Computer Records*, 37 Ariz. L. Rev. 931 (1995); and Sandra Davidson Scott, *Suggestions for a Model Statute for Access to Computerized Government Records*, 2 Wm. and Mary Bill of Rights J. 29 (1993).

[12] 5 U.S.C. § 552 (1996).

[13]*Fla. Stat.* ch. 119.011 (1) (1995). In addition, a Florida appellate court in *Seigle v. Barry* said that a records request may not be denied because the record is stored on a computer. 422 So. 2d 63 (1982).

[14]*Ga. Code Ann.* § 50–18–70(a) (1996).

[15]*Hawaii Rev. Stat.* § 92 FB3 (1992).

[16]*Ill. Comp. Stat.* tit. 5, § 140/2 (c) (West 1997).

[17]*Maine Rev. Stat. Ann.* tit.1, § 402(3) (West 1993).

[18]*Md. Code Ann., State Gov't* § 10B611 (f) (1) (ii) (1993).

[19]*Mich. Comp. Laws* § 4.1801 (2) (1997).

[20]Mo. *Rev. Stat.* § 610.026 (2) (6) (1993). See also *Deaton v. Kidd*, 932 Mo. S.W.2d 804 (Ct. App. 1996).

[21]*N.Y. Pub. Off. Law* § 86 (4) (McKinney 1988).

[22]*N.C. Gen. Stat.* § 132–6 (a) (1993).

[23]*Texas Gov't Code Ann.* § 552.002 (c) (West 1995). See also Tex. Att'y Gen. ORD-352 (1982), which states that computer tapes are public records.

[24]*Vt. Stat. Ann.* tit.1, § 316 (h) (1985).

[25]*Va. Code Ann.* § 2.1B342 (A) (4) (Michie 1994).

[26]*Wis. Stat.* § 19.32 (2) (1992).

[27]*Calif. Gov't Code* § 6252 (d, e) (West 1994); *Del. Code Ann.* tit. 29, § 10002 (d) (1991); *Idaho Code* § 9–337 (1990); *Kan. Stat. Ann.* § 45–217 (f) (1) (1994); *Ky. Rev. Stat. Ann.* § 61.870 (1) (h) (Michie 1994); *La. Rev. Stat. Ann.* § 44:1 (West 1982); *Mass. Gen. Laws Ann.* ch.4, § 7, cl. 26 (1998); *Minn. Stat.* § 13.02, subd.7 (1993); *Miss. Code Ann.* § 25–61–3 (b) (1991); *Neb. Rev. Stat.* § 84–712.01 (1) (1997); *N.M. Stat. Ann.* § 14–2–6 (E) (Michie 1988); *Ohio Rev. Code Ann.* § 149.43 (A) (B) (Anderson 1993); *Okla. Stat.* tit. 51, § 24 A.3 (1996); *Ore. Rev. Stat.* § 192.410 (4) (1993); *R.I. Gen. Laws* § 38–1–1.1 (c) (1990); *S.C. Code Ann.* § 30–4–20 (c) (Law Co-Op. 1991); *Tenn. Code Ann.* § 10–7–301 (6) (1995); *Utah Code Ann.* § 63–2–103 (18) (a) (1993); *Wash. Rev. Code* § 42.17.020 (36) (1992); *W. Va. Code* § 29.B–1–2 (5) (1993); and *Wyo. Stat. Ann.* § 16–4–201 (a) (v) (Michie 1982).

[28]*Conn. Gen. Stat.* § 1–18a (d) (1993).

[29]*Iowa Code* § 22.2 (1) (1997).

[30]*Ind. Code* § 5–14–3–2 (1993).

[31]See, e.g, *Ohio ex rel. Beacon Journal Publ'g Co. v. Andrews*, 358 Ohio N.E.2d 565 (1976).

[32]*Ala. Code* § 41–13–1 (1996).

[33]*Alaska Stat.* § 09.25.222 (3) (Michie 1993).

[34]*Ariz. Rev. Stat. Ann.* § 39.121.01.A.2 (West 1985).

[35]*Ark. Code Ann.* § 25–19–103 (1) (Michie 1993).

[36]*Colo. Rev. Stat.* § 29–1–902 (1996).

[37]*Mont.Code Ann.* § 2–6–101 (3) (1993).

[38]*Nev. Rev. Stat.* § 239.006 (1993).

[39]*N.H. Rev. Stat. Ann.* § 91–A:4 (1990).

[40]*N.J. Stat. Ann.* § 47:1A–2 (West 1994).

[41]*N.D. Cent. Code* § 44–04–18 (1978).

[42]*Pa. Const. Stat.* tit. 65, § 66.1 (West 1997).

[43]*S.D. Codified Laws* § 1–27–1 (Michie 1994).

[44]*Higg-A-Rella, Inc. v. County of Essex*, 660 N.J. A.2d 1163 (1995).

[45]311 N.H. A.2d 116 (1973).

[46]*Id.* at 117.

[47]Records custodians decide if access is necessary to the records requester. *Ala. Code* § 41–9–620 (1991).

[48]*Id.*

49*Miss. Code Ann.* § 2–61–2 (1991).

50*Hawaii Rev. Stat.* § 92F (1992).

51The court held in *Star Publishing Co. v. Pima County Attorney's Office*, 891 P.2d 899 (Ct. App. 1994), that e-mail could be considered a public record.

52*Colo. Rev. Stat.* § 24–72–204.5 (1996).

53 Op. Att§y Gen. Fla. 96 34 (May 15, 1996) states that e-mail is a public record.

54The attorney general made the determination in Maryland that e-mail is subject to public disclosure. Op. Att'y Gen. 96–016 (May 22, 1996).

55327 Mich. N.W.2d 783 (1982). See also *Mullin v. City of Detroit Police Dept.* 348 Mich. N.W.2d 708 (Ct. App. 1984).

56327 N.W.2d at 789.

57Concern for the impact of computers on privacy mentioned in the 1982 Kestenbaum decision was echoed in the U.S. Supreme Court's 1989 opinion in *Justice Dept. v. Reporters Comm. for Freedom of the Press.* In *Reporters Committee*, the Court said that a compilation in a computer database of criminal records publicly available in file cabinets in different law enforcement offices "could reasonably be expected to constitute a clearly unwarranted invasion of personal privacy" under exemption 7(c) of the federal Freedom of Information Act. However, the Court§s holding emphasized that any "third party's request for law-enforcement records or information about a private citizen can reasonably be expected to invade that citizen's privacy, and that when the request seeks no 'official information' about a government agency, but merely records that the Government happens to be storing, the invasion of privacy is §unwarranted.'" 489 U.S. 749, 781 (1989)

58528 Mass. N.E.2d 880 (App. Ct. 1988), *remanded for a second time,* 543 N.E.2d 432 (Mass. App. Ct. 1988).

59528 N.E.2d at 886.

60"When an individual's street address and make and year of automobile are known, much may be gleaned concerning his or her financial condition. If age is also factored in, such a person, particularly one of advanced years, may become the target of those who would like to share in his or her wealth." *Id.*

61660 N.J. A.2d 1163 (1995).

62660 A.3d at 1172.

63*Id.* In *Higg-A-Rella*, a private company that sold municipal tax assessment data to real estate brokers, attorneys and appraisers, was trying to buy copies of Essex County's computerized tax assessment records, which the county provided in paper form. The court said that the release of computer tapes "could trigger a high interest in confidentiality" even if the same information was available in paper form. For example, the court said, doctors could search computerized medical malpractice claims in order to avoid treating patients with a record of suing physicians.

64Some other states are blocking access to GIS systems, including Alaska, *Alaska Stat.* § 09.25.220 (1998); Arkansas, *Ark. Stat. Ann.* § 15–21–301

(1997); and Indiana, *Ind. Code Ann.* § 5–14–3–2 (Burns 1998). In Iowa, records custodians can determine the terms and conditions of access to geographic computer databases: *Iowa Code* § 22.3 (1997).

[65]This section is separate from the section discussing a requirement of access to nonconfidential data because the requirement for access-friendly computer and software can effect ease of access in other ways as well. In addition, issues of required access and the mechanical ability to segregate confidential from nonconfidential data are different issues.

[66]*Ark. Code Ann.* § 25–4–110 (d) (6) (iii) (Michie 1997).

[67]*Calif. Gov't Code* § 1713 (West 1997).

[68]*Fla. Stat.* ch. 119.01 (3) (1995).

[69]*Ind. Code* § 5–21–6–4 (1998).

[70]*Iowa Code* § 22.3A (2) (1997).

[71]*Miss. Code Ann.* § 25–61–110 (3) (1997).

[72]*Mo. Rev. Stat.* § 610.029 (1) (1997).

[73]*Neb. Rev. Stat.* § 84–1204 (1) (b) (1997).

[74]*N.C. Gen. Stat.* § 132–6.1 (1997).

[75]*Wash. Rev. Code* § 43.105–270 (1997).

[76]". . . no public agency shall purchase, lease, create, or otherwise acquire any electronic data-processing system for the storage, manipulation, or retrieval of public records unless it first determines that the system will not impair or impede the agency's ability to permit the public inspection and examination, and to provide electronic copies of such records." *N.C. Gen. Stat.* § 132.6.1 (a) (1997).

[77]*Calif. Gov't Code* § 713 (a) (West 1997).

[78]*Calif. Gov't Code* § 11713 (b) (West 1997).

[79]*Calif. Gov't Code* § 11713 (c, d) (West 1997).

[80]For example, the statute requires agencies to determine the information the public wants and needs the most, and it requires agencies to develop methods to distribute information efficiently by electronic means. *Wash. Rev. Code* § 43.105.270 (2) (c) (1997).

[81]*Wash. Rev. Code* § 43.105.270 (2) (c) (1997).

[82]Generally software is accessible to the public in accordance with Florida's broad definition of public records. *Fla. Stat.* ch. 119.011 (1) (1995). However, software that is developed and copyrighted by a public agency is not a public record. Agencies may sell or license this software and establish license fees for use. *Fla. Stat.* ch. 119.083 (2) (1995).

[83]*Maine Rev. Stat. Ann.* tit. 1, § 402 (3) (West 1993).

[84]Software is a public record unless it is "sensitive" or subject to a licensing agreement making it exempt from disclosure. *Miss. Code Ann.* § 25–61–9(6) and § 25–61–3 (c), (d) (1997).

[85]Op. Att'y Gen. No. 76–79 (Aug. 17, 1970).

[86]Alabama, Arizona, Connecticut, Delaware, Illinois, Iowa, Louisiana, Maryland, Massachusetts, Minnesota, Montana, Nebraska, New Hampshire, New Jersey, New York, North Carolina, North Dakota, Pennsylvania, Rhode Island, South Carolina, South Dakota, Tennessee, Vermont, Washington, West Virginia and Wyoming.

87*Alaska Stat.* § 09.25.220 (3) (Michie 1993).

88*Ark. Code Ann.* § 25–19–103 (1) (Michie 1993).

89*Calif. Gov't Code* § 6254.9 (West 1994).

90*Colo. Rev. Stat.* § 24–72–202 (7) (1996).

91*Ga. Code Ann.* § 50–18–72 (f) (1996).

92*Hawaii Rev. Stat.* § 92F–12 (a) (1)–(16) (Supp. 1991).

93*Idaho Code* § 9–340 (16) (1990).

94*Kan. Stat. Ann.* § 45–221 (a) (16) (1994).

95*Ky. Rev. Stat. Ann.* § 61.870 (2) (Michie 1994).

96*Mich. Comp. Laws* § 4.1801 (2) (1997).

97*Mo. Rev. Stat.* § 610.021 (10) (1993).

98*N.M. Stat. Ann.* § 14–3–15.1 and § 14–2–1 (F) (Michie 1998).

99*Okla. Stat.* tit. 51, § 24 A.S.3 (1996).

100*Utah Code Ann.* § 63–2–103 (18) (b) (iv) (Supp. 1996).

101*Va. Code Ann.* § 2.1–342 (B) (23) (Michie 1994).

102*Ohio ex rel. Recodat v. Buchanan,* 546 N.E.2d 203 (1989). See also *Ohio ex rel. Margolius v. City of Cleveland,* 584 Ohio N.E.2d 665 (1992).

103Op. Att'y Gen. No. 89–1 (Feb. 6, 1989).

104Texas Att'y Gen. ORD-581 (1990) and Texas Att§y Gen. ORD-505 (1988).

105*Ind. Code* § 5–14–3–4 (h) (11) (1998).

106*Ore. Rev. Stat.* § 192.501(15) (1993).

107Remarks by Dan Keating (research and technology editor for *The Miami Herald*), Florida Sunshine Summit, University of Florida, Gainesville, Fla., Oct. 17, 1997.

108*Alaska Stat.* § 09.25.120 (c) (Michie 1993); *Ariz. Rev. Stat. Ann.* § 39–121 (West 1991); Op. Att'y Gen. Nos. 95–031 (April 11, 1995), 94–282 (1994); *Calif. Gov't Code* § 6257 (Deering 1998); *Colo. Rev. Stat.* § 24–72–205 (4) (1996); *Fla. Stat.* ch. 19.071(a) (1995); *Idaho Code* § 9–338 (1997); *Ill. Comp. Stat.* tit. 5, § 140/6 (a) (West 1997); *Kan. Stat. Ann.* § 45–219 (c) (2) (1994); *Ky. Rev. Stat. Ann.* § 61.874 (3) (Michie 1994); *Maine Rev. Stat. Ann.* tit. 1, § 408 (West 1993); *Md. Code Ann, State Gov't* § 10–621 (1997); *Mass. Gen. Laws Ann.* ch.950, § 32.06 (1) (d) (West 1998); *Mich. Comp. Laws* § 15.234 (1) (1998); *Miss. Code Ann.* § 25–61–7 (1997); *Mo. Rev. Stat.* § 610.026.1 (2) (1993); *Mont. Code Ann.* § 2–6–110 (c) (1993); *Neb. Rev. Stat.* § 84–712.01 (1997); *N.H. Rev. Stat. Ann.* § 654:31 (1990); *N.Y. Pub. Off. Law* § 87 (1) (b) (McKinney 1988); *N.C. Gen. Stat.* § 282.303 (9) (1995); *N.D. Cent. Code* 44–04–18 (1998); *Ohio Rev. Code Ann.* §149.3 (Anderson 1996); *Ore. Rev. Stat.* § 192.444 (2)–(5) (1993); *S.C. Code Ann.* § 30–4–30 (b) (Law Co-Op. 1991); *Texas, Gov't Code Ann.* § 552.261 (West 1995); *Utah Code Ann.* § 63–2–203 (2) (c) (Supp. 1996); *Vt. Stat. Ann.* tit. 1, § 316(b) (1985); *Va. Code Ann.* § 2.1–342 (B) (4) (Michie 1994); *Wash. Rev. Code* § 42.17.300 (1992); *W. Va. Code* § 29B–1–3 (5) (1993); and *Wis. Stat.* § 19.35 (3) (1992).

Ga. Code Ann. § 50–18–71 (f) (1996) provides that agencies may charge the "actual cost of a computer disk or tape onto which the information is transferred and may charge for the administrative time involved," but the

Georgia Court of Appeals has ruled that court clerks are authorized by *Ga. Code Ann.* § 15–6–96 (1996) in at least one situation to charge a rate for records that will yield a profit. *Powell v. VonCanon,* 467 S.E.2d 193 (1996). See also *Grebner v. Clinton Charter Township,* 550 Mich. N.W.2d 265 (App. Ct. 1996).

[109] *Colo. Rev. Stat.* § 24–72–205 (4) (1996); *Neb. Rev. Stat.* § 84–712.01 (1997); *Texas Gov't Code Ann.* § 552.261 (West 1995); and *Utah Code Ann.* § 63–2–203(2)(c) (Supp. 1996).

[110] *Conn. Gen. Stat.* § 1–15 (1997); *Fla. Stat.* ch. 119.07 (1) (b) (1995); *N.C. Gen. Stat.* § 132–6.2 (a) (1995).

[111] *Fla. Stat.* ch. 119.07 (1) (b) (1995).

[112] *N.C. Gen. Stat.* § 282.303 (9) (1995).

[113] The fee schedule is as follows: 75 cents for each page up to 10 pages, 50 cents per page from 11 pages to 20 pages, 25 cents per page for more than 20 pages of copies. *N.J. Stat. Ann.* § 47:1A12 (West 1994).

[114] 660 A.2d 1163, 1181–83 (N.J. 1995).

[115] 660 A.2d at 1172–73.

[116] *R.I. Gen. Laws* § 38–2–4 (1998).

[117] *Tenn. Code Ann.* § 8–21–408 (1997).

[118] *Minn. Stat.* § 13.03, subd. 3 (1993).

[119] Nevada, Op. Att'y Gen. No. 94–6 (April 7, 1994).

[120] *N.M. Stat. Ann.* § 14–3–15.1 (A) (Michie 1998).

[121] *Wyo. Stat. Ann.* § 16–4–204 (1998).

[122] *Del. Code Ann.* tit. 29, § 10003 (a) (1991).

[123] *Ind. Code* § 5–14–3–8 (h) (1993).

[124] *Iowa Code* § 22.2 (3) (1997).

[125] Kentucky's code that allows custodians to determine reasonable fees is for determining fees for records requested for commercial use. *Ky. Rev. Stat. Ann.* § 61.874 (4) (a) (Michie 1994).

[126] *La. Rev. Stat. Ann.* § 44:32 (C) (West 1982).

[127] *Neb. Rev. Stat.* § 84–1205.02 (1998).

[128] *Okla. Stat.* tit. 51, § 24A.5.3 (1996).

[129] *Pa. Const. Stat.* tit. 65, § 66.3 (1992).

[130] Op. Att'y Gen. No. 79–6 (1979).

[131] *Neb. Rev. Stat.* § 84–712.01 (1997).

[132] *Id.*

[133] *Ariz. Rev. Stat. Ann.* § 39–121 (West 1985); Arkansas, Op. Att'y Gen. Nos. 95–262 (1995), 93–106 (1993), 92–132 (1992); *Calif. Gov't Code* § 6257 (Deering 1997); *Sargent School Dist. No. RE-33J v. Western Services Inc.* 751 Colo. P.2d 56, 61 (1988); *Town of Trumbull v. FOIC,* 5 Conn. L. Trib. No. 34 (Conn. 1979); Delaware, Op. Att§y Gen. No. 88–1028 (Dec. 2, 1988); *Fla. Stat.* ch. 119.07 (2) (a) (1995); *Ga. Code Ann.* § 50–18–72 (g) (1996); *Hawaii Rev. Stat.* § 92F–42 (13) (Supp. 1991); *Idaho Code* § 9–341(1990); *Ill. Comp. Stat.* tit. 5, § 140/8 (West 1997); *Ind. Code* § 5–14–3–6 (1993); *Iowa Code* § 246.602 (2) (1) (1997); *Kan. Stat. Ann.* § 45–221(d) (1994); *Ky. Rev. Stat. Ann.* § 61.878 (4) (Michie 1994); *La. Rev. Stat. Ann.* § 44:32B; 33A (l) (West 1982); *Maine Rev. Stat. Ann.*

tit.1, § 975-A (West 1993); *Md. Code Ann., State Gov't* § 10–614 (b) (3) (iii) (1993); *Mass. Gen. Laws Ann.* ch. 66, § 10 (a) (West 1998); *Minn. Stat.* § 13.03, subd. 3 (1993); *Miss. Code Ann.* § 25–61–9 (2) (Supp. 1996); Montana, 42 Op. Att§y Gen. 119 (1988); *Neb. Rev. Stat.* § 84–712.06 (1998); *Southern N.J. Newspaper, Inc. v. Township of Mt. Laurel,* 141 N.J. 56, 77, 660 A.2d 1173 (1995); *N.M. Stat. Ann.* § 14–2–9 (A) (1998); *N.Y. Pub. Off. Law* § 87 (2)(McKinney 1988), *N.C. Gen. Stat.* § 132–6 (c) (1993); North Dakota, Op. Att'y Gen. (Jan. 26, 1979); *Okla. Stat.* tit, 51, § 24A 5 2 (1996); *Ore. Rev. Stat.* § 192.505 (1993); *Times Publ'g Co., v. Michel,* 633 Pa. A.2d 1233, 1239 (Commw. Ct. 1993), *appeal denied,* 645 Pa. A.2d 1321 (1994); *R.I. Gen. Laws* § 38–2–2 (d) (1990); *S.C. Code Ann.* § 30–4–40 (b) (Law Co-Op. 1991); *Utah Code Ann.* § 63–2–307 (1993); *Douglas v. Windham Super. Ct.,* 597 Vt. A.2d 774 (1991); *Va. Code Ann.* § 2.1–342 (A) (3) (Michie 1994); *Wash. Rev. Code* § 42.17.310 (2) (1994); *Child Protection Group v. Cline,* 350 W. Va. S.E.2d 545 (1986); *Wis. Stat.* § 19.36 (6) (1992); *Sheridan Newspapers, Inc. v. City of Sheridan,* 660 Wyo. P.2d 797 (1983).

134*Mich. Comp. Laws* § 15.244 (2) (1994).

135*Id.*

136*Alaska Stat.* § 96.330 (b) (c) (Michie 1993).

137*Ohio ex rel. Beacon Journal Publ'g Co. v. Andrews,* 358 Ohio N.E.2d 565 (1976).

138*Bird v. Mitchell* (Cause No. 92–2786, 68th Dist. Ct. of Dallas County, July 14, 1993).

139*Seigle v. Barry,* 422 So. 2d 63 (4th DCA 1982).

140*Id.* at 63–64.

141*Id.* at 68.

142*Colo. Rev. Stat.* § 24–72–205 (3) (1996).

143*Minn. Stat.* § 13.03, subd. 3 (1993).

144*Mo. Rev. Stat.* § 610.029 (1993). Missouri's statute enables requesters to ask for customized searches, but does not require that the records custodians conduct them.

145*Mont. Code Ann* § 2–6–110 (c) (1993).

146*N.H. Rev. Stat. Ann.* § 91–A:4 (1990).

147*Ore. Rev. Stat.* § 192.440 (2) (1993).

148*R.I. Gen. Laws* § 38–2–3 (e) (1990).

149*S.C. Code Ann.* § 30–4–30 (b) (Law Co-Op. 1991).

150*Va. Code Ann.* § 2.1–342 (Michie 1994).

151*Ore. Rev. Stat.* § 192.440 (2) (1997).

152*Id.*

153*Alaska Stat.* § 29.25.220 (1) (A)–(G) (Michie 1993). Records custodians are not required to create a record that does not already exist.

154*Calif. Gov't Code* § 6252 (d) (West 1994). Records custodians are only required to provide access to records that already exist.

155*Hawaii Rev. Stat.* § 92F–11 (c) (Supp. 1991).

156*Ind. Code* § 5–14–3–6 (d) (1993). A records custodian is not required to augment computer access.

157Op. Att'y Gen. 93-ORD-118 (1993). A records custodian is not required to create a database that does not already exist.

158*Md. Code Ann., State Gov't* § 10–621 (1997). A records custodian is not required to "reprogram [an agency§s] computers or aggregate computerized data" to fulfill a request.

159*N.M. Stat. Ann.* § 14–2–8 (B) (1994). A records custodian is not required to create a record that does not already exist.

160*N.Y. Pub. Off. Law* § 89 (3). A records custodian is not required to prepare a record the agency does not already keep.

161*N.C. Gen. Stat.* § 132–6.2 (e) (1997). A records custodian is not required to "respond to a request for a copy of a public record by creating or compiling a record that does not exist."

162*Wis. Stat.* § 19.35 (1) (L) (1992). A records custodian is not required "to create a new record by extracting information from existing records and compiling the information in a new format."

163New Jersey's public records statute does not contain a provision allowing customized searches, but a 1996 state supreme court opinion held that the Newark Board of Education had a common law right to the selective copying of a database maintained by the State Health Benefits Plan. *Board of Educ. v. New Jersey Dep't of Treasury,* 678 N.J. A.2d 660 (1996). Illinois courts have also required government agencies to customize searches under certain conditions. See *Hammer v. Lentz,* 525 Ill. N.E.2d 1045 (App. Ct. 1988); *Bowie v. Evanston Community Consolidated School Dist.,* 538 Ill. N.E.2d 557 (1989); and *Family Life League v. Dept. of Public Aid,* 493 Ill. N.E. 2d 1054 (1986).

164But see *Southern N.J. Newspapers, Inc. v. Township of Mt. Laurel,* 660 A. 2d (1995) (court said that public agencies are not required "to produce new information").

165*Seigle v. Barry,* 442 So. 2d 63 (4th DCA 1982).

166The Georgia Supreme Court has held that records custodians are not required to create new programs. *Jersawitz v. Hicks,* 448 S.E.2d 352 (1994).

167In *Nungesser v. Brown,* 667 So. 2d 1036, *rehearing denied,* 671 La. So. 2d 929 (1996), the court held that agencies are not required to create a document that does not already exist.

168A custodian is not required to compile information to create a new document, according to *Ohio ex rel. Scanlon v. Deters,* 544 Ohio N.E.2d 680 (1989).

169Op. Att'y Gen. Nos. 96–044 (March 13, 1996), 95–220 (Oct. 10, 1995), 94–170 (May 31, 1994) and 92–132 (May 15, 1992).

170Op. Att'y Gen. No. 88–00079 (Dec. 16, 1987).

171A "public agency should not be permitted to require the public to exhaust massive amounts of time and resources in order to replicate the value added to the public records through the creation and storage on tape of a database containing such records. *Ohio ex rel. Margolius v. Cleveland,* 584 Ohio N.E.2d 665, 669 (1992).

172*Colo. Rev. Stat.* § 24–72–203 (1) (b) (1996).

[173]*Conn. Gen. Stat.* § 1–18a(d) (1993).

[174]*Fla. Stat.* ch. 119.083 (5) (1995).

[175]*Ind. Code* § 5–14–3–2 (1993).

[176] *Kan. Stat. Ann.* § 45–501 (1994).

[177]*Mass. Gen. Laws Ann.* ch. 26, § 7 (West 1998).

[178]*Miss. Code Ann.* § 25–61–10 (2) (Supp. 1996).

[179]*Mont. Code Ann.* § 2–6–101 (2) (1993).

[180]*N.M. Stat. Ann.* § 14–3–15.1 (1994).

[181]*N.C. Gen. Stat.* § 132.6.2 (1997).

[182]*Ore. Rev. Stat.* § 192.440 (2) (1993).

[183]*S.C. Code Ann.* § 30–4–30 (b) (Law Co-Op. 1991).

[184]*Texas Gov't Code Ann.* § 552.228 (b) (West 1995).

[185]*Utah Code Ann.* § 63–2–201 (8) (b) (1993).

[186]*Vt. Stat. Ann.* tit. 1, § 316 (i) (1985).

[187]*W. Va. Code* § 29 B–1–3 (3) (1993).

[188]Arkansas, Op. Att'y Gen. No. 95–031 (April 11, 1995); Hawaii, OIP Op. Ltr. No. 90–35, at 3 (Dec. 17, 1990).

[189]*American Fed'n of State, County & Mun. Employees v. County of Cook,* 555 Ill. N.E.2d 361 (1990); *Farrell v. City of Detroit,* 530 Mich. N.W.2d 105 (Ct. App. 1995); *Menge v. City of Manchester,* 311 N.H. A.2d 116 (1973); *Ohio ex rel. Margolius v. City of Cleveland,* 584 Ohio N.E.2d 665 (1992).

[190]*Menge v. City of Manchester,* 311 N.H. A.2d 116 (1973).

[191]*Maine Rev. Stat. Ann.* tit.1, § 408 (West 1993).

[192]*Mo. Rev. Stat.* § 610.029.1 (1993).

[193]*Alaska Stat.* §09.25.220 (1) (A) (Michie 1993).

[194]*N.J. Stat. Ann,* § 47;1A–2.1 (West 1998).

[195]*N.D. Cent. Code* §55–44.2–208 (1995).

[196]*Va. Code Ann.* § 2.1–342 (Michie 1994).

[197]*Calif. Gov't Code* § 6256 (West 1994).

[198]*Ky. Rev. Stat.* Ann. § 61.874 (2) (a) (Michie 1994).

[199]*Md. Code Ann., State Gov't* § 10–621 (1997).

[200]*Okla. Stat.* tit. 51, § 24A.5.3 (1996).

[201]Op. Att'y Gen. No. 88–00079, at 5 (Dec.16, 1987).

[202]*Wis. Stat.* § 19.35 (1) (e) (1992).

[203]Bunker et al., *Access to Government-Held Information in the Computer Age.*

[204]*N.C. Gen. Stat.* § 132–6.1(1997).

[205]*N.C. Gen. Stat.* § 132–6.1 (b) (1997).

[206]*Calif. Gov't Code* § 12184 (Deering 1997).

[207]*Texas Gov't Code* § 194.0065 (1988).

[208]*Ark. Code Ann.* § 25–27–104 (Michie 1997).

[209]*Calif. Gov't Code* § 11713 (c), (d) (West 1997).

[210]*Neb. Rev. Stat.* § 84–1204 (1) (b) (1997).

[211]*Wash. Rev. Code* § 43.105.270 (1997).

[212] *Wash. Rev. Code* § 43.105.270 (2) (1997).

[213]*Alaska Stat.* § 09.25.220 (C) (Michie 1993).

[214]*Colo. Rev. Stat.* § 24–72–203 (10) (b) (ll) (1997).

[215]*Fla. Stat.* ch. 119.01 (2) (1997).

[216]*Ind. Code* § 5–21–6–4 (4) (1998).

[217]*Ky. Rev. Stat. Ann.* § 61.874 (6) (Michie 1996).

[218]*Alaska Stat.* § 09.25.115 (f) (Michie 1997).

[219]*Colo. Rev. Stat.* § 24–72–203 (1) (b) (ll) (1997).

[220]429 U.S. 589, 650 (1977).

[221]489 U.S 749 (U.S. 1989).

[222]*Id.* at 1555.

[223]327 N.W.2d 783, 789 (1982).

[224] 60 A.2d 1163 (N.J. 1995).

[225]26 Mass. App. Ct. 415, 528 N.E.2d 880 (App. Ct. 1988), *remanded for a second time,* 27 Mass. App. Ct. 1192, 543 N.E.2d 432 (App. Ct. 1988).

3

Access and New Media Technology: Teleconferencing, Telecommuting and Public Access

Susan Dente Ross

The rise of the personal computer has transformed not only the process of government record keeping, but also the nature of governmental meetings. The smoke-filled room of yesteryear has given way to the "virtual" meeting room of cyberspace, where public officials bent on secrecy find a variety of high-tech tools to engage in the modern equivalent of an executive session. The use of advanced telecommunications devices is raising novel access issues addressed by the chapter below, which traces the use of electronic mail, teleconferencing and other media to conduct what is still the public's business. As in other areas where public access and technology collide, the courts are being asked to defend the public's right to attend public meetings—in person or via computer. The greatest challenge is to convince public officials that such technology should enhance—not hinder—access to government. Participatory democracy has its critics, who assail the ease with which the uninformed electorate can participate in civic life with little more than a click of a mouse. Beyond the hue and cry of such critics, however, lies the

> *inescapable fact that public meetings must not be closed merely be-*
> *cause they take the form of electronic meetings. The debate over*
> *teleconferencing provides a timely example of the emerging chal-*
> *lenges wrought by the Information Age.*

Citizens today have unprecedented access to classrooms and court-rooms, city halls and council chambers, that increasingly post their records and broadcast their proceedings on the Internet. Telecon-ferencing and videoconferencing allow government agencies from North Carolina to Alaska to "convene" groups across geographic di-vides and save time and money. Telecommuting, while relatively rare, promises to reduce traffic as it improves the quality of life of govern-ment workers.

But increased governmental reliance on the growing array of new media technologies offers both the greatest promise—and the greatest threat—to public access to government. In recent years governmental use of fax transmissions, e-mail, video- and teleconferencing and the Internet has raised concerns about violations of state open meeting laws.[1] E-mail has come under scrutiny by public watchdogs, "who question whether computer messaging among council members marks a return to decisions behind closed doors."[2] One journalist ar-gues that the "personal computer, keyboard and modem" are the con-temporary equivalent of the "smoke-filled rooms where politicians once traded favors for votes."[3]

Issues surrounding use of new media technologies by government are neither clear nor simple. Twenty- or 30-year-old state open meet-ing laws have not kept pace with rapidly changing technology and fail to address directly whether or when the electronic exchange of infor-mation among members of government boards creates a "meeting" to which citizens must have access. Is a board "meeting" when its mem-bers exchange e-mail or discuss business in an electronic chat room? If so, is the board legally required to provide public computers to en-able citizen access to such meetings? Or may a board meet legal re-quirements by opening the chat room to the public and providing a public e-mail box for citizens who are already on line? Does text-only access violate the rights of illiterate citizens, the blind or citizens with weak English-language skills to participate in government? Do open meeting laws require the public to be able to see and hear delibera-tions of a government agency convened at a specific time and in a spe-cific place? If so, can a board member telecommute to such a meeting?

Open meetings statutes often fail to answer such questions be-cause they do not address new media technologies that enable gov-ernment agencies to conduct business through virtual meetings.[4] As a result, citizens, journalists and elected officials across the country are struggling to reshape statutes to ensure that new media technologies improve, rather than impede, freedom of information. In the meantime, some governmental bodies spurn virtual meetings as cumbersome, costly, unnecessary and inequitable. Others apparently see technology as the latest means to evade public involvement and deliberation.

Government secrecy is not new. Government officials long have evaded public scrutiny of their actions by conducting business in back rooms, on putting greens, at social gatherings and through letters, telephone calls and teleconferences. But new media technologies provide new opportunities for access—and evasion. Systems can be designed to enhance secrecy or promote participation; officials can be trained to view public involvement as a hindrance or as a vital part of the democratic process; and open meeting laws can ignore the impact of new media technology or can be drafted to promote the right of citizens to know about their government.

This chapter presents a summary and analysis of the intricacies of statutes, court rulings and advisory legal opinions in the 50 states and the District of Columbia to determine how the different states legally enable or constrain the conduct of public business through new media technologies. The intent is to answer the following question: To what extent do state laws designed to assure open government enable new media technologies "to extend—or impede—democracy's reach?"5

Following a brief introduction to open government legislation and a section on the impact of new media technologies on society, the chapter outlines the relevant statutory provisions and their legal interpretations. The discussion is divided between those statutes that expressly permit or prohibit the use of new media technologies and the substantial number of state statutes that say nothing on the topic. The chapter concludes with recommendations for model statutory provisions.

Open Government

For nearly three decades, all 50 states and the District of Columbia have required that government bodies conduct their business in public.6 States adopted open government laws because public participation is the cornerstone of the American system of government, and neither the Constitution nor common law protects a broad public right of access to government.7   State laws reflect an understanding that open government serves the public interest in self-governance and "serve[s] as both a light and disinfectant in exposing potential abuse and misuse of power. The deliberation of public policy in the public forum is an important check and balance" on government abuse.[8]

Many state open meeting laws overtly state their purpose. For example, the Kansas statute says "a representative government is dependent upon an informed electorate, [and therefore] it is declared to be the policy of this state that meetings for the conduct of governmental affairs and the transaction of governmental business be open to the public."[9] Washington State's Open Public Meetings Act declares: "The people, in delegating authority, do not give their public servants the right to decide what is good for the people to know and what is not good for them to know. The people insist on remaining informed. . . ."[10]

But statutes differ widely on the specific means adopted to protect government openness.[11] Some offer only a brief general statement of policy and intent.[12] Others comprise scores of distinct acts detailing the rules and policies for enumerated public bodies.[13] Some states detail whether and how new media technologies may be used to conduct public business. Others provide little or no indication of the state's policy on virtual meetings and leave determinations of their legality to attorneys general and the courts. Such variations muddy the already murky determination of new media technologies' effects upon society and government.

Participatory Democracy

New media technologies have changed both the pace and the means of the communication that binds our society and facilitates involvement in government. Sociologists say the information revolution "began to [trans]form global society in the mid-1950s, increased individual disillusionment, and broke down citizen participation in government."[14] Rapid proliferation of information and elimination of common public spaces for deliberation contributed to social disintegration.[15] The move from physical to commercially mediated communities weakened the ties binding American communities and fragmented society.[16] Virtual computer-mediated communities require a mass psychological reconception of self and society.[17]

As social and economic forces eroded the tendency of citizens to seek involvement in government, increased government use of new media technologies created barriers to citizen participation.[18] Communities across the nation moved to electronically link their internal operations and to offer public services through voice mail, interactive audio and video systems, electronic bulletin boards, electronic mail systems, web pages, Gopher servers and more.[19] However, the technologies that enabled government to reach across geographic barriers excluded neighbors who lacked the wherewithal to connect to the information superhighway.[20]

Moreover, there are "serious political problems in how to structure new media in the best interest of participatory democracy."[21] Unless designed with citizen input in mind, new media technologies may undermine—not improve—citizen involvement, government accountability and community building. Today, most government systems are designed primarily to disseminate information, and citizen "input" involves selection from a paltry menu of "interaction" with a digital image.[22]

Those more sanguine about the effects of technology suggest that its deleterious effects can be constrained to protect humanity.[23] Careful public policy can direct—though not eliminate—the subversive influence of technological development.[24] Then the question becomes whether states have adopted public policies through revised open meeting laws that reflect this concern.

Statutory Provisions Allowing Use of New Media Technologies

Express Allowance

Twenty-five state open meeting statutes specifically permit government agencies to conduct public business through the use of new media technologies.[25] Some, like Alaska, allow teleconferences "for the convenience of the parties, the public, and the governmental units conducting the meetings."[26] In all, 15 states permit broad use of new media technologies. Connecticut, Kansas, Kentucky, Missouri, New Jersey, South Carolina, Utah and Vermont permit all government boards to conduct meetings "in person or by means of electronic equipment."[27]

In Colorado, public business may be conducted electronically and e-mail has the same public access requirements as physical meetings.[28] Hawaii permits meetings by video conference if all board members can see and hear each other.[29] Montana law allows government boards to convene either through "corporal [assembly] or by electronic equipment,"[30] and it affirms citizens' "constitutional right to be afforded reasonable opportunity to participate in the operation of governmental agencies prior to the final decision of the agency."[31] Similarly, North Carolina and Oregon require government agencies to provide "a location and means whereby members of the public may *listen*"[32] to virtual meetings. However, North Carolina law provides for each citizen to pay "a fee of up to $25 . . . to defray in part the cost" of providing public access.[33]

Ten states restrict how, when or why government boards may conduct virtual meetings. Some states prohibit action at virtual meetings. Others limit the frequency of such meetings. Some allow virtual meetings only as an extension of a physical meeting, and others stipulate public access provisions for virtual meetings.

California's law allows local government agencies to receive public comment and to deliberate—but not to take action—through video teleconferencing that permits both audio and visual communication among the board members and the public.[34] South Dakota also appears to limit meetings "conducted by teleconference" to the exchange of information.[35]

Virginia law constrains both the frequency and the function of electronic meetings. Virginia government bodies may conduct no more than one-fourth of their meetings "through telephonic or video equipment"[36] that extends, rather than replaces, physical meetings of members.[37] However, Virginia law also makes it illegal for a government board to conduct public business "where the members are not physically assembled" except in cases of emergencies.[38]

Iowa and New Mexico limit the use of electronic meetings to times when "meeting in person is impossible or impractical" and require that public access be provided to electronic meetings "to the extent reasonably possible."[39] Virtual meetings are limited to emergencies in Tennessee and Texas,[40] and, except in cases of emergency, no more than half the meetings of a public body may be conducted through videoconferencing in Nebraska.[41]

Oklahoma limits the use of virtual meetings to certain specifically enumerated boards and requires that all members of the government body and the public be able to see and hear each other.[42] Minnesota, which revised its statute in 1997 to permit meetings by "interactive television" or "electronic means," requires members of government agencies to participate in virtual meetings from open public sites.[43] The law also encourages public electronic access from any "remote location" and stipulates that all members of the board and the public must be able to see and hear each other.

Implied Allowance

Two state statutes suggest that use of new media technologies is permitted.[44] North Dakota's open government meeting code applies the state's notice requirements to "conference call meetings" that are not mentioned elsewhere in the law.[45] Ohio law, which defines public meetings as "*any* prearranged discussion of the public business of the public body by a majority of its members,"[46] stipulates that members attending meetings through communications equipment are not considered present and may not vote.[47]

Contextual Prohibition

Although Massachusetts law includes no reference to meetings using new media technologies, it defines a meeting as a "*corporal* convening," which appears to exclude virtual meetings.[48]

Interpretations of Statutory Provisions

Among the 25 states with explicit statutory provisions about the use of new media technologies, case law and advisory opinions have shaped the laws. Court rulings and attorneys general opinions dealing primarily with telephone calls and teleconferences inconsistently apply similar provisions of different state laws. Some states have ruled that teleconferences are not meetings; others say they are and must meet all provisions of the state open meeting law.

In Nevada, the state Supreme Court in 1998 rejected the argument that a series of fax and telephone communications constituted a meeting under state law that defines a meeting as a gathering.[49] The court held, however, that such electronic communications illegally circumvented the intent of the law. The case was brought by the state attorney general after the head of the university system Board of Regents used teleconference calls and faxes with all but one member of the board to develop a public statement critical of the excluded board member.

In Texas, a court of appeals reviewing a summary judgment in 1998 failed to determine whether the City Council of Uvalde legally established a quorum when it included a member by telephone.[50] While the court said the meeting "may have violated" the state open meeting law, it held that any violation was corrected through ratification at a subsequent legal meeting. Questions of fact surrounded whether the teleconference meeting met the state law's requirements that the telephone conversation be audible to everyone at the meeting and that teleconferences be conducted only during emergencies or when physical meetings are difficult or impossible.

Texas attorneys general have issued three rulings in the past four years that do little to clarify the legal use of teleconferences in that state. A 1998 opinion said the Dallas City Council might be subject to provisions of the state open meeting law if it never gathers a quorum "but communicates by telephone."[51] In contrast, a 1995 opinion allowed a board member to participate by telephone in a legal meeting,[52] but a 1994 ruling found that telephone participation illegally circumvented mandated public deliberations.[53]

A 1998 North Dakota attorney general opinion distinguished between permissible information gathering—which requires no public access or notification—and "multiple conversations on a particular subject . . . [that] have the potential effect of forming consensus"— that must be treated as a meeting.[54] Earlier attorneys general opinions in both North and South Dakota encouraged the use of teleconferencing and virtual meetings because "it is a matter of common knowledge and everyday experience that a variety of public and private meetings are now held both by telephone and by interactive audio visual means."[55]

Recent court rulings in Connecticut and Montana have held that discussion on telephone extensions or speaker phones constitutes a meeting under their laws, which broadly permit virtual meetings.[56] And in Georgia, prior to adoption of the state's broadly permissive provision for use of teleconferencing, the attorney general in 1994 held that a board member participating in a teleconference was present to constitute a quorum.[57]

In Kansas, the Supreme Court in 1994 said the state's broad allowance of virtual meetings is inapplicable to telephone contacts among board members.[58] In *State ex rel Stephan v. Board of County Commissioners of Seward,* the court adopted the reasoning of a 1983 Virginia Supreme Court opinion ruling that "[a] telephone conference call does not qualify" as a meeting.[59] Moreover, the Kansas court said, because "there is no common-law right of the public or press to attend the meetings of governmental bodies . . ., in the absence of a statutory prohibition, there can be no legal or constitutional objection to a governmental body transacting certain business by means of a telephone conference call. If such a call is prohibited, the prohibition must be found in legislative enactment. It cannot be done by judicial fiat."[60]

In dissent, one justice rejected the court's definition of meetings as "face-to-face relationships" and argued that any "prearranged" communication should constitute a meeting.[61] The following year, a Kansas attorney general ruled that simultaneous interactive communications via computer may constitute a meeting.[62]

The Alaska Supreme Court ruled in 1994 in *Hickel v. Southeast Conference* that Alaska's broad acceptance of new media technolo-

gies permits but does not require government teleconferencing to facilitate public meetings.[63] The following year, an attorney general
opinion stated that board members who participate in meetings by
telephone must do so at publicly noticed teleconferencing facilities
unless this causes "undue hardship."[64]

Finally, in a ruling that may apply to virtual meetings, an Ohio
appeals court held in 1998 that a physically open public meeting violated state law because "the public could not hear the business being
transacted" among board members through whispers and passed
documents.[65] Similarly, in New Mexico, a 1991 opinion of the attorney general held that telephone votes violate the open meeting act
that permits telephone participation in meetings.[66]

Statutory Silence

Twenty-three state open meeting laws fail to address how government
agencies may use new media.[67] States from Florida to Maine, New
York to Washington and Michigan to Mississippi are silent about use
of technology to facilitate or expand meetings.[68]

Few of these laws define "meeting" to clarify the law's application
to virtual meetings. For example, the Arkansas statute defines a meeting
as a meeting of a quorum.[69] In Arizona, Delaware, Illinois or Indiana,
a meeting is a gathering of members.[70] In Florida and Washington,
meetings are all meetings "at which official acts are to be taken."[71]
Idaho, Maryland, Michigan, New Hampshire, New York, Rhode
Island, West Virginia and Wisconsin define legal meetings as the "convening" of members without reference to whether convening is physical
or electronic.[72] Mississippi and Wyoming define meetings as "an assembly" of board members.[73] The meaning of such laws must be determined through opinions of the courts and attorneys general.

Interpretations of Silent Statutes

In nine states, no attorneys general opinions or court rulings provide
guidance on how the silent open meeting laws should be applied to
new media technologies (see Table 3.1). Opinions in the remain-

Table 3.1. **No legal position on new media technologies**

Alabama	Massachusetts	Washington, D.C.
Idaho	New Hampshire	West Virginia
Indiana	Washington	Wyoming

ing states suggest fundamental differences in states' views of how to balance government efficiency and access. In the absence of statutory provisions, courts and attorneys general in several states have approved the use of new media. Others have not.

Several states approve use of new media to extend physical meetings.[74] For example, a 1998 opinion of Florida's attorney general held that a member could legally participate from an appropriate public place "via electronic means" with a physically assembled quorum.[75] In 1994, the attorney general said state law allowed participation through interactive video or telephone of a member physically unable to attend a legally convened meeting.[76]

In Michigan, board representatives may attend meetings by interactive television as a means to "enhance the public's access to the meetings."[77] In a 1995 ruling, the attorney general cited *Goode v. Department of Social Services,* in which a state appellate court upheld a teleconferenced meeting and ruled that the open meeting law did not require all members to be physically present at a legally assembled physical meeting.[78]

Also in 1995, a Mississippi attorney general ruled that a telephone conference or intercom system may be used by a board member to participate in a lawfully called meeting provided there is a quorum physically present and it is done in a manner that will allow the public in attendance to hear all discussion and deliberation.[79]

Ten years earlier, the Mississippi Supreme Court had said new media technologies should not be permitted to "circumvent the [open meeting] act by preventing public disclosure of deliberation and conduct of business."[80]

Arkansas rulings also have focused on required public access to nonphysical meetings. Relying on a 1985 Arkansas Supreme Court ruling that overturned a nonpublic vote taken by a telephone poll of board members,[81] a 1997 and a 1994 state attorney general opinion said telephone discussions by two or more members of a board are meetings and must comply with all provisions of the act.[82] In addition, a 1996 opinion found the use of late night faxed meeting notices an illegal means to circumvent the intent of the law.[83]

Indeed, other states have found the need to prevent electronic circumvention of government openness is the compelling concern with new media technologies. In a 1992 ruling, the Louisiana attorney general held that telephone contact, whether serial or simultaneous, among a majority of a local ethics board illegally circumvented the state open meetings law.[84] A Louisiana appeals court had ruled in 1976 that state law required a legal meeting to be convened at "a specific time and place."[85]

In Maine, the attorney general said unequivocally in 1984 that "the practice of conducting 'public proceedings' over the telephone is inimical to the fundamental purpose" of open meetings legislation and should be considered only in cases of emergency.[86] A New York attorney general said polling of board members' opinions by telephone violates the premise of open government because "such a procedure limits the ability of the public to observe the deliberations of the public body."[87]

In stark contrast, an Illinois appellate court in 1995 permitted teleconferenced meetings and said, "[T]he absence of specific authority in the act to conduct board meetings by telephone conference does not indicate a legislative intent to prohibit such meetings."[88] The court said state law did not require members of government boards to be in each other's physical presence.[89] The Illinois court quoted extensively from a 1992 Pennsylvania Supreme Court ruling that held a "telephone conference call using a speaker telephone in a meeting open to the public" was legal under the Pennsylvania statute.[90] The court said the crucial element was the ability of the public "to personally observe the deliberation, policy formation, and decision making," not the physical assembly of the members of the public board.[91]

In Arizona, a 1991 attorney general opinion said the law broadly permitted boards to meet using new media technologies "when no reasonable alternatives exist."[92]

The most relevant Rhode Island attorney general ruling, issued in 1988, said serial telephone calls among board members did not violate the open meetings act when "no substantive discussion or vote . . . took place over the phone."[93]

However, the Wisconsin Supreme Court in 1976 held that the intent and the ability to violate the law are critical factors in determining whether nonsimultaneous and nonphysical meetings are prohibited under state law.[94] The court ruled that subquorum or serial meetings are illegal "where there is present an intent to avoid the statute, plus the ability to control or determine a decision to be made at the public session of the committee or board . . ., [or] a deliberate conspiring to violate the open meeting requirement."[95]

Some states do not believe their silent open meeting laws apply to use of new media technologies. In a 1996 opinion, a Maryland attorney general compared e-mail to traditional mail and ruled that e-mail does not constitute a meeting because there is no "convening of a quorum of a public body."[96] However, "[i]f the members of a public body are able to use e-mail for 'real time' simultaneous interchange . . ., [this] can constitute a 'meeting'" subject to all legal requirements.[97]

In 1996, the Delaware attorney general concluded that state law did not cover telephone polling of board members. The attorney general said such polls did not constitute a "gathering" or meeting covered by the law.[98]

Statutory Prohibition of Electronic Circumvention

Seven state statutes expressly prohibit the use of electronic communications to circumvent the state's commitment to open government (see Table 3.2 below). Although Nevada and Rhode Island statutes neither grant nor deny permission for virtual government meetings, both expressly prohibit electronic circumvention.[99] Louisiana also appears to prohibit electronic circumvention through its broad clause that bans chance or social gatherings and "any other means to circumvent" the state's open government provisions.[100] Six state statutes that do not address the use of new media technologies also have been interpreted to prohibit electronic circumvention of openness.

Findings

As applied, neither the express statutory provisions nor the silent statutes provide consistent guidance to government agencies on the use of new media technologies. The 27 statutes that allow virtual meetings are divided between those that view technology as a force aiding citizen involvement and those that view it as a threat to open government. Similarly divided are the 23 open meeting statutes that fail to address the use of new media technologies.

Nine states offer no legal position whatsoever on virtual meetings. In contrast, eight states interpret their silent statutes to permit

Table 3.2 . **New media circumvention of openness prohibited**

Express Statutory Ban	Ban Interpreted from Silent Statute
Hawaii	Arkansas
Louisiana	Louisiana
Nebraska	Maine
Nevada	Mississippi
Oklahoma	New York
Rhode Island	Wisconsin
South Carolina	
Tennessee	

Table 3.3.   **Use of new media technologies allowed**

Express Statutory Allowance	Implied Statutory Allowance	Allowance Interpreted from Silent Statute
Alaska	North Dakota	Arizona
California	Ohio	Arkansas
Colorado		Florida
Connecticut		Illinois
Georgia		Michigan
Hawaii		Mississippi
Iowa		Pennsylvania
Kansas		Rhode Island
Kentucky		
Minnesota		
Missouri		
Montana		
Nebraska		
New Jersey		
New Mexico		
North Carolina		
Oklahoma		
Oregon		
South Carolina		
South Dakota		
Tennessee		
Texas		
Utah		
Vermont		
Virginia		

virtual meetings,[101] while six states interpret the silence to prohibit electronic circumvention of government openness.[102]

The differences in the legal status of virtual meetings among states are not reflective of differences in express statutory commit ment to citizen access and participation in government.

Recommendations

Increasing use of new media technologies by government agencies should not be ignored. State laws designed to facilitate citizen participation and checking on government must recognize the new and changing processes of government. Strong policy statements in support of open government are essential but not sufficient. All state open government laws should include provisions recognizing the use of new media technologies in the conduct of government business and providing for citizen access to these information systems.

States need not, and should not, adopt specific chapters on virtual meetings. Virtual meetings should be treated no differently than physical meetings. States should redefine "meeting" to incorporate virtual meetings and subject them to all the requirements imposed on physical meetings. Accordingly, a meeting would be defined as any simultaneous or serial exchange of information or action related to public business by two or more members of a public board through any means. Under this definition, boards may do anything at a virtual meeting that may be done at a physical meeting, and the law makes no distinction between physical and virtual attendance of board members.

State laws also should prohibit any differences in citizen access to physical or virtual meetings. State statutes should require all meetings, virtual or physical, to provide public notice and to permit board members and the public to exchange messages. No fees should be levied on citizens who participate through new media technologies.

State laws should ensure free public access to the systems of virtual meetings both through dial-up connections to virtual government meetings and through public access terminals or screens in city halls, public libraries and other public locations. Government agencies should be required to provide copies of all printed or visual materials at all public access sites and, to the extent it is possible, on-line.

Under these guidelines, there is no reason to limit the number or frequency of virtual meetings conducted by an agency. However, states should adopt express prohibitions with severe penalties for circumvention of the act. Violations should be determined on the basis of the effect of the challenged action, not the intent of board members. Finally, exemptions from statutory requirements in cases of emergency should be clearly stipulated and narrowly construed. In this way, technology can simultaneously improve the functioning of government agencies and increase citizen access to public business.

Notes

[1] Jerry O'Brien, *State Tells Council: No More Business by Faxes*, The Providence Journal-Bulletin 1C (Feb. 8, 1996) (reporting a 1996 Rhode Island assistant attorney general ruling that the Barrington Town Council had violated the state's open meeting law by using fax transmissions to circulate among themselves a letter later sent to the newspaper editor); *Amendment to Pact*, Milwaukee Journal Sentinel 3 (Aug. 21, 1996) (reporting that the University of Wisconsin's athletic board illegally used electronic mail and phone contacts to amend a $7.9 million contract with Reebok); *Editorial: Cyber-Loophole in Open Meetings Law*, The Baltimore

Sun 18A (March 29, 1996) (reporting that Baltimore County, Md., community college board turned back $25,000 worth of personal computers they hoped would improve communications after the county's attorney ruled that e-mail messages among them would violate the open meetings law); James M. Coram, *Officials Accused of Violations*, The Baltimore Sun 1B (April 30, 1996) (reporting that a Carroll County, Md., planning commission, charged with violating the law through e-mail communications, argued that simultaneous communications in cyberspace "chat rooms" would violate the law, but e-mail exchanges did not); *Editorial: Public Access to E-Mail*, The Arizona Republic B6 (Oct. 14, 1996) (reporting concern in Phoenix about government secrecy and e-mail communications among public officials); Chris Fiscus, *New Way to Do the Public's Business Out of Public View*, The Press Enterprise (Riverside, Calif.) A15 (June 1, 1996) A15 (reporting that a Massachusetts members-only Internet bulletin board for public officials excluded the public from discussions).

2David H. Schwartz, *Online Politicians Find Privacy Elusive*, The Christian Science Monitor 3 (Dec. 3, 1996).

3Kyle Niederpruem, *E-mail New Battle for Disclosure of Public Business*, Quill 48 (Jan./Feb. 1997).

4In this context, virtual meetings occur when any new media technology permits simultaneous communication to several people who are not in each other's presence.

5Benton Foundation, *Telecommunications and Democracy*, 4 Communication Policy Briefing (1994).

6Sharon H. Iorio, *How State Open Meeting Laws Now Compare with Those of 1974*, 62 Journalism Quarterly 741 (1985).

7See, e.g., *State ex rel. Stephan v. Board of Cty. Commrs of Seward*, 254 Kan. 446 (1994); *Note: Open Meeting Statutes: The Press Fights for the "Right to Know,"* 75 Harv. L. Rev. 1199 (1962).

8Osmon, *Comment: Sunshine or Shadows? One State's Decision*, Det. Col. L. Rev. 613, 617 (1977).

9*Kan. Stat. Ann.* § 75–4317 (a) (1997).

10*Wash. Rev. Code Ann.* § 42.30.010 (1997)

11All state statutes, attorneys general opinions, and case law were searched on Lexis/Nexis during July 1998 for references to "telephon** or interactive or electronic or telecommunication* or computer or teleconferenc*** or two-way or communication equipment."

12See, e.g., District of Columbia code.

13See, e.g., California code.

14Alvin Toffler and Heidi Toffler, *Creating a New Civilization* (1995) (identifying the three waves reshaping community as: (1) systematic use of agricultural principles, (2) industrialization, (3) ascendance of information); Richard C. Harwood, *Citizens and Politics: A View From Main Street America* (1991).

15Daniel Yankelovich, *Coming to Public Judgment* (1991).

16Daniel J. Boorstin, *The Decline of Radicalism: Reflections on America Today* (1968).

[17]Howard Rheingold, *The Virtual Community: Homesteading on the Electronic Frontier* (1993).

[18]In this chapter, new media technologies refers primarily to computer-mediated communications. However, discussion also includes any electronic technology that enables real-time communication among people who are not in each other's presence (e.g., telephone, teleconference, interactive video).

[19]John Jolusha, *Virginia's Electronic Village*, The New York Times sec. 3, at 9 (Jan. 16, 1994); Martha Willman, *How to Get Around Town While Standing in Place*, Los Angeles Times J-1 (Sept. 30, 1993) Sally J. McMillan and Kathryn B. Campbell, *Online Cities: Are They Building a Virtual Public Sphere or Expanding Consumption Communities?* (unpublished paper on file with the author, 1996); Robert M. Metcalfe, *Electronic Taj Mahals Might Reduce Travel to and from Session Breaks*, 19 (4) InfoWorld 44 (Jan. 27, 1997) (noting that videoconference facilities are chronically underused).

[20]See, e.g., Benton Foundation, *Telecommunications and Democracy*. In 1994, only 11 percent of U.S. households had a personal computer with a modem.

[21]*Ibid.* (quoting Ted Becker of Auburn University).

[22]Daniel M. Weintraub, *The Technology Connection*, 44 State Legislatures 6 (June 1993); Christa Daryl Slaton, Televote: *Expanding Citizen Participation in the Quantum Age* (1992).

[23]Herbert Marcuse, *One-Dimensional Man* (1964).

[24]Andrew Feenberg, *Critical Theory of Technology* (1991).

[25]State statutes that broadly allow virtual meetings are Alaska, Colorado, Connecticut, Georgia, Hawaii, Kansas, Kentucky, Minnesota, Missouri, Montana, New Jersey, North Carolina, Oregon, South Carolina, Utah and Vermont. State statutes permitting limited use of virtual meetings are California, Iowa, Nebraska, New Mexico, Oklahoma, South Dakota, Tennessee, Texas and Virginia.

[26]*Alaska Stat.* § 44.62.310 (a), 44.62.312 (6) (1996).

[27]*Conn. Gen. Stat.* ch. 3, § 1–18 (b) (1996); *Kan. Stat. Ann.* § 75–4317 (a) (1997); *Ky. Rev. Stat. Ann.* § 61.805 (5), 61.826 (Michie 1997); *Mo. Rev. Stat.* § 610.010 (1997); *N.J. Rev. Stat.* § 10:4–8 (b) (1997); *S.C. Code Ann.* § 30–4–20 (d), 30–4–70 (b) (1997); *Utah Code Ann.* § 52–4–2 (2) (a) (1997); *Vt. Stat. Ann.* tit. 1, § 312 (a) (1997).

[28]*Colo. Rev. Stat.* § 24–6–402 (1997).

[29]*Hawaii Rev. Stat.* § 92–3.5 (a) (1997).

[30]*Mont. Code Ann.* § 2–3–202 (1997).

[31]*Mont. Code Ann.* § 2–3–101 (1997).

[32]*N.C. Gen. Stat.* § 143–318.13 (1997) (emphasis added); *Ore. Rev. Stat.* 192.670 (2) (1997).

[33]*N.C. Gen. Stat.* § 143–318.13 (1997).

[34]*Cal. Gov't Code* § 54953 (B) (1) (1997).

[35]*S.D. Codified Laws Ann.* § 1–25–1 (1997); Att'y Gen. Op. No. 89–35 (1989).

[36]*Va. Code Ann.* § 2.1–343 (Michie 1997).

[37]*Va. Code Ann.* § 2.1–343.1 E (Michie 1996).

38*Va. Code Ann.* § 2.1–343.1 F (Michie 1996).

39*Iowa Code* § 21.1, 21.8 (1) (A) (1997); *N.M. Stat. Ann.* § 10–15–1(C) (Michie 1998).

40*Tenn. Code Ann.* § 8–44–108 (1996); *Texas Gov't. Code* § 551.125 (1996).

41*Neb. Rev. Stat.* § 84–1411 (1996).

42*Okla. Stat.* tit. 25, § 307.1, 304.7 (1997).

43*Minn. Stat.* § 471.705 (1997).

44States statutes in North Dakota and Ohio imply that virtual meetings are permitted.

45*N.D. Cent. Code* § 44–04–20 (1997).

46*Ohio Rev. Code Ann.* § 121.22 (B) (2) (1996) (emphasis added).

47*Ohio Rev. Code Ann.* § 121.22 (C) (1996).

48*Mass. Ann. Laws* ch. 39, § 23B (Law Co-Op. 1996).

49*Del Papa v. Bd. of Regents of the University and Community College Sys. of Nevada,* 956 Nev. P.2d 770 (1998).

50*Torres v. City Council of Uvalde,* Texas App. LEXIS 2079 (4th Dist. April 8, 1998).

51Op. Att'y Gen. Texas LEXIS 46 (April 13, 1998).

52Op. Att'y Gen. Texas LEXIS 96 (Aug. 30, 1995) (simultaneous physical presence of quorum not necessary to constitute meeting); Op. Att'y Gen. Texas LEXIS 68 (March 24, 1994) (board members may not attend meetings or vote by telephone); Op. Att'y Gen. Texas LEXIS 65 (March 18, 1994) (board members may not attend meetings or vote by live video transmission or teleconference call except through express authorization).

53Op. Att'y Gen. Texas LEXIS 31 (finding that openness "may not be avoided by avoiding the physical gathering of a quorum in one place at one time"). See also *Hitt v. Mabry,* 687 Texas S.W.2d 791 (4th Dist. Ct. App. 1985) (requiring physical assembly of boards and finding telephone polling of members violated state statute).

54Op. Att'y Gen. N.D. LEXIS 14 (June 8, 1998).

55Op. Att'y Gen. N.D. LEXIS 86 (Oct. 11, 1995); Op. Att'y Gen. S.D. LEXIS 8 (Dec. 28, 1994).

56*Giordano v. Freedom of Information Comm.,* 36. Supp Conn. 117 (Sup. Ct., Jud. Dist. Ansonia-Milford, 1979); Bd. of Trustees, Huntley Project School Dist. No. 24, Worden v. Bd. of Cty. Comm'rs of Cty. of Yellowstone, 186 Mont. 148 (1980).

57Op. Att'y Gen. Ga. LEXIS 19 (March 16, 1994).

58*State ex rel. Stephan v. Board of Cty. Commrs. of Seward,* 254 Kan. 446 (1994).

59*Roanoke School Bd. v. Times-World,* 226 Va. 185 (1983).

60*State ex rel. Stephan v. Board of Cty. Commrs. of Seward,* 254 Kan. 446, 450 (1994).

61*Id.* at 452 (Six, J., dissenting).

62Op. Att'y Gen. Kan. LEXIS 2 (Jan. 23, 1995).

63868 Alaska P.2d 919 (1994).

64Op. Att'y Gen. Alaska LEXIS 52 (Aug. 21, 1995).

65*Manogg v. Stickle,* Ohio LEXIS 1961 (5th App. Dist. April 8, 1998).

66Op. Att'y Gen. N.M. 12 (1991).

67State statutes that are silent about permissible uses of virtual meetings are Alabama, Arizona, Arkansas, Delaware, Florida, Idaho, Illinois, Indiana, Louisiana, Maine, Maryland, Michigan, Mississippi, Nevada, New Hampshire, New York, Pennsylvania, Rhode Island, Washington, Washington, D.C., West Virginia, Wisconsin and Wyoming.

68*Ala. Code* § 13A–14–2 (1996). But see Ala. Code 11–92A–9 (f) (1996) (permitting County Industrial Development Authorities to conduct business through teleconferences and electronic communications); *Ariz. Rev. Stat. Ann.* § 38–431 *et seq.* (1996); *Ark. Code Ann.* § 25–19–102 *et seq.* (Michie 1995); *Del. Code Ann.* tit. 29, § 10001 *et seq.* (1997); *Fla. Stat.* ch. 286.001 *et seq.* (1996); *Idaho Code* § 67B2340, 67–2343 (1996); *Ill. Rev. Stat.* ch. 5, § 120/1 *et seq.* (1996); *Ind. Code Ann.* § 5–14–1.5–2 (Burns 1996); *La. Rev. Stat.* 42:4.1 *et seq.* (1996); *Maine Rev. Stat.* tit. 1, § 403 *et seq.* (1997); *Md. State Gov't Code Ann.* 10–501 *et seq.* (1996) (but see *Md. State Gov't Code Ann.* 10–211 [1996] [allowing administrative procedure hearings to be conducted by electronic means effective June 1, 1996]); *Mich. Stat. Ann.* § 4.1800 (11) *et seq.* (1996); *Miss. Code Ann.* § 25–41–1 *et seq.* (1996); *Nev. Rev. Stat. Ann.* 241.030 (1997); *N.H. Rev. Stat. Ann.* 91–A:1 (1997); *N.Y. Pub. Off. Law* § 100 *et seq.* (Consol. 1996); 65 *Pa. Cons. Stat.* 271 *et seq.* (1996); *R.I. Gen. Laws* 42–46–1 *et seq.*; *Wash. Rev. Code Ann.* § 42.30.010 *et seq.* (1997); *D.C. Code Ann.* § 1–1504 *et seq.* (1996); *W. Va. Code* § 6–9A–1 (1996) (but see *W. Va. Code* 15–5–4 (d), 18–30–5 [permitting emergency use of electronic meetings for the state Disaster Recovery Board and allowing members of the Higher Education Tuition Trust to join quorums through telephonic equipment]); *Wis. Stat.* § 19.81 (1996); *Wyo. Stat.* § 16–4–401 *et seq.* (1996) (but see *Wyo. Stat.* § 9–7–104, 21–16–703 [1996] [permitting Community Development Authority board and Higher Education Assistance Authority boards to conduct emergency electronic meetings]).

69*Ark. Stat. Ann.* § 25–19–103 (1997).

70*Ariz. Rev. Stat. Ann.* § 38–431.01 (1996); *Del. Code Ann.* tit. 29, § 10002 (e) (1997); *Ill. Rev. Stat.* tit. 5, § 120/1.02 (1996); *Ind. Code Ann.* § 5–14–1.5–2 (Burns 1996).

71*Fla. Stat.* ch. 286.001 (1) (1996); *Wash. Rev. Code. Ann.* § 42.30.020 (1997).

72*Idaho Code* § 67–2341 (1996); *Md. State Gov't Code Ann.* § 10–502 (g) (1996); *Mich. Stat. Ann.* § 4.1800 (12) (b) (1996); *N.H. Rev. Stat. Ann.* 91–A:2 (1997); *N.Y. Pub. Off. Law* § 102 (1) (Consol. 1996); *R.I. Gen. Laws* § 42–46–1 (1997); *W. Va. Code* § 6–9A–2 (1996); *Wis. Stat.* § 19.82 (1996).

73*Miss. Code Ann.* § 25–41–3 (1996); *Wyo. Stat.* § 16–4–402 (1996).

74*In re Amendments to Rule of Judicial Admin. 2.051, No. 83,927,* 651 Fla. S.2d 1185, 1190 (1995) (the court recognized the "growing use of electronic mail" by government officials and the importance of public access to the information exchanged through this medium).

75Op. Att'y Gen. Fla. LEXIS 26, Op. No. 98–28 (April 6, 1998).

76Op. Att'y Gen. Fla. LEXIS 73 (June 15, 1994). See also 1992 Op. Att'y Gen. Fla. 92B44.

77Op. Att'y Gen. Mich. LEXIS 7 (Feb. 13, 1995) at 6.

78143 Mich. App. 756 (1985).

79Op. Att'y Gen. Miss. LEXIS 600 (Aug. 31, 1995) at 3.

80*Bd. of Trustees of State Institutions of Higher Learning v. Mississippi Publ. Corp.*, 478 Miss. So.2d 269, 278 (1985).

81*Rehabilitation Hospital Services Corp. v. Delta–Hills Health Systems Agency,* 285 Ark. 397, 687 S.W.2d 840 (1985).

82Op. Att'y Gen. Ark. LEXIS 256, Op. No. 97–202 (Aug. 6, 1997); Op. Att'y Gen. Ark. LEXIS 323 (July 11, 1994).

83Op. Att'y Gen. Ark. LEXIS 141 (April 25, 1996).

84Op. Att'y Gen. La. LEXIS 228 (92–166) (1992).

85*In re Mix Board of Supervisors of Elections,* 337 La. So.2d 533, 536 (4th Cir. App. Ct. 1976. See also *Brown v. East Baton Rouge Parish School Board,* 405 La. So.2d 1148 (1st Cir. Ct. App. 1981).

86Op. Att'y Gen. Maine LEXIS 4 (84–25) (1984).

87Op. Att'y Gen. N.Y. LEXIS 62 (92–96) (1992).

88*Freedom Oil Co. v. Illinois Pollution Control Bd.,* 275 Ill. App.3d 508, 655 N.E.2d 1184 (1995).

89*Id.* at 514.

90*Babac v. Pennsylvania Milk Marketing Board,* 531 Pa. 391, 393 (1992).

91*Id.* at 395, n. 4.

92Op. Att'y. Gen. 107 (R91–036) (1991).

93Op. Att'y Gen. R.I. LEXIS 3017 (1988).

94*Lynch v. Conta,* 71 Wis. 2d 662 (1976).

95*Id.* at 703.

96Op. Att'y Gen. Md. LEXIS 18 (May 22, 1996).

97*Id.*

98Op. Att'y Gen. Del. LEXIS 21 (May 30, 1996).

99*Nev. Rev. Stat. Ann.* § 241.030 (4) (1997); *R.I. Gen. Laws* § 42–46–2, 42–46–5 (b) (1996). The remaining anti–circumvention statutes are: *Hawaii Rev. Stat.* § 92–5 (b) (1996); *Neb. Rev. Stat.* § 84–1410 (4), 84–1411 (e)(1996); *Okla. Stat.* tit. 25, § 306 (1996); *S.C. Code Ann.* § 30–4–70 (b) (1996); *Tenn. Code Ann.* § 8–44–102, 8–44–108 (c) (1996).

100*La. Rev. Stat.* 42:5 (b) (1996).

101See Arizona, Arkansas, Florida, Illinois, Michigan, Mississippi, Pennsylvania and Rhode Island.

102See Arkansas, Louisiana, Maine, Mississippi, New York and Wisconsin.

4

When Government "Contracts Out": Privatization, Accountability and Constitutional Doctrine

Matthew D. Bunker and Charles N. Davis

Governments, which by nature lack the economic efficiencies of the marketplace, are facing pressure from the public to provide better services more efficiently. In response, governments are increasingly turning to private enterprise to assume certain functions on the theory that market competition will improve service at a lower cost to taxpayers. But this shift in responsibility is confounding access laws, many of which do not address the duty of such public/private partnerships to respond to public requests for information—information critical to the role of citizens as public critics of the institutions that represent them. The result often is reduced or curtailed access and less public accountability.

Introduction

In November 1996, two convicted sex offenders scaled a prison fence outside Houston and made it 200 miles, nearly to metropolitan Dallas, before they were apprehended. The state of Texas could do nothing to punish them for escaping; in fact, state authorities had no idea the men were serving time in Texas. The escapees, convicted in Oregon, had broken out of one of 38 privately operated prisons in Texas.

In Texas and elsewhere, private prisons reflect the increased political pressure on federal, state and local governments to cut costs and streamline operations, placing renewed emphasis on the concept of privatization. A dizzying array of government agencies has engaged private entrepreneurs to perform governmental functions on a for-profit basis.

In recent years, privatization has touched nearly every area of public life. In addition to prisons,[1] hospitals,[2] schools,[3] development agencies,[4] film commissions[5] and dog racing tracks[6] have been the focus of privatization efforts. Overlooked in this rush to privatization is the threat posed to public access to government records. Records long open to public inspection now are being created, maintained and controlled by private businesses, whose goals are often at odds with the very purpose of public records laws.

In recent years, businesses assuming privatized government functions have attempted to deny the public access to a wide variety of records. For example, a private contractor transporting pupils to and from public schools in Atlanta unsuccessfully fought a request for the personnel records of its bus drivers—specifically criminal histories and driving records.[7] In San Gabriel, Calif., a waste disposal company contracted by the city filed a lawsuit against the municipality in a failed attempt to halt release of financial records needed to evaluate a rate increase city officials had granted the company.[8] Such disputes likely will increase as the privatization trend grows.

This chapter discusses various types of privatization, examines the current state of public records statutes with regard to privatized records, and analyzes one state's struggle to determine when records of a private enterprise doing business for the state are subject to disclosure under public records statutes. The focus of the chapter is on true privatization—cases in which private enterprises assume government functions—not simply cases in which private firms perform some narrow duties for government agencies. The writers conclude that current statutory definitions, combined with the inflexibility of judicial standards used to draw the line between public and private enterprise, may in some cases frustrate the public's ability to scrutinize the activities of private actors performing services for the state. To safeguard the public's right to monitor the functions of government, a bedrock principle in a self-governing society, the authors propose that courts adopt an approach borrowed from the constitutional doctrine of state action. The proposed "public function" approach would bring some measure of order to an otherwise unsettled area of public records law by embracing the notion that certain privatized activities should be treated as "public functions," despite their private appearance.

The Move Toward Privatization

The practice of private corporations providing governmental services is generating tremendous interest at all levels of government in the United States. As *The New York Times* noted in 1996: "Business does it better. That is the rallying cry on Capitol Hill and in statehouses across the country where legislators are turning over to private companies traditional government functions ranging from running jails to exploring outer space."[9]

The most common form of privatization in the United States is "contracting out." That is, functions once performed by government are delegated to private enterprises by contract. In the United States, contracting out has been applied to prisons, jails, drug treatment facilities, policing, day care, trash collection, transportation services (including road maintenance and toll road operation), food services and a variety of other services.

Proponents of contracting out argue that private enterprise, driven by marketplace competition, will provide public services more efficiently. Private firms, which in most circumstances are required to render competitive bids to win contracts, will offer greater efficiency and thus comparable or better services at a lower cost than could be provided by a government entity.

Opponents point to a number of problems associated with the practice of contracting out.[10] Bidding may not truly be competitive, creating hidden monopolies. Economies of scale, enjoyed by government entities, may be lost if duties are delegated to a number of smaller private companies. Government must still expend resources to monitor and regulate the privatized activity. Perhaps most significantly, privatization transforms the essential character of the relationship between the citizen (now the consumer) and the provider."[11] Related to this concern is the problem of accountability, which commentators on both sides of the privatization debate generally express in terms of accountability to some bureaucratic overseer.

Public Records Statutes and Privatization

The public's right of access to government records is essentially a matter of statutory law in the United States. Both the federal government, through the Freedom of Information Act (FOIA), and all 50 states have statutes creating some level of access to information and records used on behalf of the public. Unfortunately, neither the federal Freedom of Information Act nor most state records statutes explicitly allow access to the records of private entities performing public functions.

The FOIA, which allows citizens access to records of federal agencies, seems unlikely to provide access to records of privatized service providers, both because of its statutory language and its interpretation by the courts. In a 1995 study, communication law scholar Nicole B. Casarez analyzed the statute and cases interpreting the FOIA and concluded that Congress would have to amend the access statute to ensure access to the records of private prison operators.[12]

Casarez noted that federal courts' interpretation of two key FOIA terms make it unlikely that privatized government functions would be subject to the act. First, courts' definition of what constitutes a "federal agency" often has turned on the extent to which the government exercised day-to-day control over an entity.[13] Absent extensive control, or factors such as "holding a federal charter or having a presidentially appointed board of directors,"[14] private organizations are not likely to be considered federal agencies for FOIA purposes. Second, Casarez analyzed whether records of private entities could be considered "agency records," a term the statute does not define. Federal courts have held that many records in the custody and control of federal agencies, but not necessarily created by them, constitute agency records. However, this route to access is easily blocked when it comes to private prisons, Casarez suggested, because internal private prison records are unlikely to come into the possession of federal agencies and because FOIA exemptions may apply even if they do.

Casarez's analysis thus concluded that, at least in the case of private prisons, the FOIA probably would not provide news media and the public with access comparable to that for prisons run by the government. This conclusion seems applicable to other areas, too. The records of most private entities performing federal government functions probably would not be available under the FOIA as currently drafted and interpreted by the courts.[15]

The FOIA is only one public records statute, however. The writers of this chapter analyzed public records laws of all 50 states to determine whether the statutes explicitly addressed privatization.[16] Overwhelmingly, they did not. One crucial issue is just what sort of entity is subject to the law. Most state statutes define "public agency" or "public body" solely in governmental terms. Arizona's public records law, for example, defines "public body" as "the state, any county, city, town, school district, political subdivision or tax-supported district in the state, any branch, department, board, bureau, commission, council or committee of the foregoing, and any public organization or agency, supported in whole or in part by funds from the state or any political subdivision thereof, or expending funds provided by the state or any political subdivision thereof."[17] This kind of definition, with its exclusive focus on "public" entities, appears to preclude private entities performing government functions. As a result, records created by such private entities probably would not be subject to the Arizona law. Thirty-six states have similar definitions that limit the types of entities subject to public records laws.[18]

A few state statutes extend the definition of agencies subject to public access to entities that are not strictly governmental. For example, Louisiana's definition of a public body focuses on governmental entities, but includes "a public or quasi-public nonprofit corporation designated as an entity to perform a governmental or proprietary function."[19] Although broader than that of most states, this definition presumably would not include for-profit businesses that undertake government functions. A few statutes leave the definition sufficiently general that courts, if so inclined, could subject private service providers to public records laws. For example, Oklahoma's definition of a public body includes "but is not limited to" governmental bodies.[20] This statutory language would seem to give Oklahoma courts interpretive license to expand the category.[21] Six other states—Georgia, Hawaii, Idaho, Kansas, Missouri and Pennsylvania—also have statutes that allow leeway for courts to provide access to records of privatized activities.

It should be noted, of course, that statutory language alone does not settle these issues—state courts could simply reinterpret statutes to include privatized functions. It should be pointed out that the language of most statutes, which fails to address privatization, militates against a broad interpretation, particularly if courts adopt the maxim of statutory interpretation *expressio unius est exclusio alterius* (the expression of one thing is the exclusion of another). In interpreting statutes, courts often infer from the inclusion of certain items or classes of items that the legislature intended to exclude others not mentioned. To the extent that courts in many states strictly construe state access laws, records of businesses carrying out privatized functions may well be excluded.

Six states have statutory language that could easily include privatized functions. Rhode Island, for example, defines "agency" or "public body" to include the usual government units, as well as "any other public or private agency, person, partnership, corporation, or business entity acting on behalf of any public agency."[22] Florida's public records statute incorporates nearly identical language.[23] Arkansas, rather than focusing on the public body, defines "public records" to include records that "constitute a record of the performance or lack of performance of official functions which are or should be carried out by a public official or employee, a governmental agency, or any other agency wholly or partially supported by public funds or expending public funds."[24] This definition would seem to include at least some private service providers carrying out government functions. Kentucky, Texas and Utah also have statutes that might well create such access.

In summary, few state statutes seem equipped to handle the novel public records problems associated with privatization. Most seem designed to provide access only to records of government agencies. Few explicitly allow the news media and the public the right to inspect records produced by private companies performing government functions.

State Courts and Privatization

A few state courts have struggled with whether records of privatized government activities fall within the scope of public records statutes; the issue, however, has not been addressed in most jurisdictions. Plaintiffs have sought access to privatized government records ranging from expense vouchers of a metropolitan convention and visitors bureau[25] and nonprofit hospital authority records[26] to a college bookstore's book list[27] and the minutes of a dog racing association.[28] Results in these cases have been mixed.

Although a handful of state courts have adopted the view that records of private entities are publicly accessible when specified by statute or when state agencies specifically delegate their authority, few courts have encountered instances of "pure" privatization.[29] Florida is one of a few states that have developed several years' worth of precedent involving the issue.

Florida lawmakers have struggled to devise a flexible approach to bring private entities that perform government functions under its public records statute. In 1975, the Florida legislature amended its Public Records Act to apply to any entity acting "on behalf of any public agency."[30] The statute further defined "public records" as documents made "in connection with the transaction of official business by any agency."[31] Despite the seemingly clear wording of the amendment, Florida courts adopted the "traditional government function" test along with other federal precedents narrowing the scope of the Florida amendment in devising their own test. In 1989, in one of the first judicial opinions on the issue of privatized records, a Florida appellate court held that a private towing company working under a city contract was performing "a governmental function," and thus was subject to the Public Records Act.[32] The appellate court noted that the 1975 amendment clearly intended to define the types of private enterprise subject to the public records law. But the court declined nevertheless to interpret the statute according to its plain meaning, preferring to examine the nature and extent of the private entity's involvement in traditional government functions.

The Florida Supreme Court also refused to adopt the amendment's plain meaning, looking instead to federal case law to interpret the amendment. Declaring that "the statute [*Fla. Stat.* § 119.011 (2)] provides no clear criteria for determining when a private entity is acting on behalf of a public agency,"[33] the court took a different approach. In *News and Sun-Sentinel Co. v. Schwab, Twitty & Hanser Architectural Group, Inc.* the court adopted a "totality of factors" approach to evaluate whether a private entity is subject to the public records law. The court held that an architectural firm, hired by a local school board to oversee school construction, was not "acting on behalf of" a public agency. The court relied on earlier Florida cases that had applied criteria used by federal courts to determine when a private entity was an "agency" under the federal Freedom of Information Act.[34] The court reasoned that the school board had not created the architectural firm and did not control the firm's "activities or judgment."[35] Most importantly, however, the court concluded that the firm was not performing a government function because the firm had not been delegated any decision making authority by the school district.[36]

The Florida Supreme Court instructed lower courts to draw upon a list of nine factors when determining whether a private entity is "acting on behalf of" a public agency, finding six of these factors relevant to the case at hand:

1. Creation: Did the public agency play any part in the creation of the private entity?
2. Funding: Has the public agency provided substantial funds, capital or credit to the private entity or is it merely providing funds in consideration for goods or services rendered by the private agency?
3. Regulation: Does the public agency regulate or otherwise control the private entity's professional activity or judgment?

4. Decision making process: Does the private entity play an integral part in the public agency's decision making process?
5. Government function: Is the private entity exercising a governmental function?
6. Goals: Is the goal of the private entity to help the public agency and the citizens served by the agency?[37]

The Florida Supreme Court's "totality of factors" test has created a confusing mix of lower court opinions involving privatized government records.[38] Relying on both federal precedents and its own factors, the court weakened the 1975 amendment by requiring an analysis of the statutes, ordinances or charter provisions establishing the function to be performed by the private entity as well as the contractual document between the governmental entity and the private organization.[39]

For example, in 1992 a Florida attorney general opinion included a review of the articles of incorporation and other materials relating to the establishment of the Tampa Bay Performing Arts Center before concluding that the center was an "agency" subject to the public records law. The attorney general never mentioned the "acting on behalf of" language in the 1975 amendment, focusing instead on the center's governance by a board of trustees composed of city and county officials and the center's use of city property.[40]

In short, Florida's "totality of factors" test ultimately requires an analysis similar to that used by federal courts to determine whether a private entity is subject to public records law. Despite a plainly worded amendment declaring that any entity acting on behalf of a public agency is subject to public records law, Florida courts now employ contractual analysis, examining organizing statutes, ordinances and charters to determine whether an entity has become an agency. This approach seems to frustrate the legislative intent of the 1975 amendments to ensure private entities not be allowed to configure themselves as private actors if they are doing state business.

The Florida Supreme Court has stated that the broad definition of "agency" ensures that a public agency cannot avoid disclosure under the Public Records Law simply by contractually delegating to a private entity functions that would otherwise be an agency's responsibility.[41] Relying on a "totality of factors" approach, however, engenders the very sort of ambiguity the 1975 amendment was intended to remedy. Public bodies seeking "pure" privatization deals—particularly in states with no precedent on the issue—could structure contractual agreements in ways that curtail public access.

The lack of a coherent judicial doctrine addressing privatized government records will tell as courts face increased efforts by government agencies to distance themselves from day-to-day management decisions and limit their involvement in privatized enterprises to detached macro-regulation. As new forms of government—or non-government, as the case may be—emerge, the legal doctrine of privatized public records must change as well.

State Action and the Functional Approach

State and federal access laws are based almost exclusively on statutes rather than constitutions. The U.S. Supreme Court has held, for example, that the First Amendment grants almost no rights of access to government information.[42] Yet constitutional law can sometimes provide an analytic framework helpful in resolving statutory issues.

The state action doctrine holds that constitutional protections in the Bill of Rights, along with other individual liberty provisions in the Constitution, restrict only governmental conduct. When private persons or entities interfere with or abridge constitutional rights of private persons, such actions do not raise constitutional issues. Thus, for example, a public university, because of its governmental character, must respect students' First Amendment rights, while such rights generally are not enforceable against a private university. Problems sometimes arise, however, when it is not clear where government or state actions leave off and purely private actions begin.

When the state action doctrine was first articulated in the 19th century, in the context of racial discrimination, the scope of governmental action was held to be quite narrow. In the Civil Rights Cases,[43] decided in 1883, the U.S. Supreme Court suggested that the due process and equal protection clauses of the Fourteenth Amendment applied only to cases of direct action by government. Private acts of racial discrimination were largely held to be outside the reach of the Fourteenth Amendment, and thus outside the reach of the federal judiciary.

Toward the middle of the 20th century, however, the Court began to expand its definition of state action. One especially noteworthy case, *Marsh v. Alabama*,[44] decided in 1946, extended First Amendment rights to an individual arrested for distributing religious literature in an Alabama town owned by a private company. The town of Chickasaw was owned by the Gulf Shipbuilding Corporation, but was to all appearances no different from a "public" municipality, with streets, residences, businesses and sewage disposal. A member of the Jehovah's Witnesses denomination was convicted of trespassing after she refused to stop distributing religious materials. In reversing her conviction, Justice Hugo Black's majority opinion articulated a "public function" justification for the Court's finding of state action. Justice Black noted that those who operate bridges, ferries, turnpikes and other public accommodations are not entitled to complete freedom from government regulation. "Since these facilities are built and operated primarily to benefit the public and since their operation is essentially a public function, it is subject to state regulation," Justice Black wrote.[45]

In addition to *Marsh,* a number of other Supreme Court cases extended the notion of state action significantly until the 1970s, when the Court began to pull back from a broad reading of state action. For example, in *Jackson v. Metropolitan Edison Co.,*[46] decided in 1974, the Court held that a monopoly utility company was not subject to constitutional due process requirements and thus could terminate a customer's service without notice and a hearing. The Court's majority held that for a number of reasons, including the utility company's state-granted monopoly status and its provision of an essential public service, the case did not constitute state action. In denying the state action claim, the Court noted that it had, in the past, "found state action present in the exercise by a private entity of powers traditionally exclusively reserved to the State," including activities involving elections, municipal parks and the operation of a company town in *Marsh.*[47]

Similarly, in the 1978 case of *Flagg Bros. v. Brooks,*[48] the Court found no state action in the proposed sale of a woman's household goods by the warehouse that stored them. The warehouse sale, for nonpayment of rent, was authorized under New York's Uniform Commercial Code. The Supreme Court, in rejecting the state action claim, found that settling disputes between debtors and creditors was not traditionally an exclusively public function, despite the fact that a New York statute authorized the warehouse owner to sell the goods. The Court noted that the *Marsh* line of "sovereign-function cases" suggested that functions exclusively administered by states and cities were more likely to justify a finding of state action. "Among these," the Court wrote, "are such functions as education, fire and police protection and tax collection. We express no view as to the extent, if any, to which a city or State might be free to delegate to private parties the performance of such functions and thereby avoid the strictures of the Fourteenth Amendment."[49]

Legal scholar Daphne Barak-Erez has urged that a strong version of the state action doctrine be used to protect citizens' constitutional rights against privatized government service providers.[50] Barak-Erez criticized the later public function cases, such as *Jackson and Flagg Bros.*, because of the Supreme Court's limited notion of sovereign functions. Tradition should not be the sole guide, she argued, but rather "the operation of the public domain, as it is perceived today, should serve as the basic layer for the application of the state action doctrine to so-called private bodies."[51] Barak-Erez claimed that public functions should include areas such as health care, education and welfare. These categories, of course, are open to some dispute. Clearly, recent political movements toward "devolution" and smaller government suggest that no clear societal consensus exists as to what might constitute essential government functions.

Despite such disagreements, it seems clear that when government turns over functions it previously had undertaken to private companies, public oversight of the new providers would be important. This is particularly true when public awareness and public pressure could be the only way to prevent corruption and abuse by private providers. As one commentator has noted: "Consigning the provision of municipal functions to private organizations is akin to asking the wolf to guard the hen house. The private administrator will make decisions based upon what is best for the company, not what is best for the public at large."[52] While the hen house metaphor may be somewhat overstated, it seems undeniable that abuses would be lessened with openness and public accountability, especially given the disincentive government might have to expose its own bad judgment in choosing a private contractor. Although Barak-Erez did not explore access law, an analysis loosely based on her concerns can illuminate potential problems associated with laws governing public records. Again, the point is not that constitutional guarantees provide access to records, but rather that the conceptual framework of a revitalized state action doctrine can be a useful analytical tool in applying public records statutes to privatized service providers.

As a preliminary attempt at a standard, the authors suggest that a "public function" analysis could provide access to records of privatized services in the following way.[53] As an initial matter, the very fact that government is "contracting out" a service it previously performed should be treated as prima facie evidence of a public function and thus subject the new provider to public records laws. The mere fact that government once performed a function that is now contracted to private entities cannot be dispositive as to whether it should continue to be regarded as a public function, however. As legal scholar Ronald Cass put it, this would be a "conflation of positive and normative issues."[54] The authors propose that a number of factors are relevant in determining the extent to which a contracted service should be regarded as a public function. First, any private organization wielding the coercive power of state, including law enforcement and incarceration, should be subject to public records laws. As one expert on privatization has noted, "when the state deprives a private party of his or her life, liberty, or property, the state's moral authority and responsibility should be as unambiguous as possible."[55] While the quoted statement dealt with the merits of privatization in the first instance, the point is equally relevant to the public accountability of private power in this domain. Second, private entities that take on functions dealing with the public health and welfare should be subject to public records laws. Stated more generally, perhaps, the more "vital" the function, or the greater the potential for harm from abusive or inept performance of the function, the more likely it should be held to be a public function if it has once been treated as such. Clearly, fire protection, infrastructure maintenance and even education could be regarded as essential to the public health and welfare. Third, private entities should be subject to public records laws when the functions they perform particularly call for disinterested judgment: for example, the assessment and collection of taxes. This factor incorporates concerns scholars such as Paul Starr have expressed regarding "functions where the very appearance of buying and selling undermines the claim of the state to be acting impartially on behalf of the entire community. Y"[56] Even in an age of interest-group politics, one of the hallmarks of a "public function" is the notion of a government that stands neutral between competing groups within the society, an ideal to which private entities can aspire, if at all, only in the open.

The "functional" approach suggested above has some similarities to the "totality of the circumstances" approach Florida courts have taken under that state's public records law. But there are important differences as well. The extent to which a private entity is performing a governmental function is one factor considered by Florida courts, but only one, and not necessarily the most important. Florida courts also have considered whether the government "created" the private entity. Under the functional approach suggested above, this factor seems irrelevant. The pressing question is not how the private entity came into being, but how its performance is likely to affect public welfare. Florida courts have also considered the extent to which the government body regulates or controls the private entity. This factor seems beside the point as well. In fact, in certain circumstances, it could yield a result precisely the opposite of the desirable outcome. For example, private entities performing public functions that are ignored and under-regulated by government agencies may be exactly those entities that should be held more closely accountable through the application of open records laws. Official indifference may point toward the necessity of public accountability.

Conclusion

In determining whether private entities are subject to public records laws, courts have looked at a variety of factors, including the government's day-to-day control over the private entity, the entity's organizational structure and the entity's decision making authority. Such approaches ignore the reality of the privatization movement now sweeping federal and state governmental agencies: when a governmental agency delegates a public function to a private contractor, records created through the performance of a public duty that would have been subject to public disclosure can become private records solely by virtue of the contractor's non-governmental status.

Without predictable judicial or legislative standards, the public risks being shut out of the privatization process. Without public awareness, public oversight of the operation of privatized governmental operations will be inadequate. It is clear that public access often suffers once governmental operations are turned over to private entities. Private enterprises serve managers, owners and shareholders, not taxpayers. According to fundamental democratic principles, governmental services conducted by private operators should be just as accountable as services provided by public agencies. The public and the press must be able to scrutinize the activities of private actors performing governmental services, just as the public and the news media already scrutinize public activities under public records statutes.

To ensure that public access is not lost in the rush to privatize governmental services, the authors suggest that courts turn to a "public function" analysis that draws upon the constitutional concept of state action. The current judicial tests for applying public records laws to private enterprises are shaped by visions of the past. Public functions have been limited to the traditional functions of the state, preferring tradition to present realities. The challenge is to update the state action doctrine in a way that preserves the distinction between state and private actions while recognizing new forms of activity in the public sphere. Public function analysis offers the beginning of an approach for courts struggling to extend public records laws to privatized governmental functions. As the range of privatized governmental activities grows, the need to balance the public's right to know against the interests of private contractors doing business for the state will test statutes and judicial doctrine that rely on outdated notions of separation between the state and private enterprise.

Notes

[1]Gary Bowman et al., eds., *Privatizing Correctional Institutions* (Transaction Publishers, 1993).

[2]Benjamin R. Barber, *Jihad v. McWorld* 239 (1995).

[3]John Hildebrand, *Privatizing a Public School? Sharp Queries Greet Proposal in Roosevelt,* Newsday A-22 (Oct. 25, 1996).

[4]*Swaney v. Tilford,* 898 Ark. S.W. 2d 462 (1995).

[5]Jeffrey D. Zbar, *Commission With a Mission,* Variety 37 (June 10, 1996).

[6]*City of Dubuque v. Dubuque Racing Association,* 420 Iowa N.W. 2d 450 (1988).

[7]*Hackworth v. Board of Education of the City of Atlanta,* 447 Ga. S.E .2d 78 (Ct. App. 1994).

[8]*San Gabriel Tribune v. The Superior Court of Los Angeles County,* 192 Calif. Rptr. 415 (2d Dist. Ct. App. 1983).

[9]Leslie Eaton, *Public Money Foots the Bill for "Privatized" Foreign Aid,* The New York Times A-1 (Feb. 2, 1996).

[10]See Robert W. Bailey, *Uses and Misuses of Privatization,* in Prospects for Privatization 138–52 (Steve H. Hanke, ed., Proceedings of the Academy of Political Science, 1987).

[11]Paul Starr, *The Limits of Privatization,* in Prospects for Privatization 133.

[12]Nicole B. Casarez, *Furthering the Accountability Principle in Privatized and Federal Corrections: The Need for Access to Private Prison Records* 28 University of Michigan J. of Law Reform 249–303 (winter 1995).

[13]*Id.* at 273, citing *Forsham v. Harris.*

[14]*Id.*

[15]A noted FOIA treatise puts this point succinctly: "The FOIA does not apply to private companies; persons who receive Federal contracts or grants; tax-exempt organizations; or State and local governments." Justin D. Franklin and Robert F. Bouchard, *Guidebook to the Freedom of Information and Privacy Acts* 3–8 (Clark Boardman Callaghan, 1996). Another good commentary on this issue is provided by Katherine A. Meyer and Patti A. Goldman, *Agency,* in Litigation Under the Federal Open Government Laws 183–86 (Allan Robert Adler, ed., American Civil Liberties Union Foundation, 1993).

[16]The text of the statutes, current as of early 1996, was found in the State Statutes Appendix to Frankin and Bouchard, *Guidebook.*

[17]*Ariz. Rev. Stat.* § 39–121.01 (2) (1994).

[18]Although the numbers in this section suggest a degree of certainty, individual states' statutes have sufficient ambiguities and idiosyncrasies to make the figures provided here problematic. A perfect example of this uncertainty is the situation in Connecticut, discussed in the next section. Although the

Connecticut statute on the face of it offers little hope for application to privatized activities, Connecticut courts have nonetheless applied it broadly to include at least some private corporations performing public functions. In light of this, the authors can at best provide only a rough count of statutes that fit into the somewhat arbitrarily imposed categories discussed in the text. Particularly for that large majority of states in which privatization records cases have not arisen, legal predictions based on statutory language alone are fraught with uncertainty. Nonetheless, it seems worthwhile to draw some sort of order out of the statutory chaos.

[19]*La. Rev. Stat.* § 44:1 (1) (A) (1) (1996).

[20]51 *Okla. Stat. Ann.* § 24A.3 (2) (1994).

[21]It is also possible, of course, that courts faced with less open-textured statutes might nonetheless choose to read a definition broadly on policy grounds. Such a decision would depend on the court's concern with fidelity to statutory language as opposed to presumed legislative purpose.

[22]*R.I. Gen. Laws* § 38–2–2 (a) (1994).

[23]*Fla. Stat. Ann.* § 119.011 (2) (1995).

[24]*Ark. Code Ann.* § 25–19–103 (1993).

[25]*Indianapolis Convention & Visitors Bureau v. Indianapolis Newspapers Inc.,* 577 N.E. 2d 208 (1991).

[26]See, e.g., *Northwest Georgia Health System v. Times Journal, Inc.,* 461 Ga. S.E. 2d 797 (Ct. App. 1995); *Clayton County Hospital v. Webb,* 430 Ga. S.E. 2d 89 (Ct. App. 1993); *Sarasota Herald-Tribune Co. v. Community Health Corp., Inc.,* 582 Fla. So. 2d 730 (2d DCA 1991).

[27]*In the Matter of Encore College Bookstores v. Auxiliary Services Corp. of the State University of New York,* 663 N.E. 2d 302 (1995).

[28]*City of Dubuque, Iowa v. Dubuque Racing Association,* 420 N.W. 2d 450 (1988).

[29]Few cases involving instances of "pure," or large-scale, privatization exist. See, for example, *City of Fayetteville v. Edmark,* 801 Ark. S.W. 2d 275 (1990) (private attorneys acting as functional equivalent of city attorney were covered by open records act); *Connecticut Humane Society v. FOIC,* 591 Conn. A.2d 395 (1991) (statewide humane society, although performing some governmental functions, not subject to open records act); *Connecticut Bar Examining Committee v. FOIC* , 550 Conn. A.2d 633 (1988) (bar examining committee acted as arm of the state and thus certain records were subject to open records act); *Board of Trustees of Woodstock Academy v. FOCI,* 436 Conn. A.2d 266 (1980) (private school providing public secondary education for local citizens subject to open records law); *Marks v. McKenzie High School Fact-Finding Team,* 878 Ore. P. 2d 417 (1994) (school investigative panel not subject to open records statute); *Hackworth v. Bd. of Ed.,* 447 Ga. S.E. 2d 78 (App. 1994) (records of private bus company providing service for Atlanta city schools were "public records" under state open records statute); *Laine v. Rockaway Beach,* 896 Ore. P. 2d 1219 (App. 1995) (private fire department subject to open records law); *Brown v. Community College of Philadelphia,* 654 Pa. A. 2d 32 (Commw. 1994)

(community college subject to open records act). See also Op. Att'y Gen. No. 93–130, Kan. LEXIS 116 (1993) (legislatively created turnpike authority performing essential government function is subject to state open meetings and records acts); Op. Att'y Gen. Ky. LEXIS 33 (1994) (certain documents of private prison contractor subject to open records statute). Abundant case law exists on single instances of privatization or small, one-time deals between governments and private contractors. See, e.g., *San Gabriel Tribune v. City of West Covina,* 143 Calif. App. 762 (App. 2d 1983); *Alligator Towing and Recovery Inc. v. News-Press Publishing Co.,* 545 Fla. So. 2d 941 (2d DCA 1989); *State of Louisiana v. Nicholls College Foundation,* 564 So. 2d 682 (1990).

30*Fla. Stat. Ann.* § 119.011 (2) (1996).

31*Fla. Stat. Ann.* § 119.011 (1) (1996).

32*Fox v. News-Press Publishing Co.,* 545 Fla. So. 2d 941 (2d DCA 1989).

33596 Fla. So. 2d 1029 (1992).

34596 So. 2d at 1031, citing *Schwartzman v. Meritt Island Volunteer Fire Dept.,* 352 Fla. So. 2d 1230 (4th DCA 1977), *cert. denied;* 358 Fla. So. 2d 132 (1978); *Sarasota Herald-Tribune Co. v. Community Health Corp.,* 582 Fla. So. 2d 478 (2d DCA 1991).

35596 So. 2d at 1032.

36*Id.*

37596 So. 2d at 1032–36. The court said the factors include, but are not limited to: (1) the level of public funding; (2) commingling of funds; (3) whether the activity was conducted on publicly owned property; (4) whether services contracted for are an integral part of the public agency's chosen decision making process; (5) whether the private entity is performing a governmental function or a function that the public agency otherwise would perform; (6) the extent of the public agency's involvement with, regulation of or control over the private entity; (7) whether the private entity was created by the public agency; (8) whether the public agency has a substantial financial interest in the private entity; and (9) for whose benefit the private entity is functioning. 596 So. 2d at 1031.

38In Florida, as discussed earlier, the *News and Sun-Sentinel* court endorsed a multifactor test for determining when a private business is an "agency" under Florida law. Lower courts were free to draw upon nine factors that might be relevant, depending upon the facts of the particular case. In contrast, the Connecticut Supreme Court endorsed a less complicated four-factor test in *Board of Trustees of Woodstock Academy v. FOIC,* 436 Conn. A. 2d 266 (1980). Those factors are: "(1) whether the entity performs a governmental function; (2) the level of government funding; (3) the extent of government involvement or regulation; and (4) whether the entity was created by the government." 436 A.2 d at 270–71 (citations omitted). These factors are similar to some of those adopted in the Florida case, although the authors believe neither approach is ideal, as discussed in the next section.

39Op. Att'y Gen. Fla. No. 91–99 (private nonprofit corporation, leasing hospital facilities of public hospital under lease that requires that private hospital abide by public records law, is subject to public records law).

[40]Op. Att'y Gen. No. 91199.

[41]596 Fla. So. 2d 1029 (1992).

[42]See, for example, *Procunier v. Pell,* 417 U.S. 817 (1974). However, the Court has granted a narrow First Amendment right of access to criminal proceedings. See, for example, *Richmond Newspapers v. Virginia,* 448 U.S. 555 (1980).

[43]109 U.S. 3 (1883).

[44]326 U.S. 501 (1946).

[45]326 U.S. at 506.

[46]419 U.S. 345 (1974).

[47]419 U.S. at 352.

[48]436 U.S. 149 (1978).

[49]436 U.S. at 163–64.

[50]Daphne Barak-Erez, *A State Action Doctrine for an Age of Privatization* 45 Syracuse L. Rev. 1169–92 (1995).

[51]*Id.* at 1190.

[52]Shirley L. Mays, *Privatization of Municipal Services: A Contagion in the Body Politic* 34 Duquesne L. Rev. 41–70 (fall 1995).

[53]The analysis suggested here applies primarily to cases of large-scale "contracting out," which is the area the authors conclude most urgently requires public oversight. The suggested approach is almost certainly not appropriate for smaller-scale use of private businesses by government agencies, such as cases in which city councils hire consultants for a one-time project, or agencies hire professional firms to perform limited support roles, such as accounting. Such governmental use of private enterprises may also be deserving of public scrutiny, but is outside the scope of this discussion. The extent to which predominantly private businesses that do very limited business with the state should become entangled in state access laws is an immensely complicated issue. Thus, to the extent that the Florida "totality of the circumstances" test applies to such small-scale transactions, this paper expresses no opinion as to its appropriateness.

[54]Ronald A. Cass, *Privatization: Politics, Law and Theory* 71 Marquette L. Rev. 449–523 (spring 1998).

[55]William T. Gormley, *Two Cheers for Privatization, in Privatization and Its Alternatives* 310 (William T. Gormley, ed., University of Wisconsin Press, 1991).

[56]Starr, *Limits of Privatization* 133.

5

Privacy and Access: The Inevitable Collision of Competing Values

Paul H. Gates Jr.

No issue dominates the landscape of new technology like the constitutional right of privacy, which represents the inevitable clash of computerized information keeping and retrieval and the ill-defined "right to be alone." The novel issues raised by the Information Age sorely test the established privacy torts—civil torts created in the age of print dominance that have struggled to protect the rights of those caught in the spotlight of 24-hour global news gathering. The emergence of electronic hidden cameras and database technology has given rise to a new information culture in which much, if not all, of this sort of coverage of individuals rather than issues is justified under the rubric of "public interest," a broad, catchall term that has come to be associated less with what is vital for the public to know and more with whatever captures the audience's attention at the moment. The law of privacy's primary purpose, naturally, is to make a fair adjustment of the conflicting claims of the parties involved by weighing the interests for which the plaintiff demands protection against the defendant's claim of unrestrained freedom in furtherance

*of his own wishes, along with the value of those wishes. This chapter
surveys the changes in privacy law wrought by the electronic eye.*

Introduction

Web surfers who checked in on Jenni Ringley on a recent Sunday af-
ternoon saw a poorly lit shot of the 20-something woman standing in
her bedroom in a bra, pulling her hair into a ponytail. Ringley has
digital cameras scattered throughout her northwest Washington, D.C.
apartment that broadcast her life to the on-line world every two minutes, 24 hours a day, seven days a week.[1] There are costs to access,
however, and keeping up with Ringley's life requires membership—at
$15 per year. Voyeurs can duck the fee, however, by clicking on the
"guest" area when they visit, but the refresh rate is slower, as the
GuestCam site updates only every 20 minutes.

Internet exhibitionists such as Ringley notwithstanding, most
Americans treasure their privacy, often taking it for granted, but
sometimes going to great lengths to guard their private moments.
When their efforts fail, however, increasingly subjects of media
scrutiny resort to the courts, bringing civil claims of intrusion and disclosure of private facts, two torts that are commonly referred to col-
lectively as invasions of privacy. Americans routinely decry the
media's behavior in such instances, but at the same time tune in—in
huge numbers—to tabloid news programs, "reality TV" and daytime
talk shows such as *Jerry Springer* and *Sally Jessy Raphael*, exhibiting
a sort of national schizophrenia.

The blurring of the line between news and entertainment, the important and the trivial, and the related melding of politics and personality goes back at least 25 years. Richard Nixon's Oval Office tape
recordings opened the political equivalent of Jenni Ringley's bedroom
camera-as-peephole, shredding any vestiges of the belief that our political leaders spoke eloquently, focusing on weighty affairs of state.
Despite the rambling, choppy and confusing nature of the conversations between the president and his advisers revealed in the wake of
the Watergate scandal, Americans devoured the published transcripts
with a combination of fascination and revulsion.

If additional evidence of the changed definition of news were
needed, one need look no further than the blockbuster sweeps week
numbers ABC generated with Barbara Walters' prime-time soap
opera starring Monica Lewinsky. Some 74 million Americans tuned
in to the details of Lewinsky's affair with President Bill Clinton, an
audience second only to January's broadcast of the Super Bowl.[2]

Nielsen Media Research gave the broadcast a 33.4 rating and a 48 share, meaning that just under half of America's working television sets were tuned in to the program, which stuck close to the personal details of the couple's trysts and skirted larger questions about what the affair meant for the country and the presidency. In New York City, the nation's largest market, the Walters-Lewinsky interview proved the decisive factor in WABC-TV's sweeps victory over archrival WNBC-TV.[3]

Much, if not all, of this sort of coverage is justified as the "public interest," the definition of which has shifted from emphasis on issues to emphasis on individuals—throwing into stark relief the interest of "the public" as media audience and "the public" as individuals who are the focus of such attention. It is the purpose of the law of privacy, of course, to mediate between these conflicting claims.

Resolution of the conflicting claims is not made easier by the fact that the law of torts is almost by definition a struggle of social theories. The idea that private cases might embody elements important to "public policy" is by no means new to tort law,[4] but since the late 19th century, there has been a marked increase in acknowledgment that the interests of individuals might be intertwined with the interests of society in general, as seen in disputes in which both parties are private litigants.[5] The right to privacy is just such a right, a right based not on constitutional guarantees, but on notions of a social good.

The recognition of a right to privacy is often traced to the undoubtedly influential Warren and Brandeis *Harvard Law Review* article published in 1890,[6] but the famous description of the concept as "the right to be let alone" was actually coined two years earlier by Michigan Judge Thomas Cooley.[7] It was the law review article, however, that circulated the idea widely and the concept was immediately embraced by a New York Supreme Court judge in an unreported press case involving a photograph of a scantily clad actress.[8] Cooley, the New York trial judge and the two Harvard law professors were all familiar with the excesses of the press of the day, and Warren and Brandeis' argument pointedly singled it out in support of the need for some redress for those who felt unfairly targeted. Part of their argument is familiar to critics of the sensational segments of the press today:

> The press is overstepping in every direction the obvious bounds of propriety and decency. Gossip is no longer the resource of the idle and of the vicious, but has become a trade, which is pursued with industry as well as effrontery. To satisfy a prurient taste the details of sexual relations are spread broadcast in the columns of the daily papers. To occupy the indolent, column upon column is filled with idle gossip, which can only be procured by intrusion upon the domestic circle. The

intensity and complexity of life, attendant upon advancing civilization, have rendered necessary some retreat from the world, and man, under the refining influence of culture, has become more sensitive to publicity, so that solitude and privacy have become more essential to the individual; but modern enterprise and invention have, through invasions upon his privacy, subjected him to mental pain and distress, far greater than could be inflicted by mere bodily injury.[9]

Intrusion

The tort of intrusion has been described by one commentator as a "psychic trespass."[10] A common definition is the intentional invasion of the solitude or seclusion of another in his or her private affairs or concerns through either physical or electronic means.[11] In the media context, the tort arises from the conduct of journalists in obtaining information. While disclosure of private facts complaints, discussed below, concern the substance of the information revealed, intrusion concerns the means used to collect the information. The tort may also include elements of trespass, a common-law crime, but more often, in the competitive, ratings- and technology-driven news business of the late 20th century, it is intermingled with elements of disclosure. Intrusion claims may also be coupled with claims of infliction of emotional distress, where conduct is alleged to be so shocking and outrageous as to exceed all reasonable bounds of decency.

In one of the first federal decisions in the area, the U.S. Court of Appeals for the Ninth Circuit upheld an intrusion claim against reporters who used a hidden camera and hidden tape recorders, holding that the devices were not indispensable tools in news gathering and that the First Amendment does not extend immunity to news reporters who commit torts or crimes in the course of news gathering.[12] As the *Dietemann* decision makes clear, intrusion involving the press does not involve publication, but news gathering. The First Amendment issue is straightforward: When, in the course of news gathering, the press engages in conduct that would constitute intrusion if done by anyone else, does the press enjoy special immunity from liability?

First, the press does not enjoy a general news gathering immunity from intrusion. Conduct that is otherwise tortuous is not immunized from liability *solely* because it is incident to news gathering. Shortly after *Dietemann,* another federal appellate court held that the techniques used by the first "paparazzo," Ron Galella, to photograph Jackie Onassis, such as speeding dangerously close in a motorboat while she was swimming, would be tortuous if performed by anyone other than a news photographer.[13] The rule that the press enjoys no exemption from the law of intrusion is derived from the familiar case of *United States v. O'Brien*.[14]

In *O'Brien*, the Supreme Court created the benchmark against which legal rules that are not directed at the content of expression are measured: "[W]e think it clear that a government regulation is sufficiently justified if it is within the constitutional power of the Government; if it furthers an important or substantial governmental interest; if the governmental interest is unrelated to the suppression of free expression; and if the incidental restriction on alleged First Amendment freedoms is no greater than is essential to the furtherance of that interest."[15]

This lesser, or "intermediate," standard of review is significant because it permits laws that qualify for the *O'Brien* test to be evaluated against a level of review less demanding than the strict scrutiny standards normally called for under the First Amendment. Thus, when the government promulgates a rule that operates to restrict expression, but does so for reasons unrelated to the content of that expression, and the government interests at stake are, at minimum, "substantial," the regulation will normally be upheld despite that "incidental" effect of interfering with speech. The elements of the tort of intrusion are designed to protect interests unrelated to the content of expression, so therefore the less demanding standards of *O'Brien* are applicable.

There is an important qualification to that general rule, however: If the person who claims to be the victim of the intrusion is a public official, public figure or is caught up in events or issues of public concern, the degree of solitude or seclusion to which he or she is entitled may shrink. This qualification does not operate as a news gathering exception to intrusion, but instead goes to the threshold issue of what constitutes an intrusion under the circumstances. While the press has no special status that would shield it from claims of intrusion, the press, like *anyone* else, does have greater freedom to photograph a public person than a private individual and greater freedom to photograph persons involved in newsworthy events than those going about their everyday activities. Rather than a news gathering exemption to intrusion, this factor recognizes that fame, notoriety or newsworthy activity reduces the private sphere in which the subject may enforce the law against psychic trespass. The converse, however, emphasizes the important point here: that those who are private individuals involved in events of minimal concern to others enjoy the largest sphere of privacy against the prying eyes, electronic and otherwise, of both the press and their fellow citizens.

The law is well settled that under the First Amendment, the press may be prohibited from publishing material already in its possession, especially if lawfully acquired, only in extraordinary circumstances.[16] However, the press' First Amendment right of access to information is strictly limited to courtroom criminal proceedings, is a right co-equal with that of the public at large and must be balanced against other social needs.[17] The limitation on this right was foreshadowed many years earlier in a case where the U.S. Supreme Court held that there was no First Amendment right for journalists to travel to foreign countries declared off-limits to Americans by the State Department.[18]

The most recent judicial statement concerning the public's right to privacy from an overly inquisitive news media comes from the California Supreme Court in the June 1, 1998 ruling in *Shulman v. Group W Productions*.[19] In the case, the court ruled 5–2 that media personnel who make audio- and videotapes of an accident victim can be sued for invasion of privacy, but that the media cannot be sued for broadcasting private facts gathered in the pursuit of news by the "numerous mechanical devices" feared by Warren and Brandeis.[20] The case stemmed from a June 1990 accident near Riverside, Calif., in which Ruth Shulman lost control of her minivan and plunged into a drainage ditch. Both Shulman and her son, a passenger, were pinned beneath the car and had to be freed by rescuers using the "Jaws of Life." A helicopter ambulance was dispatched to the scene, carrying a nurse wearing a wireless microphone and a Group W cameraman, who videotaped the rescue, pandering to "that weak side of human nature which is never wholly cast down by the misfortunes and frailties of our neighbors."[21] The nurse's microphone picked up her conversations with the injured woman who, writhing in pain, asked to be allowed to die. Shulman, now a paraplegic, did not know the accident had been recorded until a nine-minute segment was broadcast on *On Scene: Emergency Response* more than three months later.[22] Shulman's suit was dismissed by a Superior Court judge granting summary judgment to the defendants, but an appellate court reinstated it, ruling that the lower court hadn't properly balanced the victim's privacy rights against Group W's First Amendment rights, which presented triable issues of fact.

On appeal to the state Supreme Court, the justices held that the accident was a newsworthy event as a matter of law, avoiding the need to determine whether newsworthiness is a purely descriptive term or a normative concept. By simple judicial declaration, the court avoided the thorny problem of explaining how a single-vehicle accident that injured two remained of public interest nearly 14 weeks after the fact and deserved nine minutes of airtime, including an audiotape of the conversation between the nurse and victim. The court was not without sympathy for the plaintiffs' argument, however, observing that "all material that might attract readers or viewers is not, simply by virtue of its attractiveness, of *legitimate* public interest" (emphasis in original).[23] The court also held that the camera's presence was not itself intrusion, despite the fact that the vehicle and its injured passengers were some distance off the highway, in a public area but otherwise out of view, and certainly out of hearing range, of onlookers.

The court did hold that two aspects of Group W's activities might constitute intrusion. The justices found that the cameraman's continuation of filming in the medical evacuation helicopter might present a question of intrusiveness, and that a jury might find that a reasonable expectation of privacy was violated. The state "may not intrude into the proper sphere of the news media to dictate what they should publish and broadcast, but neither may the media play tyrant to the people by unlawfully spying on them in the name of newsgathering. . . ." Absent a crime or cause of action, a "highly offensive intrusion" into private affairs cannot "generally be justified by the plea that the intruder thereby hoped to get good material for a news story."[24] Society has not yet come to the point where the public or its media representatives habitually hitch rides in air ambulances as paramedics care for injured strangers.

The justices also held that there might be a jury question in whether conversation with rescue personnel carried with it a similar expectation of privacy that was violated by recording through the hidden microphone. "A reasonable jury could find highly offensive the placement of a microphone on a medical rescuer in order to intercept what would otherwise be private conversations with an injured patient. . . . Defendants . . . took calculated advantage of the patient's vulnerability and confusion."[25] These questions will form the crux of Shulman's case when it is set for trial. The last thing an injured accident victim should have to worry about while being pried from her wrecked vehicle is whether her suffering is being recorded for the entertainment of casual television viewers. People expect uniformed medical personnel to be just that, not individuals doubling as reporters. In fact, paramedics and other emergency personnel wear uniforms precisely to distinguish their unique functions. The privacy expectations inherent in that relationship are further reinforced by the existence of the physician-patient privilege found in each state's code of evidence.

Disclosure

The tort of disclosure, which also goes by the labels "publication" or "revelation of private facts," also demands a determination of newsworthiness. Even without privacy concerns, newsworthiness is a fluid concept without objective standards. No two people have identical news judgment, leading to highly subjective interpretations in evaluating whether subject matter is important or interesting. When an individual's privacy is at stake, however, the issue comes into sharper focus and the question is cast in terms of conflicting standards: Is publication in the public interest, and if so, does that need outweigh the private individual's right to remain out of the public eye?

The conflict remains when public officials or public figures are involved, but the public interest threshold is higher for such persons who seek to prove that their privacy was invaded. The publication of a private individual's medical records would be considered beyond the pale. However, the revelation that Thomas F. Eagleton, the Missouri senator who was being considered for the 1972 Democratic vice-presidential nomination, had undergone electroshock therapy, was in the public interest. The information was certainly private and intimate, but directly related to the public's duty to appraise his fitness for the office "only a heartbeat away from the presidency."

Even though news reports may be embarrassing to those in the public eye, as in the Eagleton example, coverage of legitimate news is protected as an exercise of free speech even when it gives offense to some. The broad concept of newsworthiness affords considerable protection to journalists grounded in a strong presumption in favor of the truthful and accurate publication of information. The public interest is served best by a wide variety of information. Newsworthiness is not confined to events and facts of politics, economics and social interaction, but also includes descriptions and portrayals of how people live, work and think within their social milieu. Newsworthy figures are not only those on center stage of events, but also spectators and passers-by. In the final analysis, courts give a long leash to the values of a free press that serves diverse audiences with a variety of tastes and styles. To the extent that judicial lines are drawn, their common characteristic is offensiveness in the extreme, vulgarity, or callousness toward the human dignity of an individual whose activities are only marginally in the public interest or who lacks a close connection to a significant public issue.

In addition to the close connection required, an Illinois court has also appeared to require that there be significant reasons to single out individuals in the coverage of a significant public issue. In a 2–1 decision, the Illinois First District Appellate Court ruled that *Chicago Tribune* photographers and editors may have invaded a woman's privacy in the manner they obtained and used photographs of her dead son to illustrate a story about gang violence. The court also found that the plaintiff had made out a valid cause of action for intentional infliction of emotional distress.[26]

The facts of the case began to unfold on Dec. 30, 1992, when Laura Green's 16-year-old son was taken to Chicago's Cook County Hospital with a serious gunshot wound. *Tribune* photographers at the hospital took several photographs of emergency room doctors treating the victim without first obtaining permission from his mother, who had not yet arrived at the hospital. The doctors' efforts to revive the boy were unsuccessful and they moved his body to a private room. There, the photographers took more photos and at first barred his mother from entering the room while they did so. When she did gain entry to the room, the newspaper staffers remained and listened to her grief-stricken statements to her dead son.[27]

On New Year's Day, 1993, the *Tribune* ran a Page One story about Chicago's record homicide rate for 1992, illustrated with a picture of Calvin Green lying dead in the hospital room. The story also included statements the plaintiff made to her son's body, telling him that she loved him and that she had warned him about the dangers of street gangs and his longtime involvement with them.[28] Two days later, the newspaper published a second photo of the victim as he was being treated before his death. That photo was one that was taken without his mother's permission before she arrived at the hospital and illustrated a story about the teenage victims of gun violence. That story did not mention Calvin Green specifically.

The plaintiff's complaint sought damages for invasion of privacy and intentional infliction of emotional distress based on the articles and photographs published on the two days. A trial judge granted the defendant newspaper's motion to dismiss the complaint, but the appellate panel reversed the dismissal. *The Tribune* filed a petition for leave to appeal to the Illinois Supreme Court on Feb. 3, 1997.

The appellate panel first disagreed with the trial court's finding that the hospital room in the public hospital where the victim was moved after his death was a public place, pointing out that the general public had no right of access to the room.[29] The judges also reversed the finding that the statements the plaintiff made to her dead son were public, since she had alleged that she had previously told the reporters that she would make no statement to the press. Those comments were sufficient notice to the press that they were not to disclose her statements to the public, the court said.[30]

The newspaper did prevail in its effort to have the allegations based on the second photograph dismissed. The judges reasoned that the causes of action could be based on the plaintiff's privacy interest only and not that of her dead son. While the first day's publication did mention the plaintiff and clearly identified her as the victim's mother, the second did not.[31]

The court then turned to the issue of offensiveness. The court found that a jury could conclude that the *Tribune's* actions would be highly offensive to a reasonable person since they could find that the first day's publication was "not about an ordinary daily activity or incident . . . rather . . . an extraordinarily painful incident in plaintiff's life, when she first set eyes on her minor son after he had been shot to death."[32]

Where other courts have shied away from passing judgment on the newsworthiness of the reports that give rise to complaints, the Illinois court faced the problem head-on. *The Tribune* had argued that the subject on the offending report was the death toll from guns, gang warfare and accompanying drug use, undeniably issues of great public concern. The court, however, saw the issue quite differently: "In our view . . . the relevant inquiry is whether the photograph of plaintiff's dead son and her statements to him are of legitimate public concern." In that vein, the court found that a jury could find that the newspaper "did not need plaintiff's intimate statements to Calvin or his photograph to convey the human suffering behind gang violence."[33] A jury could find that a reasonable member of the public has no concern with the statements a grieving mother makes to her dead son, or what he looked like lying dead in the hospital. Quoting from a comment to the Restatement of Torts, the court held that the "line is to be drawn when the publicity ceases to be the giving of information to the public to which it is entitled, and becomes a morbid and sensational prying into private lives for its own sake."[34] In other words, what the court finds critical to the success of a defendant's argument based on newsworthiness is a reasonability in the nexus between reports focusing on individual anguish within the larger context of an issue whose subject matter is generally considered of important public concern.

Intrusion and Disclosure Combined

As is clear from the discussion of the foregoing cases, intrusion and disclosure are closely related and it is not unusual to find both invasion of privacy claims arising from the same set of facts. In *Miller v.*

National Broadcasting Co., an NBC camera crew following an ambulance team entered Dave and Brownie Miller's apartment without
consent to film the efforts of paramedics called to the home to try to
save the life of Dave Miller, who had suffered a fatal heart attack in
his bedroom.[35] NBC used the tape on its evening news without first
obtaining consent. Despite complaints to NBC from the widow and
the victim's daughter, the network used portions of the film in a
promo advertising a mini-documentary about paramedics.[36]

The issue on appeal was whether the plaintiff had stated a cause
of action for intrusion and disclosure. The appellate panel found that
she had:

> With respect to [Brownie Miller's] cause of action, we leave it to a
> reasonable jury whether the defendants' conduct was "outrageous."
> Not only was her home invaded without her consent, but the last mo-
> ments of her dying husband's life were filmed and broadcast to the
> world without any regard for the subsequent protestations . . . to the
> defendants. Again, the defendants' lack of response to these protesta-
> tions suggests an alarming absence of sensitivity and civility. The record
> reflects that defendants appeared to imagine that they could show or
> not show Dave Miller *in extremis* at their pleasure and with impunity.[37]

The same issue has come up again in California, with the coverage of the 1998 heroin overdose death of an aspiring actor by the "reality TV" show, *L.A.P.D.: Life on the Beat*. When police were called
to Michael Marich's Hollywood apartment, they were trailed by a
camera crew that filmed his body slumped on the living room couch.
The report also broadcast the call police made informing the victim's
parents, which they had recorded while at the scene. The parents are
suing for invasion of privacy, specifically intrusion, disclosure and intentional infliction of emotional distress, naming both the Los Angeles
Police Department and the show's producers as defendants.[38]

The segment featured the plaintiffs' attorney, Howard Rosen-
berg, who described the police department and the show's producers
as "partners in an unholy alliance" that trades access for public relations for the police department and equates tragedy with entertainment.[39] Interestingly, even CBS promoted the segment with teasers
that gave a brief glimpse of the body four days before the Monday
evening news.

Federal Case Law

Until recently, federal case law in the area had been mixed, with the
U.S. Courts of Appeal for the Fourth and Eighth Circuits approving

members of the press accompanying law enforcement officials into private residences and the Second and Ninth finding the practice to be a violation of the Fourth Amendment.[40] However, last year the Supreme Court granted certiorari in two of the cases to resolve the conflict in the circuits.[41]

In *Berger,* about 20 federal agents accompanied by a Cable News Network film crew arrived at Paul Berger's Montana sheep ranch to search for evidence of eagle poisoning, a violation of the Endangered Species Act. Berger was arrested in the raid, but was later acquitted of all charges but the relatively minor offense of improper use of a pesticide. CNN eventually used the footage of the raid as part of its coverage of government efforts to protect endangered species.

In a 3–0 decision, a Ninth Circuit panel ruled that the Fisheries and Wildlife Service officers who permitted the film crew to tag along on the raid did not have qualified immunity to do so.[42] Therefore, the court held, Berger could sue the federal authorities behind the raid. "The record . . . suggests that the government officers planned and executed the search in a manner designed to enhance its entertainment, rather than its law enforcement, value," the panel wrote.[43]

In *Wilson,* U.S. marshals, accompanied by two *Washington Post* reporters, broke into a Maryland home early one morning in April 1992 to serve an arrest warrant on Dominic Wilson. Wilson was not at home, but the officers held his father, Charles, at gunpoint face down on the floor, even though he was clearly at least 20 years older and 40 pounds heavier than the fugitive they sought. Meanwhile, one *Post* staffer took notes while the other shot still photos of Dominic Wilson's parents, who were visibly distressed, in their underwear. The photos were never published and the story never appeared in the *Post.*[44]

At trial, a federal district judge rejected the officers' assertions that allowing the reporters to enter the house didn't violate Wilson's rights. Nor did the court agree that the officers were protected by a qualified immunity, because the courts at the time had not yet established that allowing the press to accompany officers under such conditions was unconstitutional. On appeal, a divided three-judge panel of the Fourth Circuit reversed.[45] Shortly afterwards, the circuit judges voted to rehear the case *en banc,* and narrowly reversed again, 6–5, holding that the officers had not exceeded the scope of their warrant by permitting the reporters who accompanied them into Wilson's home.[46] The judges ruled that the Marshals Service media "ride-along" policy indicated the reasonable belief that keeping the public informed of the agency's activities was a duty of the agency.[47]

In *Ayeni,* the Second Circuit held that officers violated the homeowner's Fourth Amendment rights when they permitted a television crew to enter a private residence and film the execution of a search warrant. The court found the "ride-along" policy a violation and the officers' permissive decision unreasonable in the face of a federal law that prohibits any but law enforcement officers from executing warrants.[48] The court found the defendants' argument that there was no case law on this point yet in existence unpersuasive, an argument explicitly approved by the Fourth Circuit in *Wilson*.[49] The court in *Wilson* had also agreed with the Eighth Circuit decision in *Parker*, which granted officers in a similar case in St. Louis qualified immunity.[50] In that case the Eighth Circuit also agreed with the district court that the KSDK television reporters who filmed the raid acted independently of the police, who neither permitted or prohibited their entry and filming in Parker's home.[51] As a result of this decision, the homeowner was left to pursue his claim against KSDK-TV separately.

In deciding *Wilson* and *Berger* together, the Supreme Court ruled unanimously that media accompanying law enforcement officials onto private property to observe the execution of a search warrant violated the Fourth Amendment.[52] The two cases now return to federal district courts in Maryland and Montana.[53]

In his opinion for the Court, Chief Justice William Rehnquist made clear that the media's presence was not related to the objective of the warrant, and so the First Amendment claim advanced on their behalf fell short of justifying the intrusiveness of the press' activity into the protections of the Fourth Amendment.[54] The law enforcement officials had argued that it would "further their law enforcement mission to permit members of the news media to accompany them in executing a warrant. But this claim ignores the importance of the right of residential privacy at the core of the Fourth Amendment," Rehnquist wrote.[55]

The press had also argued that their presence helped protect the integrity of the warrant process and protected the officers from the subjects of the warrant. The Court dismissed the furtherance-of-justice argument, at the same time giving short shrift to the First Amendment value asserted. Rehnquist wrote that the reporters were private individuals "present for their own purposes, not to protect the Marshals, much less the Wilsons."[56]

The Court's holding makes clear that the press' coverage of law enforcement activities is now guided by the Fourth Amendment and not the needs of the "infotainment" industry, where sensationalism is increasingly confused with newsworthiness: "Surely the possibility of good public relations for the police is simply not enough, standing alone, to justify the ride-along intrusion into a public home. And even the need for accurate reporting on police issues in general," does not justify the intrusion and subsequent Fourth Amendment violation.[57]

Conclusion

Defenses to complaints about media behavior, even those that are solidly grounded in First Amendment jurisprudence, do not always square with public perception. Though the media may be on firm legal ground with regard to what they *can* do, there is often a wide gulf between that position and what a majority think they *should* do. Although the examples and arguments presented here focus largely on physically intrusive media conduct and revelations of intimate personal facts, such wrenching, headline-generating examples are hardly necessary to elicit strong feelings from poll respondents about the nature of the media's relationship with the public.

The *1992 Harris-Equifax Consumer Privacy Survey* highlighted the tension between the First Amendment rights of the press to data on individuals from public records and concerns about individual privacy. The survey found that 70 percent of the public do not believe it is right for the media to have unrestricted access to public records about people in public life or in the news.[58] This substantial majority seems to be concerned by the media's ability to gather and disseminate personal information even about newsworthy people from public records, and not only when the media collect such personal information by clandestine surveillance, misrepresentation, intrusion and other controversial journalistic techniques.

The Supreme Court's decision in *Department of Justice v. Reporters Committee for Freedom of the Press* three years before the survey may have been a harbinger of this public concern about media access to public records.[59] The unanimous decision denied the media access to individual criminal history summaries contained in centralized federal law enforcement computerized data banks. The justices reached this result even though the information contained in the individual "rap sheets" that were being sought was fully accessible to the press and public at the police stations and courthouses where the records were originally created. The Court held that comprehensive, centralized and computerized data banks of criminal histories have enhanced the potential for greater intrusiveness, even though the component elements of the records were freely available.[60]

Privacy concerns are not just about revelations of intimate tidbits that titillate and shock. Privacy concerns also inhere in the ordinary. If we accept the fact that the proliferation of advanced technology has an extraordinary ability to capture and transmit nearly every aspect of everyone's life, the question becomes one of line-drawing. How much of what we can know do we really need to know?

Even the most rabid media consumer has long forgotten the video and still images of Bill and Hillary Clinton frolicking on the beach in St. Thomas in 1997. After that family vacation there was some criticism of the press, which used telephoto lenses to capture the couple just being themselves. The White House made a few discreet comments to the effect that the press ought to have the decency to let the Clintons have a private moment. The president was the quietest of all, when days afterward in just a few words he showed both common sense and a respect for the press. When he was asked if he thought the press had invaded his privacy and where the press should draw the line, his brief response spoke volumes. Yes, he said, he thought his privacy had been invaded. Then, as for what the press should do about it, he said, "The answer to the second question is: That's why we have a First Amendment. You [the press] get to decide the answer to the second question."[61] Surely the nonjournalistic world must wonder if the news media ever do ponder the answer to the second question.

Notes

[1]http://www.jennicam.org.

[2]Associated Press national wire, March 5, 1999.

[3]129 (11) *Broadcasting & Cable* 33 (March 15, 1999).

[4]Percy H. Winfield, *Public Policy and the English Common Law*, 42 Harv. L. Rev. 76 (1928).

[5]Francis H. Bohlen, *Fifty Years of Torts*, 50 Harv. L. Rev. 725 (1937).

[6]Samuel D. Warren and Louis D. Brandeis, *The Right to Privacy*, 4 Harv. L. Rev. 193 (1890).

[7]Thomas Cooley, *Torts* 29 (2d ed 1888).

[8]*Manola v. Stevens*, reported in *The New York Times* (June 15, 18 and 21, 1890).

[9]Warren and Brandeis, *Right of Privacy*. 193, 196.

[10]Rodney A. Smolla, *Free Speech in an Open Society* 145–46 (Random House, 1992).

[11]Restatement (Second) of Torts § 652B (1977).

[12]*Dietemann v. Time, Inc.*, 449 F.2d 245, 249 (9th Cir. 1971).

[13]*Galella v. Onassis*, 487 F. 2d 986 (2d Cir. 1973).

[14]*United States v. O'Brien*, 391 U.S. 367, 88 S. Ct. 1673 (1968).

[15]*Id.* at 377.

[16]See, e.g., *Smith v. Daily Mail Publishing Co.*, 443 U.S. 97 (1979); *Florida Star v. B.J.F.*, 491 U.S. 524 (1989).

[17]*Richmond Newspapers v. Virginia*, 448 U.S. 555 (1980).

[18]"The right to speak and publish does not carry with it the *unrestrained* right to gather information" (emphasis added). *Zemel v. Rusk,* 381 U.S. 1, 17 (1965).

[19]*Shulman v. Group W Productions,* 18 Calif. 4th 200 (1998), 955 P.2d 469 (1998).

[20]Warren and Brandeis, *Right of Privacy* 193, 195.

[21]*Id.* at 196.

[22]M.L. Stein, *Privacy Suit Survives,* 131 (23) Editor & Publisher 15 (June 6, 1998).

[23]*Shulman v. Group W Productions,* 18 Caifl. 4th 200, 955 P.2d 469, 483–84 (1998).

[24]*Id.* at 497.

[25]*Id.* at 494.

[26]*Green v. Chicago Tribune Co.,* 286 Ill. App. 3d 1, 675 N.E. 2d 249 (Dec. 30, 1996).

[27]*Id.* at 3–4.

[28]*Id.* at 4. ("I love you, Calvin. I have been telling you for the longest time about this street thing. I love you, sweetheart. That is my baby. The Lord has taken him and I don't have to worry about him anymore. I accept it. They took him out of this troubled world. The boy has been troubled for a long time. Let the Lord have him.")

[29]*Id.* at 6. See also the notorious "Starving Glutton" case, *Barber v. Time, Inc.,* 159 S.W .2d 291, 295 (Mo. 1942).

[30]*Id.* at 7.

[31]*Id.* at 8.

[32]*Id.* at 9.

[33]*Id.* at 10.

[34]*Id.* at 11, quoting from the Restatement (Second) of Torts, § 652D, comment h, 391 (1977).

[35]*Miller v. National Broadcasting Co.,* 187 Calif. App. 3d 1463, 232 Calif. Rptr. 668 (1986).

[36]*Id.* at 1469.

[37]*Id.* at 1488.

[38]*Eye on America,* CBS Evening News (Jan. 4, 1999).

[39]*Id.*

[40]*Wilson v. Layne,* 141 F.3d 111 (4th Cir. 1998); *Parker v. Boyer,* 93 F.3d 445 (8th Cir. 1996); *Ayeni v. Mottola,* 35 F.3d 680 (2d Circ. 1994) and *Berger v. Hanlon,* 129 F.3d 505 (9th Circ. 1997).

[41]*Hanlon v. Berger,* 525 U.S. 981 (1998) and *Wilson v. Layne,* 525 U.S. 981 (1998).

[42]*Berger v. Hanlon,* 129 F.3d 505, 510–12.

[43]*Id.* at 515.

[44]*Wilson v. Layne,* 141 F.3d 111, 112.

[45]*Layne v. Wilson,* 110 F.3d 1071 (4th Cir. 1997).

[46]*Wilson v. Layne,* 141 F.3d 111, 115.

[47]*Id.* at 118–19.

[48]18 U.S.C. § 3105, in *Ayeni v. Mottola,* 35 F.3d 680, 686.

[49]*Wilson v. Layne,* 114 F.3d 111, 118–19.

[50]*Parker v. Boyer,* 93 F.3d 445, 447, *cert. denied,* 117 S. Ct. 1081 (1997).

[51]*Id.*

[52]*Wilson v. Layne,* 119 S. Ct. 1692 (1999).

[53]The Court ruled 8–1 that the law enforcement officers involved in the two incidents were entitled to qualify for immunity for their decision to allow the press to accompany them because the applicable law was unclear.

[54]The Fourth Amendment reads, in the pertinent part, "The right of the people to be secure in their persons, houses, papers and effects, against unreasonable searches and seizures, shall not be violated. . . ." U.S. Const, Amend IV.

[55]*Wilson v. Layne* at 1698.

[56]*Id.* at 1699.

[57]*Id.* at 1698.

[58]Alan F. Westin, *Media Access: Collision of First Amendment and Privacy Values,* 27 (17) Marketing News A17 (Aug. 16, 1993).

[59]*Department of Justice v. Reporters Committee for Freedom of the Press,* 489 U.S. 749 (1989).

[60]*Id.* at 766–71.

[61]*The Privacy Problem,* 17 (2) Electronic Media (Jan. 12, 1998).

6

Blurred Vision: The Supreme Court's FOIA Opinions on Invasion of Privacy

Martin E. Halstuk

Of the great conflicts involving access law, the clash between the ill-defined right of personal privacy and access to records kept by governmental agencies continues to bedevil courts, lawmakers and access advocates. The federal Freedom of Information Act has generated volumes of law dedicated to the central question of how to balance the competing interests of access and privacy. In this chapter, the author offers a timely review of the law of privacy in just one corner of access law—and reveals the Supreme Court's inconsistency in an area sure to dominate access law in the Information Age.

Introduction

The Freedom of Information Act (FOIA or the Act)[1] is one of the most valuable tools of inquiry for journalists and members of the public who want to know what the federal government is doing. Government agencies collect vast amounts of vital information that can serve the public interest, and the FOIA affords the public access to much of it. The statute requires that federal agencies provide any person access to all records that do not fall under one of nine exemptions.[2] Congress created the exemptions to balance the social value of the public's statutory right to know[3] with government needs to keep some information secret.

Additionally, conflicts can arise when the needs of citizens to obtain government-held information result in the disclosure of private information about other citizens. Society places great importance on privacy,[4] and the Supreme Court has recognized some implicit constitutional protection for a limited right to privacy.[5] So while the act acknowledged the critical need for citizens in a democracy to have access to government information to make informed decisions concerning self-rule,[6] Congress also recognized the importance of privacy. Thus, two of the act's exemptions[7] allow agencies to withhold information that would invade the privacy of individuals.

This chapter explores the conflict between the competing values of individual privacy and the public interest in disclosure of government information. The examination focuses on seven key Supreme Court FOIA opinions, decided between 1976 and 1997.[8] The opinions resulted from lawsuits brought by FOIA requesters after the government withheld information on grounds that the material was protected under Exemptions 6 and 7(C) of the Freedom of Information Act. The principal question posed in this analysis is whether the Court has fairly balanced the conflicting values of access and privacy within the guidelines established by Congress in the FOIA. In other words, has the Court exceeded the FOIA's plain meaning[9] and legislative intent in opinions regarding the privacy exemptions?

Along with the Supreme Court opinions that deal with the privacy question, this analysis examines the history and legislative intent of the FOIA . The first section discusses the historic roots of the FOIA to shed light on how political and social forces set the stage for the federal disclosure statute. In the second section, this chapter traces the FOIA's congressional history and explains the meaning of privacy Exemptions 6 and 7(C). The third section analyzes seven cases in which the Supreme Court addressed government refusals to disclose information on grounds that the requested material fell under the privacy exemptions.

The conclusion suggests the Supreme Court has broadly interpreted the privacy exemptions and narrowly construed the public interest served by access to government information. As a result, government has denied FOIA requesters access to information that could be used to advance the public interest in important areas such as the environment, collective bargaining by government employees and the news gathering abilities of journalists.

Historical Roots of the Freedom of Information Act

In 1966, Congress passed the Freedom of Information Act, which was amended later in significant respects.[10] The act creates a judicially enforceable policy based on a general philosophy of full disclosure of information held by government agencies.[11] The FOIA, which does not apply to state or local governments, makes agency records available to "any person" upon request[12] and places the burden of justifying nondisclosure on the government.[13] Before the FOIA was enacted, the news media and general public had no legal recourse when denied access to government information.

The Freedom of Information Act applies to records held by agencies in the executive branch of the federal government, including the Executive Office of the President, and independent regulatory agencies, such as the Federal Communications Commission, the Environmental Protection Agency and the Securities and Exchange Commission.[14] The FOIA does not apply to records held by state governments,[15] Congress,[16] the courts,[17] municipal corporations[18] or private citizens.[19] Nor does it apply to the personal staff of the president and some executive branch agencies whose sole function is to advise the president, such as the Council of Economic Advisors.[20] To help ensure access, the law requires that federal agencies publish in the Federal Register their organization plans and regulations along with procedures for the public to obtain information.[21]

Striking a Balance Between the Public's Right to Know and the Individual's Right to Privacy

In crafting the FOIA, Congress clearly recognized the crucial need for citizens to have access to government information. But legislators also understood the individual's important need for privacy and acknowledged the legal protection afforded to privacy over the years.[22] In general, definitions of privacy vary among scholars. A modern and widely accepted meaning of this right is provided by Professor Thomas I. Emerson, who wrote that the concept "attempts to draw a line between the individual and the collective, between self and society. It seeks to assure the individual a zone in which to be an individual, not a member of the community. In that zone he can think his own thoughts, have his own secrets, live his own life, reveal only what he wants to the outside world."[23]

An American court first recognized a right to privacy in 1890,[24] responding to a call for privacy protection by Samuel D. Warren and Louis D. Brandeis in a seminal article published that year in the Harvard Law Review.[25] The two authors declared that news gathering by the press too often violated the privacy of individuals. "The intensity and complexity of life, attendant upon advancing civilization, have rendered necessary some retreat from the world," Warren and Brandeis wrote, "and man, under the refining influence of culture, has become more sensitive to publicity, so that solitude and privacy have become more essential to the individual."[26]

The fundamental conflict between access and privacy arises when, in order to learn what the government is doing, private information about citizens must be disclosed. To resolve this conflict, FOIA crafters created two privacy exemptions. Exemption 6 protects personal information contained in "personnel and medical and similar files," and Exemption 7(C) protects personal information in "investigatory records compiled for law enforcement purposes."

A 1965 Senate report reflected the legislative intent behind the crafting of Exemptions 6 and 7(C): "At the same time that a broad philosophy of 'freedom of information' is enacted into law, it is necessary to protect certain equally important government rights of privacy with respect to certain information in government files, such as medical and personnel records. It is also necessary for the very operation of our Government to allow it to keep confidential certain material, such as the investigatory files of the Federal Bureau of Investigation."[27]

Nonetheless, the report also makes clear that an information policy of full disclosure underpins the Act: "Today the very vastness of our Government and its myriad of agencies makes it difficult for the electorate to obtain that 'popular information' of which [James] Madison spoke.[28] But it is only when one further considers the hundreds of departments, branches, and agencies which are not directly responsible to the people, that one begins to understand the great importance of having an information policy of full disclosure."[29]

The perspective of legislators who crafted the Act was echoed by President Lyndon B. Johnson when he signed the FOIA into law on July 4, 1966: "This legislation springs from one of our most essential principles: A democracy works best when the people have all the information that the security of the nation permits. No one should be able to pull the curtain of secrecy around decisions which can be revealed without injury to the public interest."[30]

Despite the FOIA's clear legislative intent, its wide congressional support and its endorsement by the Department of Justice,[31] the law's first few years were not as successful as its supporters had hoped. There was a general reluctance by agencies to comply with the law, rendering it, in the words of Antonin Scalia, then a law professor at the University of Chicago, "a relatively toothless beast, sometimes kicked about shamelessly by the agencies."[32] Federal agencies interpreted the exemptions broadly to justify withholding documents. Officials also used various ploys to discourage use of the act, including high fees for copying documents, long delays and bureaucratic claims that officials could not find the requested documents.[33] In great part, this state of affairs was the result of sometimes vague or even poor draftsmanship of the FOIA.[34]

Recognizing, in the words of Sen. Edward M. Kennedy, that "the doors of government would [not] be opened to the public,"[35] Congress acted to clarify and strengthen the law through a series of amendments. By early 1973—amid growing concerns about government secrecy as details of the Watergate scandal surfaced—legislators in the House and the Senate introduced a bill to put teeth in the FOIA.[36] Under the amendments:

1. Agencies were required to respond to information requests within 10 days or face a lawsuit.[37]
2. Federal district judges were permitted in camera review of top secret classified information to confirm the government's claims that the material was properly classified.[38]
3. Search and copying fees were made uniform among the agencies to avoid excessive charges.[39]
4. Requesters were allowed to describe desired records only in a general way, as long as it was sufficient to allow an agency to find the category of documents requested.[40]

Congress passed the 1974 amendments twice by overwhelming majorities, overriding President Gerald Ford's veto the second time around.[41] The 1974 amendments sharpened the FOIA, expanding protection for privacy and reshaping the law as it stands today. Although Exemption 6 was written in 1966,[42] Exemption 7(C) was not enacted until the 1974 amendments.[43] The language of Exemption 6, as crafted in the original 1966 legislation, remains intact today. Both the Senate and the House reports accompanying the FOIA said Exemption 6 required a "balancing of interests" between the individual's right to privacy and the public's interest in obtaining government-held information.[44] According to the Senate Report: "The phrase 'clearly unwarranted invasion of personal privacy' enunciates a policy that will involve a balancing of interests between the protection of an individual's private affairs and the preservation of the public's right to governmental information."[45]

In making a judgment in a privacy-interests case under Exemption 6, the courts first must determine if the records falls within the definition of "personnel," "medical" or "similar" files. Second, the courts must balance the invasion of the individual's personal privacy against the public benefit that would result from disclosure. To withhold information, the government must show the disclosure "would constitute a clearly unwarranted invasion of privacy." Likewise, the courts use a similar two-step test in deciding a privacy-interests case under Exemption 7(C). First, the documents must have been compiled for law enforcement reasons, because this exemption pertains only to investigative records. Second, government must prove the disclosure could "reasonably be expected to constitute an unwarranted invasion of privacy."

A key difference between the exemptions is evident in their statutory language: Exemption 6 calls for a *"clearly* unwarranted invasion" of privacy. On the other hand, Exemption 7 requires a less strict standard, asking an agency to show only that disclosure could *"reasonably be expected* to constitute an unwarranted invasion of privacy." The difference in language was intentional. The legislative history shows that Exemption 7(C), as originally proposed by Congress, also required a *"clearly"* unwarranted invasion of personal privacy.[46] However, the word "clearly" was dropped by the Conference Committee as a concession in negotiations with President Ford[47] to get the act approved.

By dropping "clearly," the exemption lessened the agency's burden to meet the test.[48] As a result, courts have concluded that Exemption 7(C) allows law enforcement officers more latitude to withhold records to protect privacy than is permitted under the stricter standard of Exemption 6.[49] Thus Exemption 7(C) means the public interest in disclosure carries less weight.[50]

Analysis of Cases

The Supreme Court has reviewed how lower courts balanced the public interest in access to government information against the privacy interests protected under FOIA Exemptions 6 and 7(C) in a series of cases on diverse issues. Some of these FOIA requests sought information on cadets cheating at the U.S. Air Force Academy,[51] President Nixon's so-called "enemies list"[52] and the criminal history of a reputed Mafia crime figure with ties to a corrupt Congress member.[53] In

1976, when the Supreme Court considered its first case based on government refusal to disclose information under Exemption 6, the Court established that an individual's privacy interests must be balanced against the public's interest in opening governmental operations to public view.[54]

U.S. Dept. of the Air Force v. Rose (1976)

In the leading case construing FOIA Exemption 6, *U.S. Dept. of the Air Force v. Rose*,[55] the Supreme Court reasoned that Congress sought to create a privacy exemption that would require a balancing test, which weighed the individual's right to privacy against the public interest in disclosure. The Court further held that the device adopted to strike that balance was the limited exemption where an invasion of personal privacy was "clearly unwarranted."[56]

The Court's 5–3 opinion upheld a request by student editors of *The New York University Law Review* for summaries of honor and ethics hearings at the Air Force Academy.[57] The student editors wanted the information for an article on disciplinary procedures in the service academies.[58] The Air Force rejected the request for the hearing summaries and refused to provide the documents, even with the names and identifying facts redacted.[59] The Air Force cited Exemption 6's privacy interest, asserting that disclosure would stigmatize the offenders for the rest of their careers.[60]

The U.S. District Court for the Southern District of New York granted the Air Force's motion for a summary judgment.[61] However, the U.S. Court of Appeals for the Second Circuit reversed, holding that disclosure under Exemption 6, with names and all identifying information redacted, would not subject any former cadet to public identification and stigma.[62] The Supreme Court opinion, written by Justice William J. Brennan, affirmed the Second Circuit's ruling. The Court concluded that release of disciplinary actions against the cadets—with the names of the individual cadets deleted—was in the public interest and comported with the purpose of the Freedom of Information Act.[63] Brennan wrote that the strong public interest in cheating and other violations of discipline at the Air Force Academy was obvious because obedience and reliability are important to military effectiveness.

The *Rose* majority endorsed the ruling by the Second Circuit, which said the legislative history makes it "crystal clear" that the congressional objective for the FOIA was "to pierce the veil of administrative secrecy and to open agency action to the light of public scrutiny."[64] The Court upheld the Second Circuit's view that the

FOIA's statutory language and legislative history indicate that the exemptions must be narrowly construed.[65] Brennan wrote that withholding under the exemptions applies only to information specifically stated in the exemptions, and these "limited exemptions do not obscure the basic policy that disclosure, not secrecy, is the dominant objective of the act."[66] Brennan concluded that the FOIA is "broadly conceived" to permit access to "official information long shielded unnecessarily from public view."[67]

In a situation where the government withholds information, claiming a privacy interest under Exemption 6, Brennan said Congress intended the outcome to be determined by balancing privacy interests of the individual against the public interest in disclosure.[68] This intent was consistently reflected in congressional documents. A 1965 Senate report said the term "clearly unwarranted invasion of personal privacy" enunciates a policy that involves "a balancing of interests between the protection of an individual's private affairs from unnecessary public scrutiny and the preservation of the public's right to governmental information."[69] A 1966 House report expressed the same intent in nearly identical language.[70]

Brennan cited the FOIA's statutory language and legislative history in holding that Exemption 6 did not create an absolute right to privacy concerning personnel, medical and similar files:[71] "We find nothing in the wording of Exemption 6 or its legislative history to support the Agency's claim that Congress created a blanket Exemption for personnel files."

It seems, therefore, that the *Rose* Court's prescription for balancing the privacy interest against the public interest in disclosure calls for a narrow interpretation of the FOIA exemptions and a broad construction of the public interest in knowing what the government is doing.[72] Brennan wrote that the policies underlying the FOIA are intended "to open public business to public view"[73] and allow for public access to information about government action.

It is important to note that *Rose* did not say that the purpose of the FOIA is to allow public access to government information solely to evaluate agency conduct or performance. Nor did *Rose* say that either the Act's language or legislative history suggests that such a statutory purpose exists. The absence of such language in *Rose* is significant because identifying the FOIA's purpose became a critical issue several years later in a seminal case in which the Supreme Court narrowly interpreted the statute's scope.[74] This case, *Dept. of Justice v. Reporters Committee for Freedom of the Press,* is examined later in this chapter.

After the Supreme Court concluded in *Rose* that the FOIA's statutory language and legislative history indicate that privacy Exemption

6 must be narrowly construed, there came an apparent shift in the Court's philosophy. Instead of narrowly construing the *exemptions,* the Court began to narrowly interpret *the public interest standard* in disclosure. This trend emerged in three cases in which the Court rejected FOIA requests from the news media and instead upheld government decisions to withhold information on grounds that disclosure would be an invasion of privacy.[75]

U.S. Dept. of State v. Washington Post Co. (1982)

In the first news media case, *Dept. of State v. Washington Post,* the Court considered the question of whether the term "similar files" in Exemption 6 should be interpreted to include passport information.[76] In a unanimous opinion written by Chief Justice William H. Rehnquist, the Court held that a file need not contain intimate information to qualify for withholding under Exemption 6.[77] The Court concluded, therefore, that a passport qualified as a "similar file."[78]

In *The Washington Post* case, the Supreme Court reversed the judgment of the U.S. Court of Appeals for the District of Columbia[79] and upheld the State Department's decision to withhold information sought by the newspaper.[80] In September 1979, *The Washington Post* wanted to confirm an unofficial report that two officials of Iran's revolutionary, anti-American government—Dr. Ali Behzadnia and Dr. Ibrahim Yazdi—held U.S. passports.[81] The newspaper asked the State Department for information to determine whether the report was true. The government refused, asserting that such disclosure would constitute a "clearly unwarranted" invasion of privacy under FOIA Exemption 6.

The State Department contended that passport information qualified as "similar files," and disclosure of this information would be a "clearly unwarranted invasion of privacy."[82] The government also said disclosure of the information would "cause a real threat of physical harm" to both men.[83] But the U.S. District Court for the District of Columbia ruled in favor of the newspaper, and the D.C. Circuit affirmed, holding that passport information does not qualify as a "personnel," "medical" or "similar" record because it does not contain highly personal information or intimate details about an individual.[84] However, the Supreme Court held that the term "similar files" in Exemption 6 should be interpreted to have a "broad rather than narrow meaning."[85] And under a broad interpretation, a file does not need to contain intimate information to qualify for withholding under Exemption 6.

Chief Justice Rehnquist wrote that Exemption 6's statutory language shed little light on what Congress meant by "similar files."[86]

But he said the Court found the statute's legislative history "more illuminating." And under the Court's interpretation of the legislative history, the phrase "similar files" was to have a broad rather than narrow meaning.[87] According to the Court's interpretation of House and Senate reports—which Rehnquist said did not define the phrase "similar files"—"Congress' primary purpose in enacting Exemption 6 was to protect individuals from the harm and embarrassment that can result from the unnecessary disclosure of personal information."[88]

The Court opinion gave considerable weight to the State Department affidavit, which said the two Iranians could be placed in danger if the information were disclosed: "Compliance [with *The Washington Post's* request] would cause a real threat of physical harm" to both men, who "would be in physical danger from some of the revolutionary groups that are prone to violence."[89] In recognizing this potential harm to Behzadnia and Yazdi, Rehnquist rejected the court of appeals' argument that Congress did not design Exemption 6 to direct the withholding of information on the basis of "physical security of persons stationed or residing overseas."[90]

In *The Washington Post* case, the Supreme Court took its first step in broadly interpreting a privacy exemption and narrowly interpreting the public interest in disclosure. This interpretation marked a departure from the *Rose* case, which interpreted the privacy exemption narrowly and broadly construed the public interest in disclosure. In balancing the public interest in disclosure with the privacy interests of the two Iranians, the Court did not consider an important democratic value of disclosure in this case: The information could offer the public an opportunity to assess and debate government policy in granting passport privileges—and the protection that a U.S. passport provides—to officials of foreign nations. Facilitating public discussion of American foreign policy decisions would be in keeping with the democratic principles that the FOIA was created to advance.

The Supreme Court maintained its narrow interpretation of the public interest in disclosure when it considered a second news media case. The issue concerned Exemption 7(C), the law-enforcement privacy exception. In a narrow 5–4 decision, the Supreme Court upheld the government's decision to reject a FOIA request by a journalist who wanted to gain access to FBI information.[91]

Federal Bureau of Investigation v. Abramson (1982)

In *Federal Bureau of Investigation v. Abramson*,[92] the Court held that information initially contained in records compiled for law enforcement purposes does not lose its Exemption 7(C) protection when the information is reproduced or summarized in a new document for purposes other than law enforcement.[93] The case involved reporter Howard Abramson, who, in June 1976, was investigating President Richard Nixon's alleged use of the FBI to collect derogatory information on political opponents.[94] Abramson filed a request under the FOIA for information concerning the FBI's records on individuals President Nixon believed were enemies of his administration.[95]

The FBI provided Abramson with 84 pages of documents, some intact and some with information deleted.[96] The FBI said release of the unredacted information would be an "unwarranted invasion of privacy" under Exemption 7(C).[97] Abramson brought suit in the U.S. District Court for the District of Columbia and argued that although the original records may have been compiled for law enforcement use, the summaries requested by Nixon were intended for purely political reasons. Therefore, the information should be disclosed. The district court granted the FBI's motion for summary judgment,[98] but the U.S. Court of Appeals for the District of Columbia agreed with Abramson and reversed. The D.C. Circuit held that the government had no justification to withhold the FBI summaries requested by the president because the information was provided "solely for use by the White House for purposes having nothing whatsoever to do with 'law enforcement.'"[99]

On appeal by the FBI, the Supreme Court reversed the D.C. Circuit. In an opinion written by Justice Byron R. White, the Court agreed with the court of appeals that the information withheld by the FBI was originally compiled for law enforcement purposes; that the summaries were developed pursuant to a request by the White House for information about certain public personalities; and that the summaries were not compiled for law enforcement purposes.[100] Nor was it disputed, the Court said further, that if the threshold requirement of Exemption 7(C) were met—that the documents sought were compiled for law enforcement purposes—the disclosure of the information would be an unwarranted invasion of privacy. Justice White framed the issue as whether information originally compiled for law enforcement purposes loses its Exemption 7(C) protection if summarized in a new document not created for law enforcement purposes.

Declaring that "no express answer is provided by the statutory language or by the legislative history," [101] the Court embarked on an analysis of the statute's plain language. Exemption 7(C) states that the FOIA does not apply to matters that are "records or information compiled for law enforcement purposes, but only to the extent that the production of such law enforcement records or information . . . could reasonably be expected to constitute an unwarranted invasion of personal privacy." First, the Court reasoned that the information Abramson sought consisted of a "document," namely correspondence between FBI Director J. Edgar Hoover and White House aide John D. Ehrlichman. Further, this "document" contained the summaries prepared by the FBI at the request of the White House.[102] The Court then reasoned that the summaries were compiled from a FBI "record," and this "record" was previously compiled for law enforcement purposes.[103]

Based on this analysis, which distinguished between a "document" and a "record" that may be contained in the document, the Court concluded that the FBI could withhold the information Abramson sought. The Court held that information initially contained in a record made for law enforcement purposes "continues to meet the threshold requirements of Exemption 7(C) where that recorded information is reproduced or summarized in a new document prepared for a non-law enforcement purpose"[104]—even if those records were included in a later compilation made for political reasons.[105]

Four justices dissented—Harry A. Blackmun, Brennan, Sandra Day O'Connor and Thurgood Marshall—contending that the Court majority, in effect, amended the FOIA with its overly broad interpretation. Justice Blackmun, in a dissent joined by Justice Brennan, said the Court majority ignored the plain meaning of the statutory language.[106] Blackmun said President Nixon's use of the FBI information did not meet the threshold question asked in Exemption 7(C): Are the records in question "investigatory records for law enforcement purposes?"

Justice O'Connor, in a separate dissent joined by Justice Marshall, echoed Blackmun's objections. She declared the majority opinion amounted to "judicial alteration" of the FOIA's language and intent.[107] She acknowledged there was sparse legislative history to help guide the Court, but the absence of such history is not an excuse for the Court to override "the usual presumption that the plain language of a statute controls its construction."[108] The majority, she wrote, "undertakes to rewrite the Exemption, substituting for the statutory phrase 'investigatory records compiled for law enforcement purposes' to something like 'records containing investigatory information originally gathered for law enforcement purposes.'"[109]

In concluding that the requested information should be released, O'Connor pointed to democratic political theory that underpins the FOIA's objectives to establish a general philosophy of full disclosure.[110] "It scarcely needs to be repeated," she wrote, "that Congress' objective in requiring such disclosure was 'to ensure an informed citizenry, vital to the functioning of a democratic society, needed to check against corruption and to hold the governors accountable to the governed."[111]

In the *Abramson* ruling, as in *The Washington Post* case decided in the same year, the Court majority ruled against a request by the news media to gain access to government-held information on grounds of invasion of privacy. Both cases stand as examples of Supreme Court decisions that, through narrow construction of the public interest in disclosure, not only restricted news gathering abilities of journalists but also reduced the scope of the FOIA for all who would use it. A third news media case also concerning Exemption 7(C) came before the court seven years later with similar results and even more profound consequences.

U.S. Dept. of Justice v. Reporters Committee for Freedom of the Press (1989)

The Supreme Court held unanimously in *U.S. Dept. of Justice v. Reporters Committee for Freedom of the Press*[112] that federal agencies can withhold computerized FBI compilations of "rap sheets" on private citizens even though the information might be available in public records available in local or state offices.[113] In the opinion written by Justice John Paul Stevens, the Court held that disclosure of compilations of an individual's criminal records is an unwarranted invasion of privacy under Exemption 7(C) when the request does not seek "official information" that sheds light on the conduct or performance of an agency or government official.[114]

The decision ended an 11-year effort by CBS reporter Robert Schakne and the Reporters Committee for the Freedom of the Press to obtain the FBI's rap sheet—a record of arrests, indictments, convictions or acquittals—on reputed crime figure Charles Medico.[115] Schakne was investigating Medico because Medico's company allegedly received defense contracts in exchange for political contributions to a corrupt Pennsylvania congressman, Daniel J. Flood.[116] The Pennsylvania Crime Commission had identified Medico Industries as a legitimate business dominated by organized crime figures. The FBI provided Schakne with information on three of Charles Medico's brothers, who were deceased, but the agency refused to release the requested information on Charles Medico, who was still living. Schakne brought suit in U.S. District Court for the District of Columbia, and the district court granted the FBI's motion for summary judgment, holding that the information was protected under FOIA Exemption 7(C) and disclosure would be an unwarranted invasion of Charles Medico's privacy.[117] The D.C. Circuit reversed, reasoning that the government cannot claim a privacy interest in FBI-compiled records that would be available to the public if sought from the individual law enforcement agencies.[118]

But the Supreme Court reversed the D.C. Circuit's decision and permitted the FBI to withhold the information. The Court held that the only public interest to be recognized in a balancing test against the privacy interest is that of disclosing only "official information" that directly reveals the activities of the government.[119] Justice Stevens wrote that the FOIA's "central purpose is to ensure that the government's activities be opened to the sharp eye of public scrutiny, not that information about private citizens that happens to be in the warehouse of the government be so disclosed."[120] The Court concluded that disclosure of a computerized compilation of an individual's criminal records, which do not directly reveal governmental operations or performance, is an "unwarranted" invasion of privacy because the information falls "outside the ambit of the public interest that the FOIA was enacted to serve."[121] In the Court's view, in other words, the rap sheets did not directly reveal official information about how government operates, and thus they could be withheld. The information "would tell us nothing directly about the character of the Congressman's behavior. Nor would it tell us anything about the conduct of the Department of Defense in awarding one or more contracts to the Medico Company," Stevens wrote.[122]

Stevens made a special point to note that the request was for computerized information, and that computerization of personal information poses a special potential threat to privacy.[123] The Court acknowledged that Medico's criminal history of arrests, indictments and convictions are public records, which could be available from the individual law enforcement agencies that investigated and prosecuted him. The justice emphasized, however, that Schakne sought a computerized compilation of all of this information. "The privacy interest in a rap sheet is substantial," Stevens wrote. "The substantial character of that interest is affected by the fact that in today's society the computer can accumulate and store information that would have otherwise *surely been forgotten long before a person attains the age of 80, when the FBI's rap sheets are discarded.*"[124] Stevens said there is a "vast difference between the public records that might be found after a diligent search of courthouse files, county archives and local police stations throughout the country and a computerized summary located in a single clearinghouse of information."[125]

This majority position was characterized as unsound in a concurring opinion by Justice Blackmun, joined by Justice Brennan. On the basis of Exemption 7(C)'s plain language, its legislative history and case law, Blackmun argued that the Court opinion exempting "all" rap sheet information from the FOIA's disclosure requirements was overbroad.[126] He presented a hypothetical situation in which a rap sheet disclosed a congressional candidate's conviction of tax fraud before he ran for office. The FBI's disclosure of that information could not reasonably be expected to constitute an invasion of personal privacy, much less an unwarranted invasion, because the candidate gave up any interest in preventing disclosure of this information when he chose to run for office, Blackmun said.[127]

Reporters Committee is a seminal ruling because it stands for the Supreme Court's current interpretation of the FOIA's central purpose. The opinion sets forth the principle that the statutory goal of the FOIA is limited to disclosing only official information that "sheds light on an agency's performance."[128] The statute's plain language and legislative history suggest a broader vision, however. First, the FOIA mandates broad disclosure of government documents: "[E]ach agency, upon any request for records which (A) reasonably describes such record and (B) is made in accordance with published rules stating the time, place, fees (if any), and procedures to be followed shall make the records promptly available to any person."[129] Second, an FOIA request must be granted unless the information requested falls within one of the nine statutory exemptions.[130] These specific limits to withholding are emphasized in the statute's legislative history: "There is a certain need for confidentiality in some aspects of Government operations, and these are protected *specifically; but outside these limited areas, all citizens have a right to know*"[131] (emphasis added.) Third, the government has the burden of establishing that an exemption applies, and exemptions must be construed narrowly.[132]

The *Reporters Committee* Court thus established what Professor Fred H. Cate and his colleagues called an "official information" test as a threshold to determine whether information requested under the FOIA should be disclosed.[133] In other words, although federal agencies collect vast amounts of information on virtually every facet of society, the public is entitled under *Reporters Committee* to gain access to only a limited class of information as prescribed by the Court's narrowly drawn "central purpose" of the Freedom of Information Act.[134] The consequences of the *Reporters Committee* precedent are evident in the next three privacy exemption cases to reach the Supreme Court, all concerning Exemption 6.

U.S. Dept. of State v. Ray (1991)

In deciding *U.S. Dept. of State v. Ray* in 1991, the Supreme Court concluded that the release of identifying information about Haitian refugees, who fled to the United States and were sent back involuntarily to Haiti, could be withheld because disclosure would constitute a "clearly unwarranted" invasion of privacy under Exemption 6.[135] The dispute began when a Florida lawyer, who represented Haitian nationals seeking political asylum in the United States, requested the U.S. government's files of Haitians who were returned to Haiti by American authorities.[136] The requested files contained information on interviews conducted in Haiti by the State Department with a "representative sample" of returned Haitians.[137] The interviews were conducted to determine whether the Haitian government made good on its promise not to persecute them. The State Department reported that only one or two of the returnees said they were harassed by the Haitian government upon their return.

The lawyer wanted identifying information on the interviewed Haitians so his office could contact the returnees to confirm the Haitian government was keeping its word and the United States was making good on its promise to monitor Haiti's treatment of the returnees. The lawyer wanted to follow up on the returned Haitians' treatment because he was attempting to prove in immigration proceedings that his clients faced a well-founded fear of persecution if denied asylum.. The State Department provided the lawyer with 96 pages of information, but the names of the returned Haitians—along with other identifying details such as their living conditions, children, marital status and employment status—were redacted under Exemption 6 as a "clearly unwarranted" invasion of privacy.

The lawyer brought suit against the Justice Department and the State Department to obtain the release of the uncensored files.[138] The U.S. District Court of the Southern District of Florida ordered the State Department to release the redacted information, holding that the privacy interests were minimal and were outweighed by the public interest in making sure the government protected the returned Haitians. The U.S. Court of Appeals for the Eleventh Circuit affirmed.[139] Although the Eleventh Circuit recognized there were "significant privacy interests at stake," the appeals court concluded that the privacy interests in the case were outweighed by the public interest in disclosure.[140] The appeals court reasoned the public interest would be served in finding out whether the State Department adequately monitored Haiti's compliance with its agreement not to persecute returnees and whether the U.S. government was "honest to the public" when American officials said Haiti was keeping its word.

On appeal by the State Department, the Supreme Court reversed the Eleventh Circuit's ruling and upheld the government's Exemption 6 rationale that disclosure of identifying information *was* a "clearly unwarranted" invasion of privacy.[141] Justice Stevens, writing the Court's 8–0 opinion, said the information was protected under Exemption 6 for three reasons. First, disclosure would release highly personal information about the Haitians;[142] second, disclosure would violate assurances of confidentiality given to the Haitians by State Department officials who interviewed them;[143] and third, disclosure might expose them to persecution, mistreatment or other retaliatory actions. Moreover, the Court said there was no evidence to doubt the veracity of the State Department's reports.[144]

The Supreme Court acknowledged there was a public interest in making sure the State Department protected the returned Haitians. But the Court concluded that upholding their privacy interests to keep them out of harm's way outweighed the public interest in disclosure. The Court held that public interest in disclosure of "[o]fficial information that sheds light on an agency's performance of its statutory duties," as established in *Reporters Committee*, was adequately served by the disclosure of the redacted interview summaries.[145] Additionally, the Court cited as precedent *U.S. Dept. of State v. Washington Post*—the case concerning the two Iranian officials traveling on U.S. passports—in holding that the Haitian's files were "similar files" within the meaning of Exemption 6 and thus qualified for withholding.[146] The Supreme Court further held in *Ray*, as it did in *The Washington Post* case, that disclosure of an individual's identity constituted a "clearly unwarranted" invasion of privacy if the disclosure could place an individual in danger.[147]

In terms of setting limits on the FOIA's purpose and scope, the *Reporters Committee* decision also played a major role in the next case decided by the Court, which rejected a request by unions for a list of federal employees the unions wanted to contact. But in this case, one justice voiced a strong protest against the Court's decision.[148]

U.S. Dept. of Defense v. Federal Labor Relations Authority (1994)

In *U.S. Dept. of Defense v. Federal Labor Relations Authority (FLRA)*, the Court held that releasing home addresses of government employees to union organizers would be a "clearly unwarranted" invasion of privacy under Exemption 6 because the requested information does not directly reveal the operations of the government.[149] The controversy in this case arose when two unions[150] asked the Army, Navy and Air Force to release names and home addresses of agency employees in bargaining units represented by the unions. The unions sought the information to communicate with potential members. The agencies disclosed the employees' names and work stations but refused to release their home addresses on grounds that disclosure would be an invasion of privacy.[151] The unions filed unfair labor practices charges, contending the Federal Service Labor-Management Relations Statute required the agencies to divulge the addresses. The labor statute provides that agencies must, "to the extent not prohibited by law," furnish unions with data that is necessary for collective bargaining purposes.[152] The Federal Labor Relations Authority consequently ruled the agencies must divulge the addresses.[153] The government appealed the ruling to the U.S. Court of Appeals for the Fifth Circuit.

In applying the balancing test to resolve the Exemption 6 conflict, the Fifth Circuit balanced the public interest in effective collective bargaining embodied in the labor statute against the employees' interest in keeping their home addresses private.[154] The Fifth Circuit held that furthering the "weighty" public interest of collective bargaining identified by Congress in the labor statute would not constitute a "clearly unwarranted" invasion of privacy.[155] Therefore, the Fifth Circuit upheld the FLRA's ruling that home addresses should be disclosed because the public interest in collective bargaining in this instance outweighs the privacy interests of federal employees.[156] In striking its balance, the court of appeals acknowledged the Supreme Court's decision in *Reporters Committee,* but reasoned that *Reporters Committee* had nothing to say about situations where disclosure is initially required by some statute other than the FOIA, such as the labor statute, and the FOIA is employed only secondarily.[157] In these types of cases, the court held, the federal court can consider the public interests embodied in the statute that generates the disclosure request.[158]

On appeal, the Supreme Court rejected the Fifth Circuit's argument and reversed. In an opinion by Justice Clarence Thomas, the Court held the requested employee addresses are "records" covered by the terms of the Privacy Act and, therefore, "unless FOIA would require release of the addresses," their disclosure is prohibited.[159] In the Court's view, the issue was whether disclosure of home addresses would constitute a "clearly unwarranted" invasion of privacy of the bargaining unit's employees.[160] In other words, the Fifth Circuit erred in reasoning that a balancing test could take into consideration the public interest embodied in the labor statute. Furthermore, the Court emphasized that "the only relevant 'public interest in disclosure' to be weighed in this balance is the extent to which disclosure would serve the 'core purpose of the FOIA,' which is 'contribut[ing] significantly to public understanding *of the operations or activities of the government'*" (emphasis in original).161 The Court reasoned that the relevant public interest supporting disclosure of the home address is "negligible, at best" because although disclosure might allow the unions to communicate more effectively with employees, disclosure would not "appreciably further 'the citizens' right to be informed about what their government is up to.'"162 Declaring that the individual privacy interest that would be protected by nondisclosure is "far from insignificant,"163 the Court thus concluded that the disclosure of home addresses would constitute a "clearly unwarranted" invasion of privacy.164

The Court's FLRA ruling turned entirely on the precedent established in *Reporters Committee:* Information that does not directly reveal governmental operations or performance is an invasion of privacy not permitted under the FOIA because the information falls "outside the ambit of the public interest that the FOIA was enacted to serve."165 As Justice Thomas made abundantly clear, "For guidance in [deciding FLRA], we need look no further than to our decision in *Department of Justice v. Reporters Committee for Freedom of the Press.*"166

In a concurring opinion, Justice Ruth Bader Ginsburg said she joined the majority judgment in FLRA because of the precedent set by *Reporters Committee,* but she added that she strongly disagreed with the *Reporters Committee* opinion.167 She characterized it as a "restrictive definition" of the public interest in disclosure and agreed with the Fifth Circuit's decision to release the addresses.168 She argued that Congress recognized a significant public interest in furthering collecting bargaining when it enacted the labor statute, which "unquestionably intended to strengthen the position of federal unions."169 She also noted that lower courts have held that private sector unions are entitled to receive employee home address lists from employers under the National Labor Relations Act.170 "It is surely doubtful," she reasoned, "that, in the very statute bolstering federal-sector unions, Congress aimed to deny those unions information their private-sector counterparts routinely receive."171

Justice Ginsburg wrote that the *Reporters Committee* precedent on which the Supreme Court's *FLRA* decision was based—and which she was required to follow under the doctrine of *stare decisis—* "changed the FOIA calculus" that underlies decisions favoring disclosure. She said the "core purpose" argument advanced by the Supreme

Court in *Reporters Committee* cannot be found anywhere in the FOIA's language.[172] Under the FOIA, she wrote, a requester is not required to show that disclosure would serve any public purpose, "let alone a 'core purpose' of . . . advancing 'public understanding of the operations or activities of the government.'"[173]

In pre-*Reporters Committee* days, she wrote, courts held that it was "fully consistent" with the FOIA's statutory language to judge an invasion of personal privacy as "warranted" even if the requested information is "unrelated to informing citizens about government operations."[174] She pointed out that in a 1989 Supreme Court opinion, *U.S. Dept. of Justice v. Tax Analysts,*[175] the Court required disclosure of Department of Justice compilations of district court tax decisions to the publishers of *Tax Notes,* a weekly magazine.[176] "That disclosure," Ginsburg said, "did not notably 'add to public knowledge of Government operations.'"[177]

In sum, Ginsburg rejected the FOIA "core purpose" argument and the Court's narrow reading of the public interest in disclosure, suggesting instead that the FOIA's plain meaning and congressional intent represent a broader vision—that the public is entitled to a wider range of government information than merely that information that reveals how government operates or performs its duties.[178] In her view, the Court's holdings in *Reporters Committee* and *FLRA* were not outcomes prescribed by the FOIA's plain language and legislative history. "Congress did not chart our journey's end," she wrote.[179]

The combined effect of the *Reporters Committee* and *FLRA* holdings controlled the outcome of a 1997 Supreme Court decision that also concerned a FOIA request for a list of names and home addresses held by the government.

Bibles v. Oregon Natural Desert Assn. (1997)

In *Bibles v. Oregon Natural Desert Assn. (ONDA),*[180] an Oregon nonprofit association filed a request for the names and addresses of persons who receive a newsletter published by the Bureau of Land Management. The newsletter provides information about the BLM's activities and environmental plans affecting the Oregon high desert. The Oregon Natural Desert Association, which is interested in desert preservation, wanted to find out whom the government was contacting and to whom it was directing information about the high desert.[181] The group said it wanted to provide those persons with additional information from sources that do not share the BLM's "self-interest in presenting government activities in the most favorable light."[182]

The Bureau of Land management originally refused to disclose the information. After the environmental group filed an appeal with the Department of the Interior, the BLM released the names and addresses of organizations on the mailing list, but refused to disclose similar information on individuals. The agency asserted that disclosure of such information would constitute "a clearly unwarranted" invasion of privacy under FOIA Exemption 6.[183] The environmental group brought suit in U.S. District Court for the District of Oregon, which held in favor of disclosure.[184] The district court reasoned that disclosure of the addresses could not constitute a "clearly unwarranted" invasion into the privacy of individuals who "have already opened their mail boxes to the receipt of information about BLM activities."[185]

The government appealed to the U.S. Court of Appeals for the Ninth Circuit, but the Ninth Circuit affirmed the district court's ruling.[186] The court of appeals upheld the environmental group's argument that there is "a substantial public interest in knowing to whom the government is directing information, or as ONDA characterized it, 'propaganda.'"[187] In the Ninth Circuit's view, the privacy interests claimed by the government were minimal because a majority of the individuals on the list asked to receive mailings about BLM activities.[188] The court of appeals said it considered the ruling in *U.S. Dept. of Defense v. FLRA* but concluded that the two cases were different.[189] The court of appeals distinguished *Oregon Natural Desert Assn.* from *FLRA* on the basis that government employees in the latter case had not chosen to provide the union with their addresses. The effect of disclosure on privacy in *Oregon Natural Desert Assn.* is smaller than in *FLRA,* the Ninth Circuit held, because most of the persons on the BLM's list had expressed a desire to receive mailings on subjects related to the environmental group's interests.[190]

In a two-page *per curiam* opinion, the Supreme Court reversed the Ninth Circuit and held that the Bureau of Land Management could withhold the list of names.[191] The opinion said the Ninth Circuit's decision "rested on a perceived public interest" in providing persons on the BLM's mailing list with additional information. The Court said the Ninth Circuit's holding, however, is inconsistent with the Supreme Court's ruling in *FLRA,* which held that "the *only* relevant public interest in the FOIA balancing analysis" is "the extent to which disclosure of the information would 'she[d] light on an agency's performance of its statutory duties' or otherwise let citizens know 'what their government is up to.'"[192] In reiterating its "core purpose" interpretation of the Freedom of Information Act, the Court emphasized that the ONDA request did not meet the threshold for disclosure under the statute.

The precedents established in *Reporters Committee* and *FLRA* enabled the Bureau of Land Management to avoid disclosure in *Oregon Natural Desert Assn.* As Justice Ginsburg argued in *FLRA*, disclosure of the federal employees' addresses to the unions would have been allowed pre-*Reporters Committee*.[193] Similarly, this analysis argues that the release of names and addresses of the recipients of the BLM newsletter also would have been allowed but for the precedent in *Reporters Committee*.

In *Oregon Natural Desert Assn.*, the Ninth Circuit said there is a substantial public interest in knowing to whom the government is directing information.[194] This point takes on tremendous significance in light of the fact that the federal government is the largest single producer, collector, consumer and disseminator of information in the United States.[195] "Government information is a valuable national resource," according to the Office of Management and Budget's Office of Information and Regulatory Affairs. "It provides the public with knowledge of the government, society, and economy—past, present, and future. It is a means to ensure the accountability of government, to manage the government's operations, to maintain the healthy performance of the economy, and is itself a commodity in the marketplace."[196]

With all the resources at the disposal of the federal government, it is a powerful speaker indeed. And when it comes to articulating agency policy, such as in an official agency newsletter, the government speaks in one voice. Releasing the addresses of individuals who "have already opened their mail boxes to the receipt of information about BLM activities"[197] would have been in keeping with the democratic principles behind the FOIA's policy of full disclosure—keeping the electorate informed and facilitating public debate on public issues. An important public interest could be served if the environmental group were allowed to inform the recipients of the BLM's plans for the Oregon high desert that alternatives to the government's strategies may exist. There may be differences of philosophy when it comes to how the environment is managed, and those who are interested in the future of the high desert should be allowed to know what all the options are.

Conclusion

An examination of Supreme Court opinions on the conflict between an individual's privacy interests and the public interest in disclosure of government information strongly suggests that the Court has reshaped the contours of the FOIA, as originally outlined in the statute's plain language and legislative history.[198] The leading FOIA privacy case, *U.S. Dept. of the Air Force v. Rose*,[199] said the act's basic purpose reflected "a general philosophy of full agency disclosure unless information is exempted under the clearly delineated statutory language."[200] The FOIA's congressional objective, *Rose* held, is "to pierce the veil of administrative secrecy and to open agency action to the light of public scrutiny."[201] *Rose* further held that to accomplish this goal, the courts must weigh the public interest in disclosure against the individual's right to privacy and, in doing so, privacy exemptions 6 and 7(C) must be narrowly construed.[202]

Since *Rose*, however, the Court has narrowly interpreted the public interest in disclosure and broadly construed the act's privacy exemptions, thus allowing federal agencies to deny FOIA requests for access to government information that could be used to advance the public interest in important areas. Supreme Court rulings have allowed the government:

1. To restrict the news gathering abilities of journalists, shielding questionable government activities from public scrutiny.[203]
2. To block independent attempts to confirm whether the U.S. government kept its word to safeguard human rights in Haiti.[204]
3. To make it more difficult for unions to contact federal employees even though Congress expressly endorsed the public interest in effective collective bargaining.[205]
4. To limit public debate about the government's future environmental plans for the Oregon high desert.[206]

When these cases are viewed in the aggregate, two separate problems emerge. First, Congress did not define the term "clearly unwarranted invasion of privacy" in Exemption 6. By failing to create specific guidelines for what constitutes a "clearly unwarranted" invasion of privacy, Congress has left it up to the courts to define this term, and thus made it possible for the courts to broadly construe the exemption.

The second problem, which has more serious consequences, concerns the *Reporters Committee* "core purpose" ruling. The trouble with the Supreme Court's interpretation of the FOIA's purpose is that the Court created what amounts to an "official information" test[207] as a threshold to determine whether information requested under the FOIA should be disclosed. There is nothing in the act's plain language or legislative history to support such a test.

An "official information" test based mainly on agency conduct or performance clearly conflicts with the FOIA's general policy of full disclosure, "unless information is exempted under the clearly delineated statutory language."[208] When viewed through the lens of democratic political theory underpinning the statute, such a test undermines the philosophy of the act. Citizens need information to make informed decisions when they go to the polls. True, many decisions pertaining to self-rule may concern official information about the conduct or performance of those in government. But for citizens to make informed decisions, they may also want a clear understanding of an agency's *philosophy* of governance, and philosophies can vary from administration to administration and agency to agency. An agency may operate free of misconduct and perform its functions quite efficiently, but nevertheless can execute policy that some members of the electorate might oppose.

Moreover, government-held information that does not itself directly disclose government operations or performance may lead to information that does.[209] Lyle W. Denniston said, for example, there is a significant public interest in the disclosure of information showing that someone who received defense contracts from the Pentagon was a Mafia crime figure with links to a corrupt congressman.[210] "[T]he fact that the Pentagon buys goods or services from such a person," Denniston wrote, "says a great deal indeed about the member of Congress or about the Pentagon."[211]

There are two precedents that would allow for congressional FOIA amendments to counter the effects of Supreme Court rulings that have contravened the statute's legislative intent. In 1974, Congress revised Exemption 1, the national security exemption, in direct response to a 1973 Supreme Court decision in *EPA v. Mink*.[212] In 1976, Congress amended the FOIA to clarify Exemption 3 in the aftermath of a 1975 Supreme Court decision, *Administrator, FAA v. Robertson*.[213] Under Exemption 3, the FOIA does not apply to information that has been exempted by other statutes previously passed by Congress.[214]

FOIA amendments aimed at clarifying the term "clearly unwarranted" and overriding *Reporters Committee* would serve the nation's democratic interests by reversing the backward march ordered by the Supreme Court since *Rose* was decided. Furthermore, such congressional adjustments would be in keeping with the democratic spirit of the Freedom of Information Act as envisioned by one of its principal shapers, newspaper lawyer Harold L. Cross, who said: "Public business is the public's business. The people have a right to know. Freedom of information is their just heritage. Without that, the citizens of a democracy have but changed their kings."[215]

Notes

1 5 U.S.C. § 552 (1994).

2*Id.* Briefly stated, the FOIA does not apply to matters that fall under the categories of (1) classified information and national security; (2) internal agency personnel information; (3) information exempted by statutes; (4) trade secrets and other confidential business information; (5) agency memoranda; (6) disclosures that invade personal privacy; (7) law enforcement investigation records; (8) reports from regulated financial institutions; and (9) geological and geophysical information.

3The term "right to know" has been traced to a 1945 speech by Kent Cooper, the Executive Director of the Associated Press. It was later adopted as part of the title of *The People's Right to Know,* an influential book advocating public access to government information. Harold L. Cross, *The People's Right to Know* xiv (1953).

4The Fourth Amendment, which restricts governmental searches and seizures, is the oldest constitutional right to privacy. The Fourth Amendment, more than any other explicit constitutional provision, reflects the existence of a right to privacy. See Laurence H. Tribe, *American Constitutional Law* 1390 (1988). The U.S. Supreme Court has recognized that the Fourth Amendment "protects people, not places," See *Katz v. United States,* 389 U.S. 347, 361 (1967).

5See *Griswold v. Connecticut,* 381 U.S. 479 (1965). The term privacy is not mentioned in the Constitution. According to Tribe, *Griswold* represents, among other ideas, a rule against cramped construction and permits an implied right of privacy that can be found in the Constitution's "spirit and structure" (Tribe, *American Constitutional Law* 1308–1309). In *Griswold,* the Supreme Court held that a state government may not interfere with the right of a married couple to use contraceptives. Although this case involves government limitations on personal autonomy, William O. Douglas, who wrote the opinion for the Court, spoke expansively of "zones of privacy" contained within "penumbras" of the Bill of Rights, specifically the First, Third, Fourth, Fifth and Ninth Amendments: "[S]pecific guarantees in the Bill of Rights have penumbras, formed by emanations from those guarantees that help give them life and substance. Various guarantees create zones of privacy." See 381 U.S. at 484. In 1977, the Court recognized that the constitutionally protected "zone of privacy" included two separate interests: "the interest in independence in making certain kinds of important decisions" and "the individual interest in avoiding disclosure in personal matters." See *Whalen v. Roe,* 429 U.S. 589, 599–600 (1977) (holding that a New York statute requiring physicians and pharmacies to provide copies of prescriptions to the state would not infringe on patients' privacy rights). See also *Olmstead v. United States,* 277 U.S. 438, 478 (1928) (Brandeis, J., dissenting) (dictum by Justice Louis Brandeis defining the constitutional right of privacy as "the right to be let alone—the most comprehensive of rights and the right most valued by civilized men").

6S. Rep. No. 813, 89th Cong., 1st sess. (1965), reprinted in *Freedom of Information Act Source Book: Legislative Materials, Cases, Papers* 38 (1974) (hereinafter *The FOIA Source Book*). *The Source Book of the Subcommittee on Administrative Practice and Procedure of the Committee on the Judiciary, United States Senate* is a primary source for the legislative history of the FOIA, containing congressional reports, hearings testimony and other materials.

7See 5 U.S.C. § 552 (b) 6 and § 552 (b) 7(C). The privacy interests are defined as: "(6) personnel and medical files and similar files the disclosure of which would constitute a clearly unwarranted invasion of personal privacy; (7) records or information compiled for law enforcement purposes, but only to the extent that the production of such law enforcement records or information . . . (C) could reasonably be expected to constitute an unwarranted invasion of personal privacy."

8*Bibles v. Oregon Natural Desert Assn.*, 117 S.Ct. 795 (1997); *U.S. Dept. of Defense v. Fed. Labor Relations Auth. (FLRA)*, 510 U.S. 487 (1994); *U.S. Dept. of Justice v. Reporters Comm. for Freedom of the Press*, 489 U.S. 749 (1989); *U.S. Dept. of State v. Ray*, 502 U.S. 164 (1991); *FBI v. Abramson*, 456 U.S. 615 (1982); *U.S. Dept. of State v. Washington Post Co.*, 456 U.S. 595 (1982); *U.S. Dept. of the Air Force v. Rose*, 425 U.S. 352 (1976).

9Plain meaning refers to a statute's structure and actual language, i.e., "the apparent meaning of the statutory text." See William N. Eskridge Jr., *The New Textualism*, 37 UCLA L. Rev. 621, 625 (1990).

10Congress amended the FOIA in 1974, 1976, 1986 and 1996. In 1974, Congress revised Exemption 1, the national security exemption. Congress revised Exemption 3, the withholding statutes exemption, in 1976. These exemptions are pertinent to this analysis and will be discussed later in this article. The FOIA was also amended in 1986 and 1996, but these amendments are beyond the scope of this analysis.

11See 5 U.S.C. § 552. The Court has consistently recognized this principle. See, e.g., *U.S. Dept. of Defense v. FLRA* 494; *U.S. Dept. of Justice v. Reporters Comm. for Freedom of the Press* 755; *NLRB v. Robbins Tire & Rubber Co.*, 437 U.S. 214, 220 (1978); *U.S. Dept. of the Air Force v. Rose* 360–361; *EPA v. Mink*, 410 U.S. 73, 80 (1973).

125 U.S.C. § 552 (a) (3).

13*Id.* at § 552 (a) (4) (B) (b). See 437 U.S. 214, 234, 236; 410 U.S. 73, 79, 87.

145 U.S.C. § 552 (f).

15Justin D. Franklin and Robert F. Bouchard, *Guidebook to the Freedom of Information Act* ch. 1, 21–22 (1995) (citing, e.g., *DeHarder Inv. Corp. v. Indian Housing Fin. Auth.*, 909 Ind. F.Supp. 606 [S.D. 1995]).

16*Id.* at 22 (citing *Goland v. CIA*, 607 F.2d 339, 348 [D.C. Cir. 1978]). See also *Dow Jones & Co. v. Dept. of Justice*, 917 F.2d 571, 574 (D.C. Cir. 1990) (Congress is not an "agency" for any purpose under the FOIA).

17*Id.* (citing *Warth v. Dept. of Justice*, 595 F.2d 521, 523 [9th Cir. 1979]).

18*Id.* (citing *Rankel v. Town of Greeenburgh*, 117 N.Y. F.R.D. 50, 54[S.D.1987]).

[19]Id. (citing *Buemi v. Lewis,* No. 94–4156, 1995 U.S. App. LEXIS 7816, at 6 [6th Cir. April 4, 1995]).

[20]*Id.* at 23 (citing *Rushforth v. Council of Economic Advisors,* 762 F.2d 1038, 1042–43 [D.C. Cir. 1985]). See S. Conf. Rep. No. 1200, 93d Cong., 2d sess. 15 (1974).

[21]5 U.S.C. § 552 (a) (3), (4) (Λ).

[22]Sec *supra,* note 5.

[23]Thomas I. Emerson, *The System of Freedom of Expression* 545 (1970).

[24]W. *Page Keeton, Dan B. Dobbs, Robert E. Keeton, David G. Owen, Prosser and Keeton on the Law of Torts* 850 (1984) (citing *Manola v. Stevens,* [N.Y. Sup. Ct. 1890]). Although a court had not recognized the right to privacy until 1890, "the right to be let alone" had been coined in 1888. Id. (citing T Cooley, A *Treatise on the Torts* 29 [1888]).

[25]Samuel D. Warren and Louis D. Brandeis, *The Right to Privacy,* 4 Harv. L. Rev. 193 (1890).

[26]*Id.* at 196. The article by Warren and Brandeis was highly critical of the press. They accused the press of "overstepping in every direction the obvious bounds of propriety and decency. Gossip is no longer the resource of the idle and of the vicious, but has become a trade, which is pursued with industry as well as effrontery. . . . To occupy the indolent, column upon column is filled with idle gossip, which can only be procured by intrusion upon the domestic circle."

[27]S. Rep. 813 at 38.

[28]James Madison, a major force behind the Bill of Rights, expressed strong belief in the importance of an informed society. Although writing about information in an educational context, his reasoning suggests parallel lessons for democratic society generally. He cautioned, ΛΛ popular government without popular information or the means of acquiring it, is but a prologue to a farce or a tragedy, or perhaps both. Letter from James Madison to W.T. Barry (Aug. 4, 1822), reprinted in part in *The Complete Madison* 337 (Saul K. Padover, ed 1953). *Cited in Environmental Protection Agency v. Mink,* 410 U.S. 73, 110–11 (1973).

[29]S. Rep. 813 at 38.

[30]*Statement by the President Upon Signing Bill Revising Public Information Provisions of the Administrative Procedure Act,* Weekly Comp. Pres. Doc. 895 (July 4, 1966).

[31]Former Attorney General Ramsey Clark, who served under President Johnson, characterized the FOIA's policy of full disclosure as the "transcendent goal" of the Act. *See Foreward,* Attorney General's Memorandum on the Public Information Section of the Administrative Procedures Act (1967).

[32]Antonin Scalia, *The Freedom of Information Act Has No Clothes,* Regulation 15 (March/April 1982).

[33]*Litigation Under the Federal Open Government Laws* 8 (Allan Robert Adler, ed., 1995).

[34]Criticism of the Act ranged from the subtle ("hardly . . . the apogee of legislative draftsmanship") to the blunt ("primitive and ineffective").

James T. O'Reilly, 1 *Federal Information Disclosure* para 3.01, at 3–2 (2d ed 1996).

[35]Letter to Sen. James O. Eastland, chairman, Senate Committee on the Judiciary, from Sen. Edward M. Kennedy, *The FOIA Source Book* at III.

[36]Robert P. Deyling, *Judicial Deference and De Novo Review in Litigation Over National Security Information Under the Freedom of Information Act.,* 37 Vill. L. Rev. 67, 74–75 (1992).

[37]5 U.S.C. § 552 (a) (6) (A) (i).

[38]*Id.* at § 552 (a) (4) (B); H.R. Rep. No. 1380, 93d Cong., 2d sess. 11 (1974).

[39]H.R. Rep. No. 1380, 93d Cong., 2d Sess. 7.

[40]*Id.*

[41]The first vote was 383–8 in the House and 64–17 in the Senate; Congress overrode President Ford's veto 371–31 in the House and 65–27 in the Senate.

[42]5 U.S.C. § 552 (b) 6.

[43]*Id.* at § 552 (b) 7 (C).

[44]S. Rep. No. 813 at 44; H. Rep. No. 1497 at 32.

[45]S. Rep. No. 813, 89th Cong., 1st sess. 9 at 44.

[46]120 *Cong. Rec.* 17033 (1974).

[47]Conf. Rep. No. 93–1380, 93d Cong. 2d sess. 11 (1974).

[48]O'Reilly at 17–44.

[49]*U.S. Dept. of Justice v. Reporters Comm. for Freedom of the Press* at 755–56.

[50]*Id.*

[51]*U.S. Dept. of the Air Force v. Rose.*

[52]*FBI v. Abramson.*

[53]489 U.S. 749.

[54]425 U.S. 352, 381.

[55]425 U.S. 352 (1976).

[56]*Id.* at 372, 382.

[57]*Id.* at 358.

[58]*Id.* at 354–356.

[59]*Id.* at 357.

[60]*Id.* at 377.

[61]*Id.* at 357 (citing Pet. for Cert. 35A–38A).

[62]*Rose v. U.S. Dept. of the Air Force,* 495 F.2d. 261, 263 (2d Cir. 1974), *aff'd* 425 U.S. 352 (1976).

[63]425 U.S. at 381.

[64]*Id.* at 361 (quoting 495 F.2d. at 263).

[65]*Id.*

[66]*Id.*

[67]*Id.* (citing *EPA v. Mink* at 80.)

[68]*Id.* at 373.

[69]S. Rep. No. 813, 89th Cong., 1st sess. 9.

[70]H. Rep. No. 1497, 89th Cong. 2d sess. 11 (1966).

[71]*Dept. of Air Force v. Rose* 425 U.S. at 371.

72*Id.* at 361–62.

73*Id.* at 381.

74*U.S. Dept. of Justice v. Reporters Comm. for Freedom of the Press.*

75*FBI v. Abramson; U.S. Dept. of State v. Washington Post Co.* 456 U.S.; 489 U.S. 749 (1989).

76456 U.S. at 600.

77*Id.* at 600–601.

78*Id.*

79*U.S. Dept. of State v. Washington Post,* 647 F.2d 197 (D.C. Cir. 1981).

80*U.S. Dept. of State v. Washington Post Co,* 456 U.S. at 603.

81*Id.* at 596.

82*Id.*

83*Id.* at 597, n.2.

84647 F.2d at 198.

85456 U.S. at 600.

86*Id.* at 599.

87*Id.*

88*Id.*

89*Id.* at 597, n.2.

90*U.S. Dept. of State v. Washington Post,* 647 F.2d. at 199.

91*FBI v Abramson,* 456 U.S.

92*Id.*

93*Id.* at 631–32.

94*Id.* at 618–19.

95The White House requested "name checks," which are summaries of information from FBI files, on 11 public figures. See *Abramson v. FBI,* 658 F.2d 806, 808 (1980); *FBI v. Abramson,* 456 U.S. at 620. Abramson asked for a record of written, oral or telephone requests for these "name checks." Included among the information Abramson sought were copies of correspondence between White House aide John D. Ehrlichman and J. Edgar Hoover. Id. at 618–19, n. 2.

96*Id.* at 619–20.

97*Id.*

98*Abramson v. Dept. of Justice,* Civ. Action No. 77–2206 (D.D.C. Jan. 3, 1979).

99658 F.2d at 812.

100456 U.S. at 623.

101*Id.*

102456 U.S. at 624–25.

103*Id.*

104*Id.* at 631–632.

105*Id.* at 624.

106*Id.* at 633 (Blackmun, J., dissenting).

107456 U.S. at 635, 639–40 (O'Connor, J., dissenting).

108*Id.* at 634.

109*Id.* at 643.

110*Id.* at 641.

111*Id.* at 642.

112 489 U.S. 749 (1989).

113*Id.* at 763.

114*Id.* at 772–73.

115*Id.* at 757.

116*Id.* Flood pleaded guilty on Feb. 26, 1980 to conspiracy to violate federal campaign laws and was placed on probation for a year. He was convicted of conspiracy to solicit campaign contributions from persons seeking federal government contracts. The 76-year-old Pennsylvania Democrat had resigned from the House Jan. 31, 1980. He was tried on charges of bribery, perjury and conspiracy in 1979. That trial, held in U.S. District Court in Washington, D.C., ended in a mistrial on Feb. 3, 1979, when jurors could not reach a decision after three days of deliberations. Laura Kiernan, Flood Is Placed on Year's Probation, The Washington Post A8 (Feb. 27, 1980).

117489 U.S. at 757–59.

118*Reporters Comm. for Freedom of the Press v. U.S. Dept. of Justice,* 816 F.2d 730, 740 (D.C. Cir. 1987), rev'd 489 U.S. 749 (1989).

119*U.S. Dept. of Justice v. Reporters Comm. for Freedom of the Press,* 489 U.S. at 772–73 (citing U.S. Dept. of the Air Force v. Rose, 425 U.S. at 372.

120*Id.* at 774.

121*Id.* at 775.

122*Id.* at 774.

123*Id.* at 764, 770–71.

124*Id.* at 771.

125*Id.* at 764.

126*Id.* at 780–81 (Blackmun, J., concurring).

127*Id.*

128*Id.* at 773.

129*Id.*

130*Id.* at § 552 (b); see supra, note 2.

131S. Rep. No. 813, 89th Cong., 1st sess. 5.

132*Dept. of the Air Force v. Rose,* 425 U.S. at 361–62.

133See Fred H. Cate et al., The Right to Privacy and the Public's Right to Know: The "Central Purpose" of the Freedom of Information Act 46 Admin. L. Rev. 41, 67 (1994). Professor Cate and his colleagues agree with the Supreme Court's decision in Reporters Committee. They write that in order to achieve the FOIA's intended purpose, the Court's "'official information' test should be the touchstone for disclosure." They argue further that the Supreme Court's "central purpose" test should be expanded "beyond Exemptions 7(C) and 6, and beyond FOIA exemptions altogether."

134*U.S. Dept, of Justice v. Reporters Comm. for Freedom of the Press,* 489 U.S. at 774.

135*Id.* at 175.

136*Id.* at 167–68.

137*Id.* U.S. embassy officials in Haiti interviewed 812 returnees, representing 22.8 percent of the total number of Haitians who fled over a three-year period.

138*Ray v. U.S. Dept. of Justice,* 725 Fla. F.Supp. 502, 505 (S.D. 1989).

139*U.S. Dept. of Justice v. Ray,* 908 F.2d 1549 (1990).

140*Id.*at 1555.

141*U.S. Dept. of State v. Ray* at 173–75.

142*Id.*

143*Id.* at 175–77.

144*Id.* at 179.

145*Id.* at 177–79.

146*U.S. Dept. of State v. Ray,* 502 U.S. at 173–75.

147*Id.*

148*U.S. Dept. of Defense v. FLRA,* 510 U.S. at 506–8 (Ginsburg, J., concurring).

149*Id.* at 494–95.

150Local 1657 of United Food and Commercial Workers Union represents a bargaining unit composed of employees of the Navy CBC Exchange in Gulfport, Miss. Local 1345 of American Federation of Government Employees, AFL-CIO, represents a worldwide bargaining unit composed of employees of the Army and Air Force Exchange. See id. at 490, n. 1.

151*U.S. Dept. of Defense v. FLRA,* 510 U.S. at 490–92. The government's original objection was based on the Privacy Act of 1974. The FOIA, specifically Exemption 6, emerged as the central issue because the Privacy Act does not bar disclosure of personal information if disclosure would be required under the FOIA. See 5 U.S.C. § 552a. The Fifth Circuit held that Exemption 6 was the only one of the enumerated exemptions that potentially could be applied to this case. See 510 U.S. at 490–92.

152·5 U.S.C. § 7114 (b) (4) (1988 ed. and Supp. IV).

153In enacting the labor statute, "Congress unquestionably intended to strengthen the position of federal unions." See id. at 506–8 (Ginsburg, J., concurring) (citing *Bureau of Alcohol, Tobacco, and Firearms v. FLRA,* 464 U.S. 89, 107 [1983]).

154510 U.S. at 490–92.

155*Id.*; U.S. Dept. of Defense v. FLRA, 975 F.2d 1105, 1116 (5th Cir. 1992).

156975 F.2d at 1116.

157*Id.* at 1113.

158*Id.* at 1115.

159*U.S. Dept. of Defense v. FLRA,* 510 U.S. at 494–95.

160*Id.*

161*Id.* (quoting U.S. Dept. of Justice v. Reporters Comm. for Freedom of the Press, 489 U.S. at 775).

162*Id.* at 497.

163*Id.* at 501.

164*Id.* at 489.

165*U.S. Dept. of Justice v. Reporters Comm. for Freedom of the Press,* 489 U.S. at 775.

166510 U.S. at 495.

167*Id.* at 508–9 (Ginsburg, J., concurring).

168*Id.* at 505.

169*Id.* at 506 (quoting *Bureau of Alcohol, Tobacco and Firearms v. FLRA,* 464 U.S. 89.

170*Id.* at 503 (citing *FLRA v. U.S. Dept. of Treasury, Fin. Management Serv.,* 884 F.2d 1446, 1457–1461 (D.C. Cir. 1989)).

171*Id.*

172*Id.* at 509.

173*Id.* at 507.

174*Id.* at 508.

175492 U.S. 136 (1989).

176*U.S. Dept. of Defense v. FLRA,* 510 U.S. at 507 (Ginsburg, J., concurring) (citing *U.S. Dept. of Justice v. Tax Analysts,* 492 U.S. at 156–57).

177*Id.*

178*Id.* at 505–8.

179*Id.* at 506–7.

180117 S. Ct. 795 (1997). (D. Dean Bibles is Director of Oregon Bureau of Land Management.)

181*Oregon Natural Desert Assn. v. Bibles,* 83 F.3d 1168, 1169 (9th Cir. 1996).

182*Id.* at 1171.

183*Id.* at 1170.

184*Id.* (citing *Oregon Natural Desert Assn. v. Bibles,* No. CV–93–00895–MFM [D. Ore. Dec. 6, 1993]).

185*Id.*

18683 F.3d 1168.

187*Id.* at 1171.

188*Id.*

18983 F.3d at 1172.

190*Id.*

191*Bibles v. Oregon Natural Desert Assn.,* 117 S. Ct. 795, 795 (1997).

192*Id.* (quoting *U.S. Dept. of Defense v. FLRA,* 510 U.S. at 496, and *U.S. Dept. of Justice v. Reporters Comm. for Freedom of the Press,* 489 U.S. at 773).

193510 U.S. at 506.

194*Oregon Natural Desert Assn. v. Bibles,* 83 F.3d 1168, 1171 (9th Cir. 1996).

195Management of Federal Information Resources Notice, § 7a, 59 Fed. Reg. 37,906, 37,910 (1994) (Circular AB130).

196*Id.* § 7b.

19783 F.3d at 1170.

1985 U.S.C. § 552 (1994); ee generally H. Rep. No. 1497; S. Rep. No. 813.

199425 U.S. 352 (1976).

200*Id.* at 361–62 (citing S. Rep. No. 813, 89th Cong., 1st sess. 3.)

201*Id.* (quoting *Rose v. U.S. Dept. of the Air Force,* 495 F.2d. 261, 263 [2d Cir. 1974]).

202*Id.*

203*U.S. Dept. of Justice v. Reporters Comm. for Freedom of the Press,* 489 U.S.; *FBI v. Abramson,* 456 U.S.; *U.S. Dept. of State v. Washington Post Co.,* 456 U.S.

204*U.S. Dept. of State v. Ray,* 502 U.S.

205*U.S. Dept. of Defense v. Fed. Labor Relations Auth. (FLRA),* 510 U.S.

[206]*Bibles v. Oregon Natural Desert Assn.*, 117 S.Ct. 795 (1997).

[207]See Cate, supra, note 49.

[208]S. Rep. No. 813, 89th Cong., 1st sess. 3.

[209]Glenn Dickinson, The Supreme Court's Narrow Reading of the Public Interest Served by the Freedom of Information Act, 59 U. Cin. L. Rev. 1, 191, 210 (1990).

[210]Lyle Denniston, The Press & the Law: Court Bans FOIA Probe of Central Files, Wash. Journalism Rev. 10 (May 1989).

[211]*Id.*

[212]410 U.S. 73 (1973). In deciding Mink, the Supreme Court interpreted Exemption 1 broadly and held that classified documents were exempt from judicial review. Id. at 84. Congress acted to override the Mink decision because legislators believed the Court's ruling conflicted with the general philosophy of full disclosure evinced in the FOIA. See H.R. Rep. No. 1380, 93d Cong., 2d sess. 12 (1974) and S. Rep. No. 1200, 93d Cong. 2d sess. 12 (1974). As a result, the revised national security exemption now allows for limited judicial review of documents that the government contends are classified.

[213]422 U.S. 255 (1975). In Robertson, the Supreme Court broadly construed Exemption 3, and held that the FAA administrator possessed wide discretion to withhold requested government records. Id. at 266–67. Congress disagreed, declaring that Supreme Court "misconceived" its intent. H.R. Rep. No. 880, 94th Cong., 2nd sess. pt. 1, 23 (1976). Congress revised Exemption 3 to create guidelines that strictly limit an agency executive's discretion to withhold information from the public.

[214]5 U.S.C § 552 (b) (3).

[215]Cross, supra note 3 at xiv.

Closing the Courtroom: Judicial Access and Constitutional Scrutiny After Richmond Newspapers

Matthew D. Bunker

One of the most important concerns of the public is the proper administration of justice. Public knowledge about how courts apply laws and resolve conflicts is essential to members of a self-governing society, whose ongoing support of the judicial system is of paramount importance. The legal system's very legitimacy depends on public understanding of how and why justice is done. Access to courts—at all stages of the legal process—is essential to fostering understanding and ensuring confidence. Yet pressures exist from time to time to close this process, for reasons ranging from the fundamental right to a trial by an unbiased jury, to issues of personal privacy, to purely self-serving concerns. This chapter explores the dimensions of access to court proceedings and the dangers that threaten legitimate public access.

Introduction

The First Amendment right of access to judicial proceedings is a relatively new constitutional innovation. Discovered (or, if you prefer, "created") in 1980 by the U.S. Supreme Court and nurtured by the Court in a series of cases through the mid-1980s, the right may still be in its infancy. Whether the precedents and constitutional rationale that created it will continue to be expanded by the courts or whether, in legal theorist Ronald Dworkin's phrase, the "gravitational force" of those precedents will be diminished in future years is, of course, difficult to predict.[1]

This chapter briefly summarizes First Amendment access law as it pertains to the judicial system. First, the chapter will examine the underpinnings of the doctrine as propounded by the Supreme Court. Next, it explores how some lower courts have interpreted the First Amendment access right in recent years. Finally, the chapter articulates some themes contained in recent case law that warrant attention.

Doctrinal Foundations

The conflict between the First Amendment rights of the press and public and other concerns of the criminal justice system, including defendants' fair-trial rights, is not new. The 1807 trial of Aaron Burr is one early example of the concern that uninhibited speech about criminal matters could result in prejudicial legal proceedings. Burr's lawyer claimed that jurors in that case had been prejudiced by sensational newspaper articles about Burr.

It wasn't until the 1960s, however, that the U.S. Supreme Court began serious development of a First Amendment jurisprudence to cope with the conflict. In the influential 1966 case of *Sheppard v. Maxwell*,[2] for example, the Court reversed the murder conviction of Dr. Sam Sheppard, a Cleveland surgeon, after press coverage both before and during the trial created a highly prejudicial atmosphere. Notably, the Supreme Court did not suggest direct restraints on the press, either in obtaining or reporting information, in future high-profile cases. Instead, the Court suggested measures such as sequestering the jury, continuances, change of venue and intensive *voir dire* to eliminate prejudice from the jury box. The 1976 case of *Nebraska*

Press Assn. v. Stuart made it clear that prior restraints against the press in the context of a criminal trial would face a daunting burden in order to meet First Amendment standards.[3]

Despite protection of the right to disseminate news about criminal proceedings, the Court was less enthusiastic about any affirmative right to gather news. In the 1974 cases of *Pell v. Procunier*[4] and *Saxbe v. Washington Post Co.*,[5] for example, the Court held the press had no greater right of access to prison facilities and inmate interviews than the general public. The First Amendment, it seemed, protected information already in the hands of the press, but created no affirmative right to compel government to provide that information. But as the 1970s drew to a close, the Court was on the verge of carving out a specific exception to that doctrine in the area of criminal proceedings.

The beginning of First Amendment access doctrine came with the 1980 decision in *Richmond Newspapers, Inc. v. Virginia*, in which a dispute arose concerning a closure order in a well-publicized murder retrial. After the press challenged the closure, the trial judge upheld the closure order. In arguing for the closure, the defendant's counsel cited the possibility of "leaks" to the media that might publish inaccurate information and "the fact that 'this is a small community.'"[6] The defendant was subsequently acquitted.

A plurality of the Supreme Court, in an opinion written by Chief Justice Warren Burger, held that the First Amendment required public access to the trial. This requirement sprang, in part, from the historical openness of trials in Anglo-American law. From before the Norman Conquest to colonial America, Chief Justice Burger wrote, openness was "one of the essential qualities of a court of justice."[7] The Court was less clear on why this historical fact compelled the conclusion that this state of affairs was somehow "adopted into," or became contained within, the guarantees of the First Amendment.

In addition to this historical reality, the plurality noted that access to trials encouraged public perception that trials were fair. Apart from the perception of fairness, openness in fact produced fairer trials by discouraging perjury and biased decision making. When officials, jurors and witnesses knew they were being observed by the community, presumably they would perform their roles more scrupulously. Moreover, open trials have a beneficial effect on the community. While violent crimes in particular may generate trauma and even violent reactions in affected communities, "the open process of justice serves an important prophylactic purpose, providing an outlet for community concern, hostility, and emotion."[8]

Richmond Newspapers was a genuine constitutional innovation. The plurality noted that the Court had never before found a right of access under the First Amendment. The Court's analysis nonetheless concluded that the First Amendment right to receive information, based in the speech and press clauses, and the First Amendment right of assembly combined to ensure access to places that had historically been open to the public and where access served an important functional role in ensuring fairness.

Despite the fact that the text of the Constitution did not explicitly mandate access, the Court found the right of access to be implicit in the design of the First Amendment. The plurality cited other unenumerated rights, such as privacy, as examples of important rights not found in the text of the Constitution or its amendments. Chief Justice Burger wrote that "the right to attend criminal trials is implicit in the guarantees of the First Amendment; without the freedom to attend such trials, which people have exercised for centuries, important aspects of freedom of speech and of the press could be eviscerated."[9] The Court noted that it was not abandoning previous cases denying a First Amendment right of access, such as *Saxbe v. Washington Post Co.* and *Pell v. Procunier.* Both *Saxbe* and *Pell* involved access to penal institutions, the plurality pointed out, which "do not share the long tradition of openness" associated with criminal trials.[10]

The plurality next articulated and applied the appropriate standard of review. Chief Justice Burger found that the trial judge had made no specific findings to justify the closure order and had not adequately considered alternatives such as sequestration of witnesses or jurors. In language that suggested some form of strict scrutiny, the plurality stated that "[a]bsent an overriding interest articulated in findings, the trial of a criminal case must be open to the public."[11]

Justice William Brennan, in a concurrence, wrote that the Court need not, in the case at hand, decide what interests would be sufficiently compelling to justify closing a criminal trial. Justice Brennan also noted additional justifications for open trials not mentioned by the plurality, including the notion that open trials would assist in locating key witnesses unknown to the parties by bringing the proceedings to the attention of those witnesses.

A year after *Richmond Newspapers,* the Court extended its newly minted access right and struck down a Massachusetts statute mandating closure in cases involving sexual assaults against minors. In *Globe Newspaper Co. v. Superior Court,*[12] a Massachusetts trial court had closed the trial of a defendant charged with the rape of three minor females. Globe Newspaper appealed the closure order to the Supreme Judicial Court of Massachusetts, which chose to defer consideration of the constitutional claim until the U.S. Supreme

Court's decision in *Richmond Newspapers*—then pending—was reached. After the Court decided *Richmond Newspapers,* the Massachusetts high court held that the traditional openness of criminal trials did not apply to rape cases.

On appeal, a majority of the Supreme Court ruled the statute unconstitutional. Massachusetts asserted two interests the state claimed justified the mandatory closure rule. First, the state sought to protect minors who had been sexually assaulted from the trauma and humiliation that might result from an open trial, and thus protect their psychological well-being. Second, the state hoped to encourage victims of sexual assault to come forward—something an open proceeding would presumably discourage. As to the interest in protecting minors from trauma and humiliation, the Court found it to be "compelling" but not sufficiently narrowly tailored. Psychological harm and trauma to the victim from public proceedings could be addressed on a case-by-case basis rather than by a blanket rule. A trial court could determine in each case the gravity of potential harm based on "the minor victim's age, psychological maturity and understanding, the nature of the crime, the desires of the victim, and the interests of parents and relatives."[13]

Moreover, the majority asserted, the state's interest in encouraging sexual assault victims to come forward was based on an unsupported premise. The Court stated that no empirical data supported the notion that closing proceedings increased minor victims' willingness to report sexual assaults. Moreover, it was unlikely that closure alone would encourage victims to come forward, particularly because the press in Massachusetts could easily and legally learn the victim's identity and obtain a transcript of the testimony given during the closed proceeding. In addition, the majority stated, the notion of encouraging victims to come forward "proves too much," because it could easily apply to victims of many different crimes, not simply those involving sexual assault.[14] But the notion of encouraging victims to come forward by providing closed proceedings, which might apply to any criminal case, "runs contrary to the very foundation of the right of access recognized in *Richmond Newspapers:* namely, 'that a presumption of openness inheres in the very nature of a criminal trial under our system of justice.'"[15]

The Court expanded the First Amendment right of access to encompass *voir dire* in 1984. In *Press-Enterprise Co. v. Superior Court of California*[16] (which has since become known as *Press-Enterprise I*), a California trial court had closed most of the *voir dire* proceedings in a rape and murder trial. Both after the jury was chosen and after the trial concluded, Press-Enterprise Co. sought transcripts of the *voir dire* proceedings. The trial judge denied these requests based on the privacy interests of the jurors.

Chief Justice Burger's opinion in *Press-Enterprise I* apparently assumed the Court was deciding not merely the right of the press to obtain the transcripts, but the right of the press to be physically present at the proceeding. After a historical excursion that determined that *voir dire* was traditionally an open proceeding, the Court stated that a presumption of openness "may be overcome only by an overriding interest based on findings that closure is essential to preserve higher values and is narrowly tailored to serve that interest."[17] In addition, the Court held that trial courts should make specific findings concerning the interest served by closing *voir dire*.

On the basis of the trial court record, the Court found that the trial court had not made adequate findings to warrant closure. Neither had the trial court adequately considered alternatives to closure, the Court wrote. The Court stated that a compelling interest in juror privacy might be established "when interrogation touches on deeply personal matters that a person has legitimate reasons for keeping out of the public domain."[18] Such a compelling interest might exist, for example, in the case of a juror who had been a rape victim. In a concurrence, Justice Thurgood Marshall urged that a trial court be required to use the least restrictive means available to advance a compelling interest in closing *voir dire* proceedings. For example, Justice Marshall suggested that transcripts of juror responses be released while concealing juror identity in cases in which privacy interests were "compelling." "Only in the most extraordinary circumstances can the substance of a juror's response to questioning at *voir dire* be permanently excluded from the salutary scrutiny of the public and the press," Justice Marshall wrote.[19]

The Court continued its expansion of First Amendment access in 1986 in a case involving a preliminary hearing in a California trial court. In *Press Enterprise Co. v. Superior Court*[20] (*Press-Enterprise II*), a nurse was accused of murdering 12 patients by injecting them with lethal doses of a heart drug. The horrific nature of the case naturally attracted great interest from the national media. On a motion by the defendant, the trial judge excluded the press and public from the preliminary hearing in the case. The trial court claimed the closure was designed to protect the defendant's Sixth Amendment fair-trial rights. After the preliminary hearing ended and the defendant was bound over for trial, the court refused to release transcripts of the proceeding, again based on the possibility of prejudicing the defendant's fair-trial rights.

The California Supreme Court upheld the closure, basing its decision on two grounds. First, the state high court said earlier U.S.

Supreme Court cases such as *Press-Enterprise I* and *Globe Newspaper Co.* applied only to actual trials. Second, the state Supreme Court reasoned that the closings in *Press-Enterprise I* and *Globe* had been based on privacy rights of victims and potential jurors, presumably a weaker interest than the fair-trial rights central in *Press-Enterprise II*.

On appeal, the U. S. Supreme Court reversed the California high court. The Court noted that the right of access issue could not be decided exclusively based upon characterization of the preliminary hearing as an event completely separate and distinct from the trial. "[T]he First Amendment question cannot be resolved solely on the label we give the event, i.e., 'trial' or otherwise, particularly where the preliminary hearing functions much like a full-scale trial,"[21] the Court reasoned.

Consistent with its earlier access decisions, the Court looked to both history and function to determine if the First Amendment right of access attached. First, the Court asked whether the proceeding was one that had historically been open to the public. The *Press-Enterprise II* Court found that preliminary hearings had indeed traditionally been open. Second, the Court considered "whether public access plays a significant positive role in the functioning of the particular process in question."[22] In this case, the Court determined that California preliminary hearings functioned as a kind of "mini-trial" in which criminal defendants could, among other things, cross-examine witnesses, present evidence and be represented by counsel. As a result, public access to the preliminary hearings promoted all of the positive attributes of open proceedings discussed in *Richmond Newspapers*. These included protecting against biased proceedings, providing a public perception of fairness and creating a cathartic community release in the face of violent crime. In addition, the Court pointed out that "the preliminary hearing in many cases provides 'the sole occasion for public observation of the criminal justice system.'"[23]

Because the preliminary hearing in *Press-Enterprise II* was found to have met the history and function inquiries, the Court said a qualified First Amendment right of access applied. The Court next stated the appropriate standard for deciding whether the qualified access right would trump competing interests. That standard was the "higher values" test from *Press-Enterprise I*, supplemented with the following required findings: "First, there is a substantial probability that the defendant's right to a fair trial will be prejudiced by publicity that closure would prevent and, second, reasonable alternatives to closure cannot adequately protect the defendant's fair trial rights."[24] Because the lower court had adopted a less rigorous standard—the "reasonable likelihood" of prejudice test—the *Press-Enterprise II* Court reversed the lower court. The Court reasoned that a mere risk of prejudice was not sufficient to support closing a hearing to which the First Amendment right of access applied. In addition, the lower court had simply not explicitly considered whether alternatives such as careful *voir dire* might reduce the impact of any prejudicial publicity.

Thus, *Richmond Newspapers* and its progeny have created a significant new First Amendment right—the right of access to criminal proceedings. Lower courts have extended this right to related matters such as civil cases, as the next section will discuss. As noted earlier, however, the First Amendment right of access creates only the right to be physically present in the courtroom, not the right to enter with audio- and videorecording devices. The Court's 1981 ruling in *Chandler v. Florida*[25] only *allowed* states to experiment with cameras in court; it made clear that the Constitution did not *mandate* such access.

The Evolution of First Amendment Access

The Supreme Court has not decided further significant First Amendment access cases after the quartet of decisions beginning with *Richmond Newspapers* and ending with *Press-Enterprise II*. Thus it has been left to lower courts to flesh out the doctrine and decide its outer limits. The following section will discuss some of the important lower court decisions in this still evolving area of the law. As one commentator has pointed out, the Court's quartet of access cases has resulted in lower court decisions extending the right of access to "suppression hearings, bail hearings, sentencing hearings, change of venue hearings, plea hearings, contempt hearings, pretrial ex parte recusal hearings, post conviction proceedings, parole revocation proceedings, parole release hearings, executions, bench conferences, chambers conferences, juvenile proceedings, court martials, civil case proceedings, preliminary injunction proceedings, and closure proceedings."[26] Because there are literally hundreds of state and federal cases dealing with these issues, this section will attempt to single out a few noteworthy recent examples.[27] It should be noted that the following brief survey cannot claim to be representative of all First Amendment access cases, at least in part because the cases are so context-specific and often turn on minor factual or procedural distinctions that make broad generalizations difficult. Nonetheless, it is hoped that the discussion that follows will illuminate at least some of the important recent issues.

Since *Richmond Newspapers*, few courts have closed even portions of an adult criminal trial itself. For example, a 1992 federal district court decision used creative measures to avoid closing portions of the trial of a doctor accused of impregnating his female fertility patients. The prosecution in the case, *U.S. v. Jacobson*,[28] sought closure to protect the children from learning their true paternity. Although the court ruled that the welfare of the children in this context was indeed a compelling interest, it nonetheless chose to use a number of measures short of closure to protect the children. These measures included providing pseudonyms for the testifying parents and deleting their names from the trial records. The court also excluded sketch artists from the courtroom.

The criminal cases that arose from the Oklahoma City federal building bombing generated some interesting access decisions dealing with pretrial criminal proceedings and records. For example, in *United States v. McVeigh*,[29] the U.S. Court of Appeals for the Tenth Circuit upheld the trial court's sealing of documents that included portions of Terry Nichols' suppression motion, an accompanying exhibit concerning a statement Nichols made to authorities and portions of both Nichols' and Timothy McVeigh's motions for severance, along with exhibits.

The news media challenged the sealing orders, asserting rights of access both under the First Amendment and the common law. The Tenth Circuit's opinion noted that numerous other courts had extended the First Amendment right of access to court records and documents, something the Supreme Court has not explicitly done. However, the Tenth Circuit declined to decide whether there was a First Amendment right of access to the documents. Because the Tenth Circuit found that the trial court's closure order would have met the standards of *Press-Enterprise II*, thus making the sealing constitutionally permissible, the court found it unnecessary to decide whether the First Amendment right in fact attached. The court also assumed that if First Amendment access were not mandated, no access under the common law would attach.

For example, as to the documents filed as part of the suppression motion, the appeals court found that, hypothetically, the First Amendment right of access would apply. This was so because a suppression hearing, at which a trial court decides whether evidence will be admissible at trial, was both historically open and a critically important point in the pretrial proceedings. Thus, a suppression motion met the "experience and logic" test of *Press-Enterprise II*.

Nonetheless, although the First Amendment right of access hypothetically would have applied, the right would not extend to evidence that had been ruled inadmissible, as the documents sought in this case were. As the Tenth Circuit wrote, "Access to inadmissible evidence is not necessary to understand the suppression hearing, so long as the public is able to understand the circumstances that gave rise to the decision to suppress. Moreover, suppressed evidence, by definition, will not be admissible at trial, and thus press access to such evidence will not play a significant positive role in the functioning of the criminal process, as that evidence is simply irrelevant to the process."[30] In addition, the Tenth Circuit maintained that access could cause serious harm because it would bring to the attention of both the jury pool and the public incriminating evidence that could not be considered in the case. The appellate court followed this same reasoning as to some inadmissible notes of a Nichols' interview with authorities.

The Tenth Circuit also decided that even if the First Amendment access right applied to the severance documents, the trial court had properly sealed them. The court reasoned that parties seeking severance—that is, separate trials—must reveal a good bit of their own trial strategy and attempt to shift some of the blame to the other defendant. Defendants could not make these arguments fully and candidly if they were to be released to the public, imperiling a fair trial at some later point in the proceedings. "Granting general access to such documents would create a Hobson's choice between the need to obtain severance and the need to protect the client's interest in avoiding prejudicial pre-trial publicity," the court wrote.[31]

Finally, the Tenth Circuit noted the trial court had made adequate findings to support its sealing orders and that the orders were narrowly tailored to serve the compelling interest at stake—the fair-trial rights of the defendants. Alternatives were few, the appeals court noted, because measures such as change of venue, extensive *voir dire*, continuances and juror admonishments were being, or had already been, used in the case.

In another 1997 case related to the Oklahoma City bombing trial, a New York federal district court unsealed a search warrant and related documents, although the court redacted some information based on privacy concerns. In *In re Buffalo News*,[32] the warrant had been issued for the home of William McVeigh, father of Timothy McVeigh, and Jennifer McVeigh, Timothy's sister. Both Timothy and Jennifer McVeigh challenged the unsealing, Timothy McVeigh on the basis that it would undermine his fair-trial rights and Jennifer McVeigh because it would invade her privacy. Interestingly, although William McVeigh did not oppose the unsealing, nevertheless the court, "based on the opposition of Jennifer McVeigh, considered his privacy interests in the matter."[33]

The *Buffalo News* court ruled that Timothy McVeigh's opposition to the unsealing failed to meet the "substantial probability" standard of *Press-Enterprise II*. The court, with little elaboration, suggested that careful *voir dire* could screen out biased jurors and that
McVeigh's opposition was based on mere "conclusory assertions" regarding the impact of the unsealing on his trial.

The *Buffalo News* court did, however, redact portions of the material sought in order to protect the privacy of William and Jennifer
McVeigh. Citing Second Circuit precedent, the court noted that because neither William nor Jennifer were targets of the investigation,
the First Amendment right of access was subject to qualification to
protect their "intimate relations." In the case of Jennifer McVeigh,
that exception applied to the titles of books taken from her bedroom
during the search. In the case of William McVeigh, the exception applied to his account, given in the affidavit in support of the warrant,
of his children's political views. Both of these portions of the documents should be redacted, the court ruled. "There can be no better
example of the zone of privacy a person residing in our society should
enjoy than what books he or she chooses to read," the court wrote.
"Further, it cannot be gainsaid that information a parent learns from
a child regarding the child's beliefs is knowledge derived from an intimate relationship.[34]

The *McVeigh* court to the contrary, a number of recent lower
court decisions have held that pretrial criminal proceedings should be
fully accessible under the First Amendment. A Connecticut appeals
court vacated a closure order in a 1997 case in which the trial court
had excluded the press and public from part of a pretrial hearing on
the defendant's motion to dismiss. The case, *State v. Kelly*,[35] involved
the second trial, after a mistrial, of Alex Kelly on charges of kidnap-
ping and sexual assault. The trial court, on its own motion, closed a
portion of the hearing, which centered on allegations that the prosecution had improperly leaked prejudicial information to the media.

The state appeals court pointed out that the trial court had not
adequately explained how closing the hearing would help assure an
unbiased jury pool. The hearing concerned the *source* of statements
made to the press, not the truth of the statements. "The hearing
would primarily concern whether there was prosecutorial misconduct
involved in leaking information to the press and whether that involvement would warrant dismissal of the charges against the defendant," the appellate court wrote. "It is unclear how this hearing
would be prejudicial to the defendant. . . ."[36]

Although the trial court's closure order did discuss the inadequacy of alternatives such as extensive *voir dire* and admonitions to

the jury, the appeals court found the trial court's discussion both of the potential for prejudice and the inadequacy of possible alternatives to be "conclusory." This was particularly so given that any prejudicial statements that may have been leaked had already been disseminated in the press. The trial court itself had admitted as much by stating that the "cat is out of the bag."[37]

Finally, the appeals court noted that questions of misconduct by the prosecution would suggest that the hearing should be open. Such issues, which involved the public's confidence in the integrity of the judicial system, should, if possible, be adjudicated in the open.

In another pretrial proceedings case, this one from 1988, a New York state appellate court reversed the closure of a plea bargain hearing in *New York Times Co. v. Demakos*.[38] In *Demakos*, *The Times* sought to prohibit a trial judge from holding closed plea proceedings in a sensational case in which a group of white youths had attacked three African American men in Queens. When *The Times* learned that two of the defendants were negotiating plea agreements, the paper sought information from the judge, who refused to respond either to questions about the process or to a request for a hearing on the closure. One defendant eventually pleaded guilty in the judge's chambers and the court sealed a transcript of the proceeding.

Finally, as a second defendant was preparing to enter into a plea bargain, the judge agreed to a hearing on the closures. At the hearing, at which neither the prosecution nor defense counsel argued in favor of closure, the judge denied *The Times'* application to open the proceedings because the fair-trial rights of the remaining defendants would be jeopardized. According to the appellate court, "this determination consisted of conclusory statements lacking any factual basis whatsoever."[39]

The appellate court overturned the closure order, finding that the First Amendment presumption of openness was not overcome in *Demakos*. The court described the numerous advantages of openness set forth in *Richmond Newspapers*. These included the power of public proceedings in helping to assure that the justice system operates fairly and the community therapeutic value in seeing justice done.

In the case at hand, the appellate court stated that the judge had not only failed to make adequate findings, but had initially refused to provide the newspaper with a hearing to press its claim. Moreover, when the trial court eventually did hold a hearing on the second defendant, the trial court did not present sufficient reasons to justify its conclusion that closure was necessary to protect the fair-trial rights of the remaining defendants. Vague and conclusory statements, without more, could not overcome the constitutional right of access, the appellate court held. The appellate court further noted that the trial judge had, in fact, eventually been able to seat an impartial jury for the remaining defendants through careful jury selection. Finally, the appellate court pointed out, public and media attention to the crime had been so intense that any additional publicity generated by an open plea proceeding could not have been presumed to have any significant effect on potential jurors. "It is difficult to discern," the appellate court wrote, "how public access to [these] plea proceedings would cause such prejudice to the remaining defendants' right to a fair and impartial jury as to warrant the categorical denial of the constitutional right of access of the public and the press. This is particularly so where it is apparent that at least one of the attorneys for a defendant to be tried voiced opposition to the closed sessions because of a concern of the prejudice to his client of 'partial' and speculative media reports of the closed proceedings."[40] For these reasons, the appellate court held the proceeding should have been open and ordered the release of the transcript of the previously closed proceeding.

Lower courts have had mixed reactions to First Amendment access claims in civil proceedings, although most have recognized some kind of presumptive access right. A 1996 California appellate court decision recognized a First Amendment right of access to civil proceedings in *NBC Subsidiary (KNBC-TV), Inc. v. Superior Court*.[41] The case involved a high-profile suit by actress Sondra Locke against film star Clint Eastwood for a variety of torts based upon Eastwood's alleged promises to assist Locke in developing motion picture projects. The trial court excluded the press and public from the proceedings at all times when the jury was not present. The order was designed to shield the jury from hearing, through the media, about excluded evidence and other items that would not otherwise come to their attention. The trial court asserted that its primary duty was to ensure an impartial jury for the litigants, and that the information from proceedings when the jury was not present "is the type of information that ends up in tabloids, that faces everybody that walks . . . into the grocery store to buy their groceries."[42] The trial court also pointed out that it would make the information available at the end of the case, and that the closure order "is a very, very small intrusion on the 1st Amendment, and in essence it's not an intrusion on the 1st Amendment. It is a slight delay."[43]

The appellate court held that the First Amendment right of access applied to civil trials, noting that the question was one of first impression in California. The court reasoned that both history and functional considerations supported the right as applied to civil proceedings.

After this initial conclusion, the appellate court found that the lower court had not justified its closure order under the *Press-Enterprise I* standard requiring "an overriding interest based on findings that closure is essential to preserve higher values and is narrowly tailored to serve that interest.[44] The appellate court noted that the simple fact that jurors might be exposed to inadmissible evidence through media reports was not sufficient to justify closure. Alternatives such as careful *voir dire* and admonitions to disregard news reports could be used to protect the fairness of the proceedings. The court also ruled that the delay in releasing the information violated the First Amendment. In this part of its opinion, the appellate court somewhat confusingly—and less than accurately—compared the delay with a prior restraint, such as that in *Nebraska Press Assn. v. Stuart*.[45] In any event, the appellate court concluded that "absent appropriate findings, delayed disclosure does not meet the mandate of the First Amendment."[46]

Not all recent cases have supported open civil proceedings, even when a First Amendment right of access was recognized. In an unusual case, *Doe v. Santa Fe Independent School District*,[47] a federal district court in Texas held that closure as to the general public—but not the press—could be used to protect the anonymity of minor plaintiffs. The plaintiffs—three adults and three minors—were challenging certain religious practices in the public school system. The court reasoned that if the general public were allowed in court during the trial, the plaintiffs' identities would become known widely. The court pointed out that the minor plaintiffs were more vulnerable to intimidation and violence if their identities became known than the adult plaintiffs were.

While recognizing a First Amendment right of access to the proceedings, the court cited *Globe Newspaper* for the proposition that protecting the physical and psychological well-being of a minor was a compelling interest. As a result, the court issued a novel order in which the trial was open throughout to those with media credentials, but was closed during the minors' testimony to members of the general public without press credentials. The court further allowed certain school district representatives to be present throughout the trial, but ordered them on pain of criminal contempt not to disclose the plaintiffs' identities.

Some courts have been less willing to open proceedings and documents related to settlements in civil suits. For example, in *United States v. Town of Moreau*,[48] a federal district court in 1997 held that settlement conferences and documents related to an environmental action brought against General Electric Company could be closed. A local newspaper had challenged the closure of the proceedings and documents based on the public need to monitor any negotiated settlement. The court first rejected First Amendment access based on the history or tradition inquiry, noting that it was "beyond argument that none of the forms of access sought by the proposed intervenors have ever been traditionally open to the public."[49] As to common-law access, the court reasoned that settlement negotiations carried out in public would result in a failure to settle. While noting the newspaper's argument that the public would be presented with a settlement that was a "fait accompli," the court nevertheless stressed the need to reach settlement behind closed doors: "In a perfect world, the public would be kept abreast of all developments in the settlement discussions of lawsuits of public interest. In our world, such disclosure would, as discussed above, result in no settlement discussions and no settlements."[50]

Recent juvenile proceedings have resulted in some closures and some open hearings, although overall the trend in juvenile proceedings seems to be toward more openness. In one 1994 case, decided under the federal Juvenile Delinquency Act, the Third Circuit held that judges should decide whether to close juvenile proceedings on a case-by-case basis. In *United States v. A.D.*,[51] the Third Circuit reasoned that the statutory scheme of the Juvenile Delinquency Act should be interpreted in light of the constitutional goals behind *Richmond Newspapers* and its progeny. In particular, the court pointed out that mandatory closure of juvenile hearings was unconstitutional. A 1995 First Circuit case, however, questioned how First Amendment standards should apply in juvenile cases. In *United States v. Three Juveniles*[52]—another case decided under the Juvenile Delinquency Act—the First Circuit pointed out that the tradition of closure in juvenile proceedings, and the rehabilitative purpose behind such closure, made the First Amendment questions involved more uncertain. The First Circuit seemed unconvinced that the *Richmond Newspapers* line of cases applied to juvenile proceedings at all. Even if that were the case, the court suggested, the closure of proceedings in the juvenile context could meet the relevant First Amendment test with relative ease.

Trial judges seem to be expressing more consideration of the privacy interests of jurors in recent years, to the detriment of access rights. Once a device to protect jurors from physical harm, anonymous juries have been used in numerous cases without any such threat to protect jurors' privacy. As one influential publication noted: "Anonymous juries were used in both Oklahoma City bombing prosecutions in federal court in Denver, the trial of the Branch Davidian survivors in Waco, Oliver North, and World Trade Center bombers."[53] The judge in the Unabomber trial also ordered that the identities of jurors in that case be confidential, although the defendant, Ted Kaczynski, pleaded guilty before the trial began. A 1994 Eleventh Circuit opinion suggested that use of anonymous juries should be used only in rare cases.[54]

In addition to anonymous juries, bans on post-trial juror interviews have been the subject of a number of cases. In a 1997 case, *United States v. Cleveland,*[55] the Fifth Circuit upheld a trial court order barring the media from interviewing jurors in a racketeering case about their deliberations. The Fifth Circuit held that the order was a valid one designed "to prevent a substantial threat to the administration of justice—namely, the threat presented to freedom of speech within the jury room by the possibility of post-verdict interviews."[56] Moreover, the Fifth Circuit held that the order was narrowly tailored, even though it was unlimited in duration. The order applied only to the jurors themselves, not relatives or friends, and furthermore applied only to questions about deliberations, not questions about jurors' general reactions to the verdict. The Fifth Circuit also noted that the order did not prevent jurors from speaking out on their own initiative.

In contrast to *Cleveland,* in one 1998 California case, a state appellate court ruled that the trial judge had gone too far in protecting juror privacy. In *Contra Costa Newspapers, Inc. v. Superior Court,*[57] the trial court had ordered that "the press" have no contact with jurors since the jurors had indicated by raising their hands that they did not wish to discuss their deliberations. The appellate court vacated the order, noting among other things that no media entity had been served with any subpoena or summons that would even establish the jurisdiction of the trial court. Aside from jurisdictional issues, the appellate court noted that news gathering and dissemination was a constitutionally protected activity that could not be interfered with absent a compelling interest furthered in a narrowly tailored manner. In this case, the appellate court noted, the order "contained no time or scope limitations and encompassed every possible juror interview situation."[58]

Conclusion

The law of access to court proceedings and records is still a work in progress, as is so much of constitutional law. From the cases examined in this chapter, a few themes warrant further attention.

First, although the courts routinely cite and purport to apply the constitutional tests derived from *Richmond Newspapers* and its progeny, the actual application of these tests varies tremendously in different courts and access contexts. As this writer has explored in more detail in another work,[59] although lower courts are ostensibly applying some variation of strict scrutiny, these determinations are fraught with uncertainty in any given case. The actual "measurement" of the strength of interests opposing access is often performed in what appears to be a purely intuitional manner, with some conclusory statements serving as the sole justification in the opinion. Although it appears unlikely, some sort of guidance from the Supreme Court as to exactly what might constitute a "compelling" or "overriding" interest in this context could create more certainty and consistency in these often highly questionable determinations.

Second, while *Richmond Newspapers* and its progeny were largely concerned with fair-trial considerations, quite a few recent cases focus on privacy concerns. While privacy in the abstract is certainly a good thing in many circumstances, the talismanic invocation of the term "privacy" to trump important First Amendment interests is questionable. The range of interests served by open access to proceedings and records—including increased fairness and accountability, increased public trust in the process, the identification of perjury and bias in witnesses and potential jurors, and the like—are so important that the level of justification for privacy-related closures should be quite high. At the very least, courts should make some important conceptual distinctions about what exactly are protectable privacy interests. For example, protecting the confidentiality of Timothy McVeigh's sister's reading material, as discussed earlier, would seem to go to the heart of many notions of privacy. Some information about people's lives certainly deserves the designation "private," when it concerns aspects of their lives that are central to preserving the integrity of the "self" that most of us wish to maintain out of the view of others. The books we read, the entertainment programming we consume, the intimate conversations we have with loved ones all seem to fall into this intuitively private zone. This justification is particularly strong when that information is at best tangential to a public criminal proceeding. On the other hand, withholding the names of citizens who serve on juries in important criminal cases (where there is no serious danger of retaliation) may be carrying matters too far. Criminal trials in our system are and should be public events, and those who participate in them should have no reasonable expectation of avoiding all public scrutiny. That scrutiny serves valuable purposes, as the Supreme Court has recognized.

Finally, serious consideration should be given to downplaying or eliminating the "history" portion of the "history and function" inquiry that is the prerequisite to First Amendment access. Some better-reasoned opinions already seem to have done so.[60] First, the historical inquiry becomes increasingly irrelevant as contemporary procedural innovations change the way both civil and criminal cases are conducted. It makes little sense to ask about the provenance of openness in connection with, for example, a suppression hearing, a proceeding with which 18th-century jurist William Blackstone had no acquaintance. Second, and more importantly, even if historical analogues exist, there seems to be no legitimate reason to restrain First Amendment access law with the dead hand of the past. Unless one is laboring under some sort of quasi-originalist interpretive philosophy, the coherence of which is doubtful, tradition is simply not a meaningful standard for determining what the First Amendment requires. The historical closure of certain proceedings may or may not be justified by substantive reasons, but the simple descriptive fact of that history should carry no constitutional weight. Consider, for instance, the case of juvenile proceedings. There may certainly be important normative arguments in favor of closure, including the familiar ones dealing with rehabilitative concerns and stigmatization. These claims, which may or may not be sufficient to overcome access rights in individual cases, exhaust the realm of meaningful argument against access. It simply adds nothing for the proponent to add: "Oh, and by the way, we've always done it this way."

First Amendment access is an important constitutional innovation. Since the Supreme Court seems disinclined to revisit it, it is all the more important that access advocates not give up the fight in the lower courts.

Notes

[1]Ronald Dworkin, *Taking Rights Seriously* (1977).
[2]384 U.S. 333 (1966).
[3]427 U.S. 539 (1976).
[4]417 U.S. 817 (1974).
[5]417 U.S. 843 (1974). See also *Houchins v. KQED*, 438 U.S. 1 (1978).
[6]448 U.S. 555 (1980).
[7]*Id.* at 567, quoting *Daubney v. Cooper*, 10 B. & C 237, 240, 109 Eng. Rep. 438, 440 (K.B. 1829).
[8]*Id.* at 571.
[9]Id. at 580, quoting *Branzburg v. Hayes*, 408 U.S. 665, 681 (1972).
[10]*Id.* at 576, n. 11.

[11]*Id.* at 581.

[12]457 U.S. 596 (1981).

[13]*Id.* at 608.

[14]*Id.* at 610.

[15]*Id.* at 610, quoting *Richmond Newspapers,* 448 U.S. at 573.

[16]464 U.S. 501 (1984).

[17]*Id.* at 510.

[18]*Id.* at 511.

[19]*Id.* at 520–21 (Marshall, J., concurring).

[20]478 U.S. 1 (1986).

[21]*Id.* at 7.

[22]*Id.* at 8.

[23]*Id.* at 12 (citation omitted).

[24]478 U.S. at 14.

[25]449 U.S. 560 (1981).

[26]Thomas F. Liotti, *Closing the Courtroom to the Public: Whose Rights Are Violated?* 63 Brooklyn L. Rev. 501, 533 (1997) (citations omitted).

[27]For more encyclopedic treatment of court-related access law, see, e.g., id. See also C. Thomas Dienes, Lee Levine and Robert C. Lind, *Newsgathering and the Law* and Dan Paul and Richard J. Ovelmen, *Access,* 2 Communications Law 1125 (1997).

[28]785 Va. F.Supp. 563 (E.D.1992).

[29]119 F.3d 806 (10th Cir. 1997).

[30]*Id.* at 813.

[31]*Id.* at 814.

[32]969 N.Y. F.Supp. 869 (W.D. 1997).

[33]*Id.* at 870, n. 1.

[34]*Id.* at 871-72.

[35]695 A,2d 1 (Conn. App. 1997).

[36]*Id.* at 3.

[37]*Id.* at 4.

[38]137 A.D.2d 247, 529 N.Y.S.2d 97 (1988).

[39]529 N.Y. S.2d at 99.

[40]*Id.* at 101.

[41]49 Calif. App. 4th 487 (1996).

[42]*Id.* at 492.

[43]*Id.* at 492–93.

[44]*Id.* at 502 (quoting 464 U.S. 501, 510).

[45]427 U.S. 539 (1976).

[46]49 Calif. App. 4th at 505.

[47]933 Texas F.Supp. 647 (S.D. 1996).

[48]979 N.Y. F.Supp. 129 (N.D. 1997).

[49]*Id.* at 133.

[50]*Id.* at 136.

[51]28 F.3d 1353 (3d Cir. 1994).

[52]61 F.3d 86 (1st Cir. 1995).

[53]*The Privacy Paradox,* The News Media and the Law 10 (Spring 1998).

[54]*United States v. Ross,* 33 F.3d 1507 (11th Cir. 1994).

[55]128 F.3d 267 (5th Cir. 1997).

[56]*Id.* at 270.

[57]61 Calif. App. 4th 862 (1998).

[58]*Id.* at 868.

[59]Matthew D. Bunker, *Justice and the Media: Reconciling Fair Trials and a Free Press* (Erlbaum 1997).

[60]See, e.g., Application of the Herald Co., 734 F.2d 93 (2nd Cir. 1984).

8

Anonymous Juries: Justice in the Dark

Sandra F. Chance, Esq.

People in an open society do not demand infallibility from their institutions, but it is difficult for them to accept what they are prohibited from observing.

Chief Justice Warren Burger

The constant conflict between the people's right to know and the criminal defendant's Sixth Amendment right to a fair trial is well chronicled in the legal literature. However, as part of a dangerous new trend, juries in high-profile cases are being routinely shrouded in secrecy, and public confidence in the judicial system is at stake. Judges are increasingly impaneling anonymous juries, concealing the selection process and identity of the people who sit in judgment of their fellow citizens. By authorizing use of anonymous juries, judges are shielding jurors' identities—and masking the face of justice. The chapter below highlights yet another cutting-edge issue in access law—one sure to grow in importance as trial coverage leaps from print to television to the Internet.

The Court of the Star Chamber was England's infamous secret court. Trials were held in secret, without a jury. Defendants often were taken from their homes in the dead of night, without explanation. The secret court routinely used torture to force confessions and cloaked the accuser's identity. Ultimately, the court's justice was meted out in secret as well. Eventually, word spread about the outrages of this secret tribunal and the court was abolished in 1641.[1]

With the abolition of the Star Chamber, public trials, with jurors selected in open court, became the cornerstone of the English legal system. Open jury selection was adopted in colonial America and was common practice when the Constitution was adopted.[2] In the early days of jury development, the identity of jurors was well known. In fact, potential jurors could be disqualified if they were not from the same neighborhood.[3]

Historically, jurors have played a critical role in the criminal justice system, deciding not just guilt or innocence, but also life or death. In addition, jurors serve as a safeguard against the wrath of a ruthless prosecutor or the tyranny of a corrupt judge.[4] Jurors represent the public, bringing the public's values and common sense to the legal process. Jurors also learn about the criminal justice system.[5]

However, in a disturbing development, juries in high-profile cases are often veiled in secrecy. More and more, juries are anonymous[6]—chosen in secret and their identities unknown—although it is they who judge their peers. The implications are worrisome, particularly with regard to public confidence in the judicial system. Jane Kirtley, former head of the Reporters Committee for Freedom of the Press, now the Silha Professor of Media Ethics and Law at the University of Minnesota, has called the trend a "growing epidemic of secrecy."[7]

The debate, centuries old, focuses on competing constitutional rights. Courts have traditionally balanced the First Amendment rights of the news media,[8] the public's First Amendment right to attend criminal trials[9] and judicial proceedings,[10] including *voir dire*, with a criminal defendant's Sixth Amendment right to a fair trial. Recently, courts have added the amount of publicity and a juror's right to privacy to the constitutional mix.

High-profile cases present extraordinary challenges to judges, who must balance these competing constitutional rights, ultimately ensuring a defendant's right to a fair trial. Judges presiding over the most notorious cases during the past decade have resorted increasingly to a once-rare remedy, impaneling anonymous juries.[11] Anonymous juries were used in the criminal trials of O.J. Simpson; Theodore Kaczynski, known as the Unabomber; Timothy McVeigh, convicted in the Oklahoma City bombing case; Terry Nichols, convicted of conspiring with McVeigh in the Oklahoma City bombing; British au pair Louise Woodward, convicted of manslaughter in the death of baby Matthew Eappen; the Branch Davidians, convicted of murdering federal marshals; and in the federal civil rights trial of four police officers convicted of beating Rodney King.

By authorizing use of anonymous juries, judges are shielding jurors' identities—and masking the face of justice.

High-Profile Cases Increasingly Use Anonymous Juries

In the wake of the O.J. Simpson trial, judges are increasingly concerned about public perception that the criminal justice system is not working properly. In an attempt to alter that perception, they are attempting to control the message the public receives by shutting down access to information.[12]

For example, in 1998, after a public defender said threats had been made against witnesses in the Unabomber case and the prosecution complained about extensive news coverage, U.S. District Judge Garland Burrell Jr. ordered that jurors' names be kept secret until the conclusion of Theodore Kaczynski's trial.[13] A coalition of newspaper and broadcast companies challenged the order.[14] Without a demonstrated, credible threat to juror safety, there was no support for this extraordinary measure, according to the media companies' lawyer. Kaczynski, a 55-year-old former University of California at Berkeley professor, pled guilty to killing two people during his 17-year anti-technology crusade before the trial began, so the jury was never used. An appeal is pending.[15]

In perhaps the most secret legal proceeding in recent memory, an anonymous jury was impaneled for the trial of Timothy McVeigh. The jurors' identities were known only to the judge, the attorneys and the defendant.[16] McVeigh, 28, a Persian Gulf War veteran, was charged in the worst act of terrorism on U.S. soil, the 1995 bombing of the Alfred P. Murrah Federal Building in Oklahoma City that killed 168 people and injured 500.[17] In sealing their identities, the judge admitted he was not concerned that jurors would be threatened. Rather, he was concerned that once people knew the jurors' identity, they would try to influence the jurors' decision.[18] In addition to sealing their identities from the public and press,[19] the judge had a partition erected in the courtroom to shield them from public view.

The media vehemently objected to the extreme measures, calling the restrictions "appalling,"[20] and filed a suit challenging the restrictions. The media's requests were denied.[21] McVeigh was convicted, but according to at least one critic, the judge ignored 20 years of Supreme Court precedent establishing that the First Amendment requires a presumption that criminal trial proceedings be open to public scrutiny.22 Unfortunately, this case may serve as the prototype of how justice should be done. Would the severe restrictions on access be so readily embraced if McVeigh had been acquitted?

Anonymous jurors also were seated in the racially charged trials involving the beatings of Rodney King and Reginald Denny. In these cases, even the defendants did not know their jurors' identities.23 The original Rodney King beating trial, in which four white police officers were acquitted, also used an anonymous jury. Once the trial was over, jurors' names were released. The jurors received death threats following the verdict, which prompted one of the worst riots in California history.

Not surprisingly, the judge in the federal civil rights trial of the four police officers impaneled an anonymous jury.24 Most of the time, however, anonymous juries are not justified and are a defensive reaction to harsh criticism of the judicial process.

Some legal experts say this trend toward secrecy is a legacy of the O.J. Simpson trial.25 Judge Lance Ito impaneled an anonymous jury in the 1994 murder trial of O.J. Simpson.26 The jurors' identities were shielded from the attorneys, the defendant, the public and the press.27 The judge did not explain his decision, but some court watchers speculated the secrecy was intended to dampen publicity about the case and shield the potential jurors from overzealous reporters.28 This case put the criminal justice system under a microscope and many Americans did not like what they saw. It also demonstrated one of the problems with anonymous juries. One juror was dismissed and replaced after an investigation showed she failed to acknowledge she had once been a victim of domestic violence, even though she had filed a complaint with police accusing her husband of shoving her, threatening her and forcing her to have sex.29 Had her identity been known, chances are the critical information would have been exposed during *voir dire*. The court's time would not have been wasted and a potential mistrial or miscarriage of justice would not have been such a distinct possibility.

In some cases, such as the 1997 New Jersey trial of Jesse K. Timmendequas, the man accused of killing 7-year-old Megan Kanka, an anonymous jury seems unnecessary and contrary to the American justice system's aversion to trials by secret panels. Timmendequas' crime was reported widely by national news organizations and spurred passage of laws across the country to protect children from child molesters. Without any evidence of danger to jurors, the judge refused to make public the list of the jurors until the trial was complete, and threatened to jail reporters who interviewed them in the two days after their verdict.30 Again, without evidence of danger, an anonymous jury was used in the trial of British au pair Louise Woodward, accused of murdering 8-month-old Matthew Eappen.[31] Unfortunately, in these and other cases, concern over jurors' privacy is trumping the First and Sixth Amendments and the sanctity of our criminal justice system is at risk.

History of Anonymous Juries

The first anonymous jury was used in New York City in the late-1970s in the federal trial of a notorious drug kingpin, Nick Barnes.[32] Following the lead of the U.S. Court of Appeals for the Second Circuit in *United States v. Barnes,* judges have impaneled anonymous juries in organized crime, drug trafficking or gang-related cases where there were serious threats to jurors' safety or a demonstrated willingness by the defendant to interfere with the justice system.[33]

In recent years, particularly after the O.J. Simpson trial, judges have been expanding those precedents and shielding identities of jurors even when the risk of physical harm is not present, especially in high-profile cases.[34] Despite the Supreme Court's repudiation of an across-the-board presumption that serving on juries results in invasions of privacy, courts are increasingly willing to seal jurors' identities to protect them from "harassment" or "annoyance" by the media.[35] However, generalized concerns about media harassment and intrusion on jurors' privacy are not legitimate interests, according to the Supreme Court in *Press-Enterprise Co. v. Superior Court of California,* commonly known as *Press-Enterprise I.*[36]

An anonymous jury is a drastic measure that should be undertaken only under limited and carefully delineated circumstances, warns one federal circuit court of appeals.[37] Recently, courts have seemed eager to ignore this warning, especially in cases where there is substantial media coverage and public interest. Only specific findings based on concrete threats to privacy should be allowed to trump the First Amendment.

Constitutional Conflicts

Courts using anonymous jurors must consider a number of competing constitutional rights, including the First Amendment right of access. Courts considering anonymous juries also have struggled with balancing the defendant's Sixth Amendment right to a fair trial and a juror's right to privacy.

The First Amendment Right of Access to Criminal Trials, Voir Dire *and Pretrial Hearings*

The U.S Supreme Court recognized a First Amendment right of access to criminal trials in the 1980 landmark case, *Richmond Newspapers, Inc. v. Virginia.*[38] Before beginning the fourth murder trial of John Stevenson, the frustrated trial judge, who had presided over the three previous failed trials, closed the courtroom. This closure violated the public's right to attend the trial, according to the Supreme Court. While the First Amendment does not explicitly mention a public right to attend criminal trials, the right is implicit in protections that ensure free communication about the government, the Court reasoned.[39] The Court based its decision, in part, on this country's long tradition of openness in the judicial system. Also, according to the Court, public trials serve a number of important interests. Public trials discourage perjury and official misconduct during the proceedings and inspire public confidence in the criminal justice process. This helps defuse community outrage after major crimes.

Following the decision, which guaranteed a right of public access to criminal trials, it was the Supreme Court's decision two years later, in *Globe Newspaper Co. v. Superior Court,*[40] that began to give shape and meaning to this right. In *Globe,* the Court invalidated a Massachusetts statute that automatically excluded the public and news media from courtrooms during testimony by minors in sex offense cases. In doing so, the Court established the standard that must be satisfied before the First Amendment right of access could be restricted.[41] The *Globe* Court admonished lower courts considering restricting access to construe the public right of access broadly because "it permits the public to participate in and serves as a check upon the judicial process, an essential component in our structure of self-government."[42] To aid courts in their analysis, the Court set out a two-tiered analysis judges must apply before limiting public access. The first level involves determining whether a right of access attaches to a particular proceeding. Courts should ask two questions. First, has the public historically had access to such proceedings? Second, does public access serve a useful function? If these two conditions obtain, the qualified First Amendment right of access applies.[43]

Once a right of access has been determined, the court proceeds to the second part of the analysis and must identify a compelling interest sufficient to warrant closure and overcome the First Amendment right of access.[44] The Supreme Court applied this newly crafted test two years later and extended the First Amendment right of access to the process of jury selection.[45]

Access to Voir Dire

Since the development of the jury system, the process of jury selection, including the questioning of jurors known as *voir dire,* has always been open to the public. In 1984, the Supreme Court said: "The value of openness lies in the fact that people not actually attending trials can have confidence that standards of fairness are being observed; the sure knowledge that anyone is free to attend gives assurance that established procedures are being followed and that deviations will become known."[46]

In *Press-Enterprise I,* the Supreme Court reversed a trial court judge who had closed the entire *voir dire* proceedings in a rape case to protect jurors' privacy. In extending the qualified First Amendment right for the public and news media to attend criminal trials to the *voir dire* process, the Court warned that closing proceedings must be rare and only for reasons clearly shown to outweigh the value of openness. Applying this analysis to the *Press-Enterprise I* facts, the Supreme Court held the public and news media have a right to be present during jury selection. In legal jargon, this is known as a "qualified" right. It can be denied only after a judge finds "that closure is essential to preserve higher values and is narrowly tailored to serve that interest."[47] In addition, the Court in *Press-Enterprise I* reasoned that the right of access to criminal *voir dire* exists under the First Amendment, as jury selection has historically been public, and that openness serves the First Amendment. The Court discussed two reasons for closing *voir dire:* protecting the defendant's Sixth Amendment right to a fair trial and protecting a specific juror's privacy.

Protecting Jurors' Privacy

Serving on a jury is not automatically an invasion of a juror's privacy. In *Press-Enterprise I,* the Supreme Court shed light on when a juror's right to privacy might justify restrictions on access to *voir dire.* The Court stressed that the right of privacy belongs to the juror, who must assert the right. Moreover, the right to privacy is implicated only when the questions asked at *voir dire* probe into sensitive areas of a juror's life.

In his concurrence, Justice Harry Blackmun stressed that the Court did not, and had never, found that jurors automatically have a right to privacy. "Despite the fact that a juror does not put himself voluntarily into the public eye, a trial is a public event," according to Justice Blackmun.[48] Thus, while a prospective juror has an interest in sheltering embarrassing personal information from the news media and the public, the juror has no interest in preventing the public from simply knowing the juror has been called to serve on a jury. According to the Supreme Court, each case must be considered on its own merits, and measures limiting public access to information about jurors can be no more restrictive than absolutely necessary to protect a compelling privacy interest.[49] During the past decade, judges have seized on this language and have impaneled anonymous juries as a way to protect jurors' privacy. However, the courts have expanded the definition of privacy far beyond what the Court in *Press-Enterprise I* intended as a "compelling privacy interest." These courts also have failed to adequately balance the public's fundamental First Amendment right to observe the justice system at work.

Additionally, judges who are concerned about publicity but unable to stop news organizations from publishing what they know are trying to control news reports by seating anonymous juries, thus limiting the information available to reporters.[50] The greater the publicity, the more likely prosecutors are to call for an anonymous jury. However, as one defense lawyer argues, "The best guarantee of a fair trial is publicity."[51]

The Sixth Amendment Right to a Fair Trial by Jury

Jurors have been called the "conscience of the community."[52] The right to a trial by an impartial jury is a fundamental tenet of this country's judicial system, guaranteed by the Sixth Amendment.[53] An essential element of a fair trial is the presumption of innocence.[54]

In *Press-Enterprise I*, the Supreme Court said protecting a defendant's constitutional right to a fair trial also may justify closing *voir dire*.[55] However, many defense lawyers have argued that anonymous juries actually violate a criminal defendant's Sixth Amendment right. They contend that anonymous juries should be impaneled only when there is concrete evidence of jury tampering or a credible threat to jurors' safety.[56] Criminal defense lawyers say anonymous juries deprive defendants of their constitutional rights to both a public trial before an impartial jury and the presumption of innocence.[57] In one of the early anonymous jury cases, the defendant challenged its use, claiming the process was unconstitutional and gave jurors the impression the defendant was dangerous and a threat to their safety.[58] While the Second Circuit recognized the importance of the presumption of innocence, it ruled that the goal of protecting jurors justified the burden placed on the defendant's constitutional right.[59] The court held, however, that the practice would not be constitutional in all cases; it would pass constitutional muster only when there was "strong reason" to believe jurors needed protection and the court had taken "reasonable precautions" to minimize the impact of anonymity on the jurors' views.[60] Despite the strenuous opposition of defense attorneys, every federal circuit that has considered the question has upheld the constitutionality of anonymous juries.[61] However, no court has held the practice constitutional under routine circumstances. Rather, anonymous juries are constitutional only in limited circumstances and generally are limited to exceptional cases where there is clear evidence that juror safety may be in danger.[62]

Courts have upheld anonymous juries after considering the following factors: (1) the defendant's involvement in organized crime; (2) his or her participation in a group with the capacity to harm jurors or past attempts to interfere with the judicial process; (3) the potential punishment faced by the defendant; (4) the degree of publicity the trial has received; and (5) the possibility of juror harassment.[63] Where these factors have not been present, at least one court has overturned a conviction by an anonymous jury.[64]

Standards for Seating Anonymous Juries

The Second Circuit of the U.S. Court of Appeals, which includes New York, has been the most active federal circuit supporting use of anonymous juries. The Second Circuit established a two-prong test before courts could constitutionally seat anonymous juries.[65] First, a court must have a strong reason to believe the jury needs protection and second, reasonable precautions must be taken to minimize the effect that such a decision might have on the jurors' opinions of the defendants.[66] This standard was adopted in subsequent cases where defendants were alleged to be members of organized crime families that possessed the means to harm jurors and had a history of jury tampering.[67]

In 1985, a federal judge in New York developed the standard for determining whether jurors need protecting. In *United States v. Persico*,[68] the court balanced the government's interest in protecting jurors with the defendants' interest in obtaining a fair trial. The court considered the following factors: (1) whether the defendants are alleged to have engaged in "dangerous and unscrupulous conduct," with particular consideration of whether such conduct was part of a "large-scale organized" criminal enterprise; (2) whether defendants have engaged in past attempts to interfere with the judicial process; and (3) whether there has been a substantial degree of pretrial publicity such as to enhance the possibility that jurors' names would become public and thus expose them to intimidation by the defendants' friends or enemies or harassment by the public.[69] In 1996, the U.S. Court of Appeals for the Fifth Circuit adopted the *Persico* test and considered publicity as a factor when it approved an anonymous jury over the vehement objections of defense lawyers in the trial of 11 Branch Davidians, accused of killing four federal agents during a raid on the Davidians' compound outside Waco, Texas.[70] The appellate court said the "enormous amount of world-wide media attention generated by the case, the emotionally charged atmosphere surrounding it, and the prospect of publicity militates in favor of jury anonymity to prevent exposure of the jurors to intimidation or harassment."[71] For an anonymous jury to be constitutional, courts must minimize the effect an anonymous jury has on the jurors' opinion of the defendants.[72] Courts have done this by administering extensive questionnaires, by increased latitude in questioning during *voir dire*[73] and by admonishing jurors with a cautionary instruction.[74]

It is somewhat ironic that judges often mislead jurors during these cautionary instructions, often blaming extensive news coverage for the anonymity, even when the true concern lies with the jurors' safety and possible retribution by the defendant.[75] Judges work hard to gain the trust and respect of jurors, yet they often are willing to fabricate the reason for shielding their identities.[76] While the defendant receives the benefit of the presumption of innocence this instruction provides, jurors are instructed to fear and distrust the news media without good cause.

At least one court has refused to participate in this subterfuge. In *United States v. Scarfo*,[77] the trial judge decided to be frank with the jury impaneled to hear testimony about organized crime. The judge explained that the anonymous selection procedure was being used "as a precautionary measure to make sure that both sides get a fair trial," but that he believed there was no reason for the jury to be apprehensive that they or their families would be endangered. The jurors also were told the anonymous selection procedure was not to be interpreted as a reflection on the defense.

The Case for Anonymous Juries

There is considerable public support for anonymous juries.[78] Proponents argue that anonymous juries "alleviate juror fear, enhance the participation of citizens in jury service, increase the reliability of the voir dire process, improve the quality of jury deliberations and ensure the fairness of the criminal verdicts."[79] In addition, proponents argue that without appropriate protections regarding their identities, jurors may be reluctant to serve in a given case.[80] Anonymous juries will encourage more prospective jurors to report for duty.[81] Jurors will be more honest if they are anonymous because they will feel safer.[82] Finally, anonymous jurors will be protected from public intimidation and pressure to reach a particular verdict.[83]

Anonymous Juries Threaten Justice

The routine use of anonymous juries threatens the integrity of the criminal justice system, which depends on public access, according to the Supreme Court. Access to judicial proceedings enhances public confidence in their fairness, promotes public respect for the system, ensures that uniform procedures are used, encourages truthful *voir dire* testimony, uncovers juror bias, provides an outlet for community rage and functions as a check on state abuses of power.[84] Critics say that in most cases anonymity is a gross overreaction to extraordinary situations, especially where jurors are being protected not from retaliation, but from the news media.[85] Anonymity also limits accountability, an important pressure on jurors to do the right thing.[86] And, finally, secrecy in the criminal justice system inhibits the public's ability to ensure fairness of the process.

Journalists are not the only opponents of anonymous juries. Defense attorneys often oppose them as well. They say anonymous juries create the impression the jurors have something to fear.[87] In addition, they argue that veiling the identity of the jurors strips the defendant of the presumption of innocence.[88] Also, these attorneys believe it is harder to select a jury when they do not have access to their names.[89] Finally, a number of judges have criticized use of anonymous juries.[90] One judge worries that anonymous juries "would be a breeding ground for problems," allowing jurors to lie about their qualifications to get onto a jury.[91]

The integrity of the criminal justice system has been threatened by the use of anonymous jurors. In addition to the juror in the O.J. Simpson criminal trial who was removed once her background of domestic violence became known to the judge, an anonymous juror was able to fix the trial of John Gotti, reputed organized crime boss and head of the Gambino family. Following what had become almost standard procedure in mob-related cases, a federal judge in New York impaneled an anonymous jury to ensure they would not be threatened or corrupted by the defendants.[92] No one but the court clerk knew the jurors' names, address, employers or anything else that might identify them. The judge even carried the jurors' questionnaires home with him every night.

However, unbeknown to the prosecution and the judge, one juror was a former roommate and close personal friend of a gang member. In an effort to solidify his position with the Gotti organization, this gang member reported his friendship with the juror to defendant Gotti. The jury acquitted Gotti and his co-defendants and one of the jurors received $60,000 from Gotti via his juror friend. Many people outside the courtroom knew about the connection between the juror and the gang member and, had jurors' identities been public, they could have alerted officials.

Anonymity thus is no guarantee jurors will not be threatened. In the 1989 heroin trafficking trial of Gene Gotti, John Gotti's brother, an anonymous juror was excused after he reported he was threatened by a man he later identified as a member of the Gambino crime family.[93] A Florida judge was forced to declare a mistrial following the murder conviction in the highly publicized case of a Canadian tourist after he learned that one anonymous juror was acquainted with the defendant's family.[94] Had these jurors been identified, someone in the community probably would have become aware of the situation and brought it to the court's attention, thus avoiding an extraordinary waste of judicial time and resources.

States Respond to Calls for Anonymous Juries

Despite objections from defense lawyers and media groups, state courts around the country are seating anonymous juries. In fact, two judges in southern Los Angeles County offered anonymity to all jurors involved in criminal cases.[95] The public defender's office challenged the practice, claiming it created the impression jurors have something to fear from defendants. A year later, a state Superior Court ruling forbade blanket use of anonymous juries and ordered jurors' names to be made public.[96]

In its first case where an anonymous jury was an issue, a Wisconsin appellate court upheld the trial court's decision to use an anonymous jury in 1996.[97] While acknowledging that Wisconsin statutes guarantee court proceedings are open to the public,[98] the appellate court said that in the appropriate case and with the proper exercise of discretion, as in the case at hand, an anonymous jury was proper.[99]

Defense lawyers have been more successful fighting anonymous juries on the state level.[100] For example, the Massachusetts Supreme Court has ruled that anonymous juries violate the state's constitution, holding that it puts defendants at an unfair advantage.[101] New Jersey also weighed in against use of anonymous juries, holding that the risk of prejudice to the defendant could not be overcome by the judge's instructions to the jurors, which were not likely to be "truthful and efficacious."[102]

Trial courts in New York have recently split on the issue of anonymous juries. In April 1998, a Brooklyn trial court justice refused to impanel an anonymous jury, holding that jury selection must be open to the public in the state's first case under its 1995 death penalty law.[103] A year earlier, a Staten Island judge held that a state court could seat an anonymous jury if it could be "predicted" that a defendant would tamper with justice. Citing a New York statute that requires jurors' names and addresses to be disclosed to a defendant, the judge held that where a defendant presents a clear threat to either the safety or integrity of the court, as in this case, he forfeits the right to know the jurors' identities.[104]

Prophylactic Measures

The First Amendment requires that before closing any phase of the *voir dire* process, including impaneling an anonymous jury, courts must consider each case on its own merits.[105] In addition, measures limiting information about jurors must be no more restrictive than absolutely necessary to protect a compelling interest.[106] Clearly, measures that call for routine use of anonymous juries violate these constitutional requirements.

Rather than mounting an assault on the First Amendment by seating an anonymous jury in cases where publicity is the primary concern, judges should consider alternative preventive measures to ensure a fair and public trial. For example, judges should conduct an in-depth inquiry during *voir dire* about the effects of the news media and publicity on the juror's ability to be fair and impartial. They might be surprised.

In one case, *Gannett Co. v. Delaware*,[107] the trial court asked prospective jurors whether they could perform their duties fairly and impartially if their names were made public. Only five of 76 potential jurors stated they felt they could not be fair to the defendant if their names were publicly announced.[108] If we trust jurors to make life and death decisions, jurors should be trusted to answer these questions truthfully, and if jurors can be impartial if their identities are known, judges must avoid the routine use of anonymous juries in high-profile cases.

Conclusion

The prospect of allowing defendants to be tried before jurors whose names will never be disclosed conjures up images of hooded judges and secret tribunals. This procedure is antithetical to this country's history of openness in the criminal justice system and should be used with great caution and circumspection.

While the Supreme Court has refused to rule on the practice of shrouding the jurors in anonymity, the Court has repeatedly stressed that openness in the criminal justice system has a special value. Openness, and the publicity it invites, serve at least two distinct functions, according to the Court. It enhances the basic fairness of the criminal trial and it enhances the *appearance* of fairness, essential to public confidence in the system. Fairness and the appearance of fairness are impaired when judges cloak jurors in a veil of anonymity. When the public is aware the law is being enforced, there is more confidence in the criminal justice system. Anonymity impairs a jury's sense of responsibility to the public and the public's faith in the jury.

Closure proceedings must be rare. The court must make a specific finding that a compelling governmental interest outweighs the value of openness and the procedure for closure must be carefully fashioned to meet these specific interests and not be broader than absolutely necessary.

Prospective jurors have neither an actual nor reasonable expectation that what occurs in court will be kept private. Generalized concern about juror privacy cannot be allowed to override the rights of the public and the news media to know who's making the decision in jury trials. Only specific findings based on concrete threats to the jurors or the administration of justice should be allowed to trump the First Amendment.

Notes

[1] J.H. Baker, *An Introduction to English Legal History* 10 (1971); See also C.H.S. Fifoot, *English Law and Its Background* 86 (1993).

[2] Jack Pope, *The Jury,* 39 Texas L. Rev. 426 (1961).

[3] *Id.* at 437–39. In addition, jurors were required to have knowledge about the dispute. Ignorance of the facts resulted in being excused from the venire.

[4] Robert Lloyd Raskopf, *A First Amendment Right of Access to a Juror's Identity: Toward a Fuller Understanding of the Jury's Deliberative Process,* 17 Pepperdine Law Rev. 357 (1990).

[5]*Gannett Co. v. Delaware*, 571 Del. A.2d 735, 761 (1990) (Walsh, J., dissenting).

[6]A jury is "anonymous" when the trial court withholds, or bars the revelation of, information that would identify the jurors. *United States v. Crockett*, 979 F.2d 1204, 1215 (7th Cir. 1992), *cert. denied*, 507 U.S. 998 (1993).

[7]Jane Kirtley, *Hiding the Identity of Potential Jurors*, American Journalism Review 50 (June 1997).

[8]The news media, which under the First Amendment are guaranteed the right to attend criminal trials and judicial proceedings, have always been deemed a surrogate for the public that cannot attend trials daily.

[9]*Richmond Newspapers Inc. v. Virginia*, 448 U.S. 555 (1980) (public, including press, has a First Amendment right to attend criminal trials).

[10]*Globe Newspaper Co. v. Superior Court*, 457 U.S. 596 (1982) (First Amendment protects right of access to trial testimony of minor sex offense victims); *Press-Enterprise Co. v. Superior Court*, 464 U.S. 501 (1984) (*voir dire* examination of prospective jurors should ordinarily be open to the public and press) (hereinafter *Press-Enterprise I*); *Press Enterprise v. Superior Court*, 478 U.S. 1 (1986) (First Amendment right of access attaches to pretrial hearings) (hereinafter *Press-Enterprise II*).

[11]Trial judges seal identifying information about jurors, including their names, addresses, places of employment, ethnic backgrounds and religion. See *United States v. Crockett*.

[12]Jane Kirtley, *Lessons From the Timothy McVeigh Trial I*, Media Studies J. 11 (winter 1998).

[13]John Howard, *Judge Orders Anonymous Jury in Unabomber Case*, Austin American-Statesman A12 (Oct. 4, 1997).

[14]William Glaberson, *Courts Under Challenge for Anonymity of Juries*, The New York Times A20 (Dec. 22, 1997). A three-judge panel of the 9th U.S. Circuit Court of Appeals in San Francisco heard the media's appeal on May 12, 1998. At least one of the judges questioned the need for evidence of danger to the jurors and appeared to support jury anonymity in all well-known cases. See also *California Briefly*, The Orange County Register A4 (May 13, 1998).

[15]Emelyn Cruz Lat, *Lawyers Cull Unabomb Pool*, The San Francisco Examiner A-2 (Dec. 22, 1997).

[16]Kevin Johnson, *The Secret Trial of Timothy McVeigh*, USA Today 1A (April 24, 1997).

[17]*Jurors Selected in Trial of McVeigh; Judge Continues Efforts to Keep Identities Secret*, St. Louis Post-Dispatch, A6 (April 23, 1997).

[18]Nolan Clay, *Bomb Jury Selection to Enter Last Phase*, The Daily Oklahoman 1 (April 22, 1997).

[19]*Id.* Judge Matsch said, "It's not an anonymous jury. The lawyers in the case and Mr. McVeigh know who the jurors are. . . . But their names are not going to be made public."

[20]Kevin Johnson and Tony Mauro, *The Secret Trial of Timothy McVeigh: Judge Hides Jury From Public Eye, Gags Lawyers and Imposes Unheard*

of Restrictions; Critics Say Strict Measures Hurt Tradition of Open Court, USA Today 1A (April 24, 1997).

[21]*United States v. McVeigh,* 964 F. Supp. 313 (D. Colo. 1997).

[22]Kirtley, *Lessons From the Timothy McVeigh Trial* at 13.

[23]Robert Worthington, *L.A. Beatings Test Concept of Jury Anonymity,* The Chicago Tribune 1 (Feb. 15, 1993).

[24]*Id.*

[25]Steve Berry, *"Legal Experts See an Increasing Trend by Judges to Seal Court Records, Issue Gag Orders and Otherwise Restrict Access; At Issue Is the Effect . . .,"* The Los Angeles Times B1 (May 24, 1998).

[26]*Jurors' Names Reportedly to Be Secret,* Atlanta Journal and Constitution A6 (Sept. 16, 1994).

[27]*Id.*; see Bill Boyarsky, *The Spin: Shielding Simpson's Jury Selection in Name of Efficiency,* The Los Angeles Times B1 (Sept. 18, 1994).

[28]*Jurors'* Names.

[29]Don Babwin, *Before the Verdict, Fear Prowls the Jury Room,* The Press-Enterprise B1 (Aug. 23, 1995).

[30]Glaberson, *Courts Under Challenge.*

[31]Bill Hutchinson, *Twelve to Decide the Fate of Nanny,* The Boston Herald 14 (Oct. 7, 1997).

[32]504 F.2d 121 (2d Cir. 1979).

[33]*United States v. Edmond,* 730 F. Supp. 1144 (D.C. Cir. 1990); *United States v. Scarfo,* 850 F.2d 1015 (3d Cir. 1988); *United States v. Edwards,* 823 F.2d 111 (5th Cir. 1987), *rehearing denied;* 828 F.2d 772, *cert. denied;* 485 U.S. 934 (1988); *United States v. Persico,* 832 F.2d 705 (2d Cir. 1987); *United States v. Thomas,* 757 F.2d 1359 (2d Cir. 1985); *United States v. Tutino,* 883 F.2d 1125 (2d Cir. 1989); *United States v. Gotti,* 1992 U.S. Dist. LEXIS 11400 (2d Cir. 1992).

[34]Kirtley, *Hiding the Identity of Potential Jurors.*

[35]Glaberson, *Courts Under Challenge;* see also Janet Elliott, *In San Antonio Federal Courts, A Double Dose of Jury Secrecy,* Texas Lawyer 1 (Jan. 10, 1994) (quoting judge's order that "media attention would increase the chance that the jurors's names would become public and they could be exposed to harassment."); *United States v. McVeigh,* No. 96–CR–68, 1997 U.S. Dist. LEXIS 6304 (D. Colo. May, 5, 1998); *Newsday, Inc. v. Goodman,* 159 N.Y. A.D.2d 667 (App. Div. 1990); *United States v. Darden,* 70 F.3d 1057 (8th Cir. 1995); *United States v. Ross,* 33 F.3d 1507 (11th Cir. 1994), *cert. denied,* 115 S. Ct. 2558 (1995); *United States v. Persico,* 621 N.Y. F. Supp. 842 (S.D. 1985).

[36]464 U.S. 501 (1984).

[37]*United States v. Krout,* 66 F. 3d 1420, 1427 (5th Cir. 1995), *cert. denied,* 116 S. Ct. 963 (1996).

[38]448 U.S. 555 (1980) (right to attend criminal trials is implicit in the guarantees of the First Amendment).

[39]*Id.* at 575.

[40]457 U.S. 596 (1982).

[41]*Id.* at 605.

[42]*Id.* at 605–07.

[43]*Id.* at 606, *Press-Enterprise II*, 478 U.S. 1, 8 (1986).

[44]457 U.S. at 605–07.

[45]*Press-Enterprise I*, 464 U.S. 501 (1984).

[46]*Id.* at 508.

[47]*Id.* at 510.

[48]*Id.* at 514, n.1.

[49]*Id.* at 510.

[50]See Glaberson, *supra* note 14.

[51]See Wendy Benjaminson, *Shroud of Secrecy Increasingly Veils Trials in Texas,* The Houston Chronicle A-1 (March 13, 1994).

[52]*Witherspoon v. Illinois,* 391 U.S. 510, 519 (1968); *United States v. Spock,* 416 F.2d 165 (1st Cir. 1969); *United States v. Derrigan,* 417 F.2d 1002 (4th Cir. 1969), *cert. denied,* 397 U.S. 910 (1970).

[53]U.S. Const. amend. VI.; *Estelle v. Williams,* 425 U.S. 501 (1976) (writing for the majority, Chief Justice Burger stated that the right to a fair trial is a "fundamental liberty secured by the . . . Fourteenth Amendment").

[54]*Id.* at 503. ("The presumption of innocence, although not articulated in the Constitution, is a basic component of a fair trial in our criminal justice system.")

[55]464 U.S. 501, 510–513.

[56]Eva M. Rodriguez, *When Jurors Dare Not Speak Their Names,* Legal Times 1 (May 9, 1994).

[57]Abraham Abramovsky, *Juror Safety: The Presumption of Innocence and Meaningful Voir Dire in Federal Criminal Prosecutions—Are They Endangered Species?,* 50 Fordham L. Rev. 30 (1981).

[58]*United States v. Thomas,* 757 F.2d 1359 (2d Cir. 1985); *United States v. Scarfo,* 850 F.2d 1015, 1026 (3d Cir. 1988).

[59]*Thomas,* 757 F.2d at 1364–65.

[60]*Id.* at 1365.

[61]David Weinstein, *Protecting a Juror's Right to Privacy: Constitutional Constraints and Policy Options,* 70 Temple L. Rev. 1, 26. See also *United States v. Darden,* 70 F.3d 1507, 1532 (8th Cir. 1995); *United States v. Edmond,* 52 F.3d 1080, 1090–91 (D.C. Cir. 1995); *United States v. Ross,* 33 F.3d 1507, 1519 (11th Cir. 1994), *cert. denied,* 115 S. Ct. 2558 (1995); *United States v. Crockett,* 979 F.2d 1204, 1215–17 (7th Cir. 1992); *Scarfo,* 850 F.2d 1015, 1021–26.

[62]*United States v. Krout,* 66 F.3d 1420, 1427 (5th Cir. 1995), *cert. denied,* 116 S. Ct. 963 (1996); See also *Globe Newspaper Co.,* 920 F.2d 88, 97–98 (1st Cir. 1990); *United States v. Colon,* 834 N.Y. F. Supp. 78, 82–86 (S.D. 1993).

[63]*Darden,* 70 F.3d at 1532; *Ross,* 33 F.3d at 1520.

[64]*United States v. Sanchez,* 74 F.3d 562, 564–65 (5th Cir. 1996).

[65]*Thomas,* 757 F.2d 1359 (2d Cir. 1985).

[66]*Id.* at 1365.

[67]See, e.g., *United States v. Tutino,* 883 F.2d 1125, 1132 (2d Cir. 1989), *cert. denied,* 474 U.S. 819 (1985), *and cert. denied,* 479 U.S. 818 (1986);

United States v. Vario, 943 F.2d 236, 239 (2d Cir. 1991), *cert. denied,* 502 U.S. 1036 (1992).

68621 F. Supp. 842 (S.D.N.Y. 1985).

69*Id.* at 878.

70Kathy Fair, *8 Women, 4 Men Seated for Branch Davidian Jury,* The Houston Chronicle A19 (Jan. 12, 1994).

71*United States v. Branch,* 91 F.3d 699 (5th Cir. 1996). The procedure drew sharp criticism from protesters outside the courtroom, including members of a group called the Fully Informed Jury Association. The group's co-founder expressed concern that the government could have brought in a busload of FBI agents dressed in street clothes to serve as jurors. See Scott W. Wright, *Protests, Media Again Surround Cult,* Austin American A1 (Jan. 11, 1994).

72David Weinstein, *Protecting a Juror's Right to Privacy: Constitutional Constraints and Policy Options,* 70 Temple L. Rev. 1, 26. See also *United States v. Darden,* 70 F.3d 1507, 1532 (8th Cir. 1995); *United States v. Edmond,* 52 F.3d 1080, 1090–91 (D.C. Cir. 1995); *United States v. Ross,* 33 F.3d 1507, 1519 (11th Cir. 1994), *cert. denied,* 115 S. Ct. 2558 (1995); *United States v. Crockett,* 979 F.2d 1204, 1215–17 (7th Cir. 1992); *Scarfo,* 850 F.2d 1015, 1021–26.

73See Rodriguez, *When Jurors Dare Not Speak Their Names.* In the federal trial of the officers accused of violating Rodney King's civil rights, U.S. District Judge John Davies allowed lawyers to use a jury questionnaire of more than 50 pages.

74*Tutino,* 883 F.2d 1125, 1133; *Scarfo,* 850 F.2d at 1017; *Thomas,* 757 F.2d at 1365, n. 1; *United States v. Pasciuti,* 803 N.H. F. Supp. 499, 503 n. 5 (D. 1992); *Edmond,* 730 F. Supp. at 1151.

75*Thomas,* 757 F.2d at 1365, n. 1. The *Thomas* Court suggests the following cautionary instruction: "Your identities will remain anonymous . . . to ward off curiosity and seekers for information that might otherwise infringe on your privacy and it will aid in insulating and sheltering you from unwanted and undesirable publicity and embarrassment and notoriety and any access to you which would interfere with preserving your sworn duty to fairly, impartially and independently serve as a juror."

76757 F.2d at 1365, n. 1, *Tutino,* 883 F.2d at 1133; *Pasciuti,* 803 N.H. F. Supp. 499, 503, n. 5 (D. 1992); *Edmond,* 730 F. Supp. at 1151.

77*Scarfo,* 850 F.2d 1015, 1021.

78A 1995 survey in *Glamour* magazine reported that 84 percent of the primarily young, working women survey supported the use of anonymous juries in all criminal cases. *Should We Protect the Identity of Jurors in Criminal Trials?* Glamour 159 (March 1995); Jurors *Should Serve Anonymously in All Criminal Trials, Say 84% of Young Women Surveyed,* PR Newswire (Feb. 13, 1995); Nancy J. King, *Nameless Justice: The Case for the Routine Use of Anonymous Juries in Criminal Trials,* 49 Vand. L. Rev. 123, 127 (1996).

79King, *Nameless Justice* at 125.

80*State v. Britt,* 203 Wis. 2d 25 (Ct. App.).

[81]King, *Nameless Justice* at 138.

[82]Don DeBenedictis, *Anonymity Now Shields Jurors' Identities; Defense Lawyers Question Legality, Wisdom of Allowing Secrecy in All Cases,* 80 A.B.A. 16 (Nov. 1994).

[83]*Id.* at 137.

[84]*Press-Enterprise II,* 478 U.S. 1, 12–13; *Press-Enterprise I,* 464 U.S. 501, 508–509; *Globe Newspaper,* 457 U.S. 596, 606; *Richmond Newspapers,* 448 U.S. 555, 569; *Gannett Co. v. DePasquale,* 443 U.S. 368, 383 (1979); *Gannett Co. v. Delaware,* 571 Del. A.2d 735 (1990) (Walsh, J., dissenting).

[85]Melissa Block, *Anonymity for Juries,* NPR, Morning Edition, Transcript No. 97122210-210 (Dec. 22, 1997).

[86]Catherine Gewertz, *Courthouse Makes Blanket Use of Juror Anonymity,* The Los Angeles Times A1 (July 25, 1994); see also Don DeBenedictis, *Anonymity Now Shields Jurors' Identities.*

[87]Rodriguez, *When Jurors Dare Not Speak Their Name.*

[88]Abramovsky, *Juror Safety;* see also supra note 82.

[89]*United States v. Barnes,* 604 F. 2d 121, 168 (2d Cir. 1979) (Meskill, J., dissenting), *cert. denied,* 464 U.S. 907 (1980); *Commonwealth v. Angiulo,* 415 Mass. 501, 520 (1993) (lack of written findings on necessity of anonymous jury and failure to protect defendant's due process rights results in reversal of murder conviction and remand for retrial); Abramovsky, *Juror Safety* at 49, see also Don DeBenedictis, *Anonymity Now Shields Jurors' Identities.*

[90]Babwin, *Before the Verdict.*

[91]*Id.*

[92]Marcia Chambers, *Sua Sponte,* The National Law Journal 17 (Nov. 30, 1992).

[93]Kim Wessel, *Jurors' Privacy Falls to Defendants' Rights,* The Courier-Journal B1 (Sept. 15, 1996).

[94]Radio TV Reports (Sept. 24, 1993).

[95]Catherine Gewertz, *Judge Halts His Blanket Use of Jury Anonymity in Bellflower,* The Los Angeles Time B3 (Jan. 10, 1995).

[96]*Id.*

[97]*Wisconsin v. Britt,* 203 Wis. 2d 25 (Ct. App.).

[98]*Wis. Stat.* § 757.14. (1997).

[99]Britt, 203 Wis. 2d at 35 (Ct. App.).

[100]Rodriguez, *When Jurors Dare Not Speak Their Name.*

[101]*Commonwealth v. Angiulo,* 415 Mass. 502 (1993).

[102]*New Jersey v. Accetturo,* 619 N.J. A. 2d 272, 273 (Super. Ct. Law Div. 1992).

[103]http://www.rcfp.org/NMU/980406h.html.

[104]Bill Alden, *Reasons Defined for Allowing Anonymous Jury,* New York L. J. 1 (June 18, 1997).

[105]*Press-Enterprise I,* 464 U.S. at 510.

[106]*Id.*

[107]571 A.2d 735 (Del. 1990).

[108]*Id.* at 739.

9

The Threat From Within: Balancing Access and National Security

Wallace Eberhard

I don't think we need an Official Secrets Act—we are partly there already.

—Ford Rowan

Public and news media access to government information has been frustrated by a number of factors, as the preceding chapters have shown. Invariably, courts and legislatures have had to balance competing societal interests, ensuring both the needs of an informed citizenry and the needs of representative government to protect rights of individuals as well as government's own legitimate interests. Among the most important government interests is national security—protecting information the disclosure of which could undermine the nation's very existence. The very importance of this interest, however, makes policing its abuse all the more difficult for advocates of legitimate access.

What a complex people we Americans are. Public pronouncements supporting free speech and press rights abound. News media and public interest groups commit both moral authority and resources to defend critical constitutional rights. Meanwhile, the federal government has amassed awesome executive authority and Congress has passed legislation that prohibits access to people, places and records under the banner of national security. As one scholar has noted: "Today, over three million government officials and industry employees can classify information. In 1995 alone, over 3.6 million documents were classified top secret, secret or confidential (the Pentagon accounting for approximately 50 percent of all classified documents, the Central Intelligence Agency 30 percent, and the Justice Department 10 percent.)"[1] At the same time, a general air of openness in the United States makes it easy to gather a small mountain of information about matters related to national security. Large parts of most military installations are open to the public. Local telephone books list military units and their locations. While a wall of secrecy surrounds many national security and military plans, the Government Printing Office offers for sale basic technical manuals dealing with American weaponry, tactics and operations.

It is true the United States has no Official Secrets Act. Note the capitalization, usually used with an implied air of democratic superiority over the mother country, Great Britain. That nation has such an act, which is more draconian in many respects than similar laws and regulations on this side of the Atlantic.[2] But after surveying a wide body of literature, law and comment on national security, Ford Rowan's[3] comment about a de facto U.S. "Official Secrets Act" appears to be a grim, difficult and sometimes foreboding truth. Piecemeal and incrementally, the journalist or citizen who wants access or information may run into roadblocks in surprising places.

Laws and regulations related to national security have grown over time, instituted for one purpose or another, malevolent or sound, depending on the viewpoint and the era. Secrecy under the rubric of national security is controversial, expensive, inefficient, pervasive and probably out of control. Millions of documents are classified yearly— one estimate is that 19,000 documents are classified every working day. The need to protect some information is not questioned, but government policy in this area is best described as "in disarray," as one critic put it. It inhibits oversight of the executive branch by the legislative, keeps useful technology from development in the private sector and may indeed reach beyond the domain of government to classification of private research with *possible* national security implications.[4]

A full exposition of arguments for and against secrecy and re-striction in their many forms is beyond the scope of this chapter, but the central philosophical questions for American democracy are these: Can and should an open society protect its secrets?[5] How many restrictions and of what nature must we accept, and in what particu-lar circumstances?

International Concern About National Security and A Free Flow of Information

The American public hardly can escape notice of something called "the global economy." From workers to scholars to soldiers, we pay increasing attention to what goes on beyond the two great oceans that separate but no longer insulate us from other nations. At the same time, little attention is paid to access issues related to national security in other nations of the world. ARTICLE 19, the International Center Against Censorship, makes these matters its business. The center, lo-cated in London, recently convened a meeting of experts in South Africa to establish a model document on international censorship. The result was published under the title *The Johannesburg Principles on National Security, Freedom of Express and Access to Information.*[6] The principles realistically recognize that governments will try to pro-tect secrecy, for base or noble reasons, and will try to frame clear lim-its on the reasons for secrecy as well as limiting what may be classi-fied. Two of the principles addressed individual rights and government responsibilities:

> Principle 11: General Rule on Access to Information
> Everyone has the right to obtain information from public authori-ties, including information related to national security. No restriction on this right may be imposed on the ground of national security unless the government can demonstrate that the restriction is prescribed by law and is necessary in a democratic society to protect a legitimate national security interest.
> Principle 12: Narrow Designation of Security Exemption
> A state may not categorically deny access to all information related to national security, but must designate in law only those specific and narrow categories of information that it is necessary to withhold in order to protect a legitimate national security interest.[7]

One of the other principles protects individuals against punish-ment for disclosing information if there is no harm to national secu-rity or if the public interest in disclosure outweighs the harm from disclosure. The body of principles—25 in all—represents a global concern for the suppression of information by government, and calls on the rule of law to narrow reasons for restricting information and to protect the rights of individuals inherent in any free society.

Access to Places

This section deals with the federal government's ability to tell citizens where they may not go (and when) in the name of national security. Discussion of access in war or conflict situations, however, is covered separately later in this chapter.

Simply put, government has considerable power to restrict access to federal property in times of war or peace. This is a bit paradoxical. A tourist or reporter would find no armed guards at the entry to most military installations these days. Those interested in seeing how paratroopers win their coveted "jump wings" can drive through Fort Benning, Ga., without concern—as long as they observe traffic laws and signs that clearly indicate restricted areas that are off-limits to unauthorized personnel. One simple reason installation commanders have authority is safety, both for visitors and for federal personnel, in and out of uniform. It is one thing for a tourist or a car full of relatives to watch training activities at Fort Benning from the safety of the roadside. It is another matter to wander among the trainees and instructors. Consider the responsibility placed on the commander of Fort Sill, Okla., the nation's foremost training center for artillery personnel. Night and day the distant din of artillery fire is heard at Fort Sill. Howitzers wheel through the post regularly on their way to and from training areas. The commander would be negligent if he or she did not insist on flying red flags and setting up roadblocks manned by soldiers to keep unwary tourists from wandering into areas where thousands of high explosive rounds are fired for training.

It is also clear that courts will uphold the rights of the installation commanders to restrict access to all or parts of a post or base, despite a general policy of open access to most places most of the time. As one pair of analysts wrote: "The primacy of the military mission is, and must be, at the core of the military persona. All other issues, all other concerns, pale before this central principle. The installations on which our military material is stored, our weapons systems are developed, and our soldiers, sailors, marines and airmen are trained and exercised must be preserved for the uses to which they are lawfully dedicated. The focus of installation commanders must be to channel human and material resources to the military mission."[8]

The power of military commanders to restrict access extends to First Amendment activity that could not normally be limited in other public forums. A letter may bar a specific individual from a military installation, even though others may come and go freely.[9] Civilians who want access to an installation to engage in political activity may be excluded,[10] and the broad power to exclude civilians for security reasons was spelled out by a court in *Cafeteria and Restaurant Workers Union v. McElroy*.[11] Put another way, as the U.S. Supreme Court stated in *Greer v. Spock*, the basic purpose of military installations or related civilian agencies, such as the CIA, is to "provide for the common defense."[12] This holding would no doubt extend to many non-wartime settings. It covers political protests on military installations and the threat of terrorist attacks on such installations, federal buildings, and one of the symbols of the American republic, the White House.[13]

The government's right to declare federal property off-limits to all but essential personnel is embedded in various laws and leads to what might best be described as curious confrontations between access and secrecy. Take, for example, the case of the fabled Area 51, perhaps the most secret of secret military reservations. Located in central Nevada, Area 51 is an Air Force base where futuristic aircraft are developed and tested, including the famous Stealth bomber capable of eluding enemy radar. A civilian tour guide, who once led the curious to a ridge overlooking the sprawling base, had his entrepreneurship cut short when the government took control of an additional 4,500 acres next to the base that included the vantage point he had used to satisfy his customers' curiosity. And the widow of an employee who died of either too much alcohol or exposure to hazardous chemicals found government lawyers turning his lawsuit into what has been described as something out of a Cold War spy novel, replete with sealed motions, "confidential hearings, blacked-out docket sheets, and classified briefs."[14] The attorney for the widow said the plaintiffs were "in the rather unenviable position of suing a facility that doesn't exist on behalf of workers who don't officially exist."[15] The case revived the problem of confronting government on a historic principle borrowed from English common law—the ability to claim exemption from disclosure of information because of an inherent right to protect military and state secrets.[16]

The right of the executive branch to control access to places was, indeed, written into a major piece of environmental law. The president is permitted to exempt a government facility from disclosure requirements of the Comprehensive Environmental Response,

Compensation and Liability Act[17] and the Emergency Planning and Community Right-to-Know Act of 1986[18] to protect national security interests, but must report the exemption to Congress with 30 days.[19] The provision thus provides a rationale for government legally to fence out environmental cleanup and protection advocates who want information about what government has done on militarily sensitive bases.[20]

One of the most recent—and firmest—restatements of the right to control access to government property emerged near the end of the Gulf War. Many Americans have viewed the mournful homecoming of American dead, civilian and military, at Dover Air Force Base in Dover, Del. The base has been a solemn stage for ceremonies honoring soldiers killed in Lebanon in 1983 and during the 1989 invasion of Panama. The open access policy changed shortly before the beginning of Desert Storm, the "shooting war" part of the Gulf War. Dover AFB was closed to the public and to journalists, even though ceremonies had been open to both for years. The Defense Department said the change was to shift "these events to sites closer to the families of the deceased and provide that the families would exercise veto power over press coverage,"[21] thus invoking a privacy interest on the part of these families. At the same time, there was "no change in the pre-existing policy allowing civilians to witness other activities on the base, including outgoing transport of military personnel and supplies to the Persian Gulf, as long as such access was consistent with any other applicable restrictions."[22] JB Pictures and other organizations challenged the new policy on First Amendment grounds, arguing that leaving open some base activities that were viewed as positive to the armed forces headed to the Gulf amounted to "viewpoint discrimination." The somber, negative images of the flag-draped caskets of the dead coming home were kept from their cameras' view. A federal circuit court affirmed a lower court ruling that upheld the access restrictions. The court accepted the government's argument based on privacy of the families involved, and rejected JB Pictures' reasoning that First Amendment rights to speak were abrogated. The news organization and others supporting the case were, according to the court, "primarily concerned with carrying a message *from* Dover," rather than somehow trying to speak out at the ceremonies.[23]

Access to Records

This writer was comfortably settled in for a week of research at the Franklin D. Roosevelt Presidential Library at Hyde Park, N.Y. The archives are magnificent and rich in the FDR period, the setting picturesque and restful with its overlook of the Hudson River, and the archivists helpful in locating material within the millions of documents entrusted to their care. My interest was in the development of censorship policy in the pre-World War II period. Many items, particularly copies of FBI reports to the White House, still carried "restricted" labels of one kind or another. Blessedly, the archivist on duty in the reading room declassified a document with an intriguing label (now forgotten). It is not always so easy.

The mountain of classified documents under federal control did not rise up, volcano-like, overnight. The glut of protected documents and the ability of thousands of government employees to classify them are the product of the United States' emerging role as international leader and of crises such as the Great Depression and two world wars in which American industrial and military power tipped the balance. The legal basis for protecting records under the national security rubric is found in the Constitution and bits and pieces of federal legislation. The president is vested with the power to command the armed forces and conduct foreign policy. Congress must fund and enact specifics in both areas. Along the way, each branch of government has acted independently in ways that keep both the scope and details of many national security matters from the public. Presidents conduct foreign policy as openly or secretly as they wish, often acting and then telling Congress and the people what they have done. Often the telling is separated from the action by a considerable time gap. Congress is no less secretive when it believes it is acting in the national interest. Huge chunks of the federal budget—often called a "black budget" because it reveals no dollar figures or specifics—are kept secret in war and peace. During World War II, for instance, weapons projects such as the development of the atom bomb were completed with only a few in government knowing the end product. And in peacetime, details of the Central Intelligence Agency's budget and its operations are closely guarded, known only to the current administration and a select few in Congress, which controls the purse strings.[24]

Although presidents since Washington have kept secrets from the public and Congress under the guise of conducting foreign policy, the first executive order authorizing federal officials to classify military information did not come about until 1940, when President Roosevelt issued such an order to protect national security.[25] He based his authority on the Espionage Act of 1938. The act provided for presidential protection of "vital military and naval installations or equipment."[26] President Truman expanded that authority, citing the powers vested in him "by the Constitution and statues, and as President of the United States."[27] That action drew criticism for its vastly expanded classification authority without any plan for review of classification actions.[28]

President Eisenhower backtracked from Truman's policy when he took office in 1953, putting limits on the number of agencies that could classify, narrowing the categories of classification and instituting internal review systems.[29] Yet the chorus of criticism grew, leading to the first major federal legislation relating to government records. Although the Freedom of Information Act of 1966 included a specific exemption for national security information, it provided a mechanism for access to non-national security documents.[30] Amendments to the federal FOIA in 1974 gave a toehold to document seekers in the area of national security. The amendments permitted courts to determine, in closed session, whether requested documents were "properly classified" and exempt—or the reverse. The review to determine whether classification was "proper" is weighted in favor of those who classify, and the history of the use of this amendment bears this out.[31]

The sum total of this abbreviated history: a withholding system ripe with opportunities to classify for political, rather than national security, reasons; an annual total of "classification actions" reaching nearly seven million in one recent year; a backlog of declassification, purported to take place automatically after 50 years but not always tended to; and a list of public issues ranging from nuclear energy to covert action in small nations to the investigation of the Gulf War syndrome of diseases wrapped in distrust and secrecy.[32] Some tentative steps to limit classification, reduce the backlog of classified documents and make more information available to the public were taken by President Clinton, and Congress had under consideration in early 1999 legislation designed to curb excesses in the classification system.

Enter Technology 1: Satellites and Access

The Founding Fathers, men both brilliant and practical, cannot be faulted for not anticipating technological developments when they met to draft the Constitution. One of those developments enables us to see virtually every square yard of earth from bunkers in Washington or elsewhere. This technology accelerates knowledge in the Information Age, but also poses problems for national security and, inevitably, the news media.

One commentator has described the field of remote sensing from outer space as a "First Amendment time bomb."[33] Many peaceful, useful applications of remote sensing are obvious. Weather, crop development and pollution can be monitored worldwide, contributing to local safety and national and international economies in a variety of ways. But the same satellites also pose problems for national security, individual privacy and nation-state sovereignty.[34]

Commercial remote sensing took hold rapidly after the launch of the first Landsat satellite by NASA in 1972 and initially had a resolution of 80 meters. That means an object with a dimension of that size could be identified. As the resolution capability has improved, objects of smaller dimensions can be identified, increasing concerns of the federal government about spying on restricted federal reservations from space. A resolution of five meters is desirable for the best commercial uses and also provides an excellent look at classified facilities not accessible by land.[35] Both commercial development and national security concerns were addressed when Congress passed the Land Remote Sensing Commercialization Act of 1984 (the Landsat Act).[36] Commercial development under the act requires that the seller and purchaser of the imagery must protect national defense and foreign policy interests. The Commerce Secretary cannot issue a license for commercial remote-sensing ventures until the Department of Defense reviews it for national security and the State Department examines the area of maintaining foreign relations.[37] A clear definition of "national security" is not provided in the Landsat Act. The legislative history of the act also indicates that Congress gave little consideration to the implications of news uses of satellite imagery on national security.[38] Both commercial and news uses of satellite imagery also would fall under the Espionage Act.[39] Its provisions provide for criminal prosecution of those who gather defense information that may threaten national security, provide a foreign government with U.S. national security information, photograph defense installations, distribute or sell photographs of this type or broadcast classified information.[40] The Espionage Act is not a prior restraint; instead it relies on prosecution after publication or broadcast. Though seldom used against journalists in times of war or peace, it remains both a legal and moral concern for journalistic institutions.

Satellite and remote sensing imagery have legitimately employed national security reasons since the 1960s, in the wake of the downing of the U-2 spy plane over the Soviet Union. American hostages held by Iran in Tehran were located by satellite, and remote sensing helped plan the 1986 U.S. air raid on Libya. A dozen satellites with a resolution of up to six inches were employed to locate Iraqi forces in the Gulf War, assess air strike damage and plan attacks. When General Norman Schwarzkopf knew that Iraq had been denied access to remote images because of United Nations sanctions, he began to move Army units into position for the ground war.[41] The Gulf War also began to test potential intrusion by the news media into national security matters. In the years before that war, news agencies purchased imagery from various agencies, including one operated by the French known as "SPOT," because of their superior resolution. SPOT officials quickly restricted access to its imagery after the buildup of coalition forces began but news agencies found images elsewhere to give them their own view of the potential battlefield. The difficulties and dangers of "misanalysis and deception" became apparent when ABC bought imagery from a Soviet satellite firm in September 1990. It showed the allied buildup in Saudi Arabia but no corresponding increase of Iraqi forces in occupied Kuwait. Though this observation contradicted Bush administration statements, ABC withheld its photos and evaluation, for a variety of reasons, including gaps in the satellite coverage. In short, their satellite reporters in the sky provided incomplete and conflicting evidence that did not lead to a broadcast. But the same images ABC obtained provided detailed information on the kind and number of aircraft parked at the U.S. airbase at Dhahran, information that certainly would have been useful to Saddam Hussein.[42]

To summarize, the playing field is uncertain and the out-of-bounds lines unclear. Government maintains control of imagery from its own satellites and to some extent the images of commercial satellites. But the United States has no monopoly on eyes in the sky; imagery is for sale from a number of world sources. And while there was fierce debate over news media access, or lack thereof, during and after the war, little attention has been focused on satellite imagery as part of that or future wars. Indeed, the time bomb is ticking.[43]

Enter Technology 2: The Internet and Access

The Internet explosion has presented the nation with a new set of First Amendment issues not concerned with national security issues: pornography and obscenity, copyright, and protecting minors and unsuspecting viewers from offensive material, for starters. The ubiquitous nature of Internet access around the globe has led one analyst, William Arkin, to suggest that: "The Internet is going to have an impact on military and media operations. It already has; it already is a national security issue. If the Gulf War was the CNN war, then the next war is going to be the Internet war. While the media will utilize the Internet, in some ways the Internet will become an alternate form of communications for talk about the news. And the military will use the Internet to circumvent the news media."[44]

Internet challenges could be formidable in a future war, and current problems abound in trying to maintain crypto-security for classified information transmitted via e-mail and the Internet for government purposes. Consider these:

1. A rush by civilians to be on-line for war news might overwhelm the Internet, thus hobbling government communication in a critical moment.
2. An official government Internet site, if not overwhelmed, might turn an official source into an opportunity for public disinformation, deception and extensive one-on-one government propaganda efforts.
3. Reporters unwilling to go along with any voluntary or mandatory restrictions on transmission from the battlefield can hunt for an Internet connection in another area and transmit material that might jeopardize the course of a battle.
4. Hackers, whether motivated by the challenge or for purposes of espionage, could intercept classified information flowing between command centers and the battlefield. (Indeed, the problem of breaking into Defense Department computers has cropped up periodically in recent peacetime settings.)
5. Addition of a high-resolution camera attachment to a laptop computer turns all reporters—not just broadcast journalists—into potential broadcasters from their "sites," that is, wherever the journalists happen to be at the moment.[45]

And, publicly at least, the government has not advanced any discussion of policies that govern use of the Internet in wartime or times that look like war. How will we regulate this new communication tool to protect national security interests without complete control of all means of transmission used by journalists and citizens?

Prior Restraints: Media and Individual

Issues of prior restraint have both confusion and misunderstanding built into them. Those who have been drawing comfort from some mythic notion that, except in time of war, government may not restrain an individual or news medium from saying or publishing what it wishes must think again. Despite the notion—and reality—that free expression has broad cultural and legal support in the United States, individuals are daily restrained from and occasionally punished for publication of material without government approval. Magazines, book publishers and newspapers have all had their presses stopped or pages altered because of real or asserted national security interests. Two cases provide sobering examples of stopping presses in the name of national security—the Pentagon Papers and the *Progressive* H-bomb secret case.

The Pentagon Papers[46]

The Vietnam War produced crisis, strain, bloodshed and conflict of tragic proportions. As the war, an eight-year attempt by American forces to stem the southward advance of the North Vietnamese, plodded toward an end, *The New York Times* and other publications obtained "leaked" copies of a hefty government compilation of documents covering the history of the war. The leaker was Daniel Ellsberg, employed by the RAND Corporation, an important West Coast think tank with considerable government financing for research projects. The problem was that the documents—dubbed the "Pentagon Papers"—were classified. There was (and is) potential for imprisonment and/or fines for anyone who passed classified material to unauthorized persons. The case was a genuine test of two important, competing interests. Could government censor what it thought was important and properly classified material that was about to be published if such publication posed dangers to military operations and American service men and women? Or was the press free to print what it had obtained, worrying only about actions that might be brought against it after publication?

Free press rights won the day. The presses rolled and the public was offered a chance to examine the twisted and uncertain policy path followed as an effort to shore up a fledgling but autocratic democracy grew into massive U.S. intervention with the eventual loss of more than 50,000 American lives.

But the Supreme Court decision in the case, despite the victory for the press, may be a weak and uncertain legal reed to rely on in future cases. There were five separate opinions, revealing no strong consensus on the rationale that permitted the Court to agree to lift the temporary restraining order in force during appeals. The closest thing to legal reasoning that could prove useful in future cases might be found in a sentence from the opinion of Justice Potter Stewart, joined by Justice Byron White. They wrote that an injunction is appropriate only if disclosure "will surely result in direct, immediate, and irreparable damage to our Nation or its people.[47] As at least one commentator has suggested, "It is almost impossible to say in the abstract how the holding should be applied to actual controversies."[48] The lead counsel for the United States in the case in the Southern District of New York and the Second Circuit of the U.S. Court of Appeals views the generally triumphant nature of the Pentagon Papers decision as loaded with misconceptions.[49] Whitney North Seymour Jr. maintains that the object of the government action was not to shroud history with secrecy but to protect current operations in Vietnam as American forces were reduced in number and negotiations to repatriate American prisoners of war crept on.[50] He points out that a concurring opinion, joined by Stewart and White, showed reservations about the Court's actions. "I do not say that in no circumstances would the First Amendment permit an injunction against publishing information about Government plans or operations. Nor, after examining the materials the Government characterizes as the most sensitive and destructive, can I deny that revelation of these documents will do substantial damage to public interests. Indeed, I am confident that their disclosure will have that result."[51]

Indeed, Seymour claims the government lost the battle (the case) but won the war (by keeping certain classified material from publication).[52] And it is worth remembering that six of the nine justices in the Pentagon Papers case suggested that *The New York Times* and *The Washington Post* might be subject to prosecution for violating the Espionage Act.[53]

U.S. v. Progressive[54]

The Progressive magazine traces its roots to Robert LaFollette of Wisconsin, champion of what has been dubbed the Progressive movement at the turn of the century. What this small-circulation, liberal-in-orientation magazine set out to do led to a prior restraint order that lasted six months until the government voluntarily withdrew the case. A reporter for *The Progressive*, Howard Morland, an Emory University science graduate, had developed a manuscript the editors titled: *The H-bomb Secret: How We Got It—Why We're Telling It*. Morland and the editors maintained they had used easily accessible, nonclassified books and articles to outline how an H-bomb works and how it is built. The government obtained the restraining order when it learned of the impending publication, maintaining that the secrecy provisions of the Atomic Energy Act had been broken and that publication would endanger national security. Erwin Knoll, *The Progressive*'s editor, maintained that the information was available "in almost any library, from a tour of nuclear weapons facilities . . . and from interviews [Morland] conducted as a reporter receiving on-the-record information."[55] The Atomic Energy Act was overly broad, he maintained, resulting in whimsical and arbitrary classification that throttled debate on issues involving atomic energy.[56]

The scientific community weighed in with a split decision on the national security implications of publishing the article. Ray E. Kidder, a Lawrence Livermore Laboratory physicist, said the article's material was "deductible from information widely available to the public by a person having an unexceptional knowledge of physics and without access to classified information." And, Kidder added, the design details "not deductible from the public record are not of such a nature that their disclosure would significantly influence the national security."[57] But a physicist at Cornell University, Hans A. Bethe, said the article contained information not in the public record or available to other than those involved in government weapons programs. Publishing the manuscript, he said, "would substantially hasten the development of thermonuclear weapon capabilities by nations now having such capabilities."[58]

The secrets—if that's what they were—contained in the Morland piece began to leak. A computer programmer in California wrote an 18-page, single-spaced letter to a number of major newspapers, outlining essentially what was in the still-restrained Morland article. The publication of the letter on Sept. 18, 1979, by *The Chicago Tribune* seemed to be the beginning of the end of the government's case. The government withdrew, in a victory for *The Progressive* and an unrestrained press. Still, the issues raised by both Knoll and the government were never resolved and lie waiting for a possible future case.[59]

These two cases represent a lingering warning that government may in certain circumstances try to stop or alter publication under existing law in peacetime. Another three cases illustrate the ability of the government to restrict the right of individuals to publish or speak because of conditions imposed upon them for government employment—*Marchetti*, *Morison*, and *Snepp*.

U.S. v. Marchetti[60]

Victor L. Marchetti was a Central Intelligence Agency employee who had signed the usual nondisclosure agreement when he accepted the job. He would not publish anything containing classified information without clearance from the agency. The agreement seems to be a timeless one for CIA employees. It applies during employment and after resignation or retirement. So when Marchetti and John Marks wrote a book titled *The CIA and the Cult of Intelligence*[61] after Marchetti left federal service, the agency obtained an injunction blocking publication. The government wanted 339 passages excised from the work. En camera negotiations among the judge, government attorneys and Marchetti and Marks' lawyers restored all but 27 of the 339 passages. The published book makes clear where the offending passages were removed, with large blank spaces marked simply with "DELETED" to soberly remind the reader that the nondisclosure agreement Marchetti signed resulted in pre-publication censorship in peacetime. Of that closed-door battle to keep as much material in the book as possible, Marchetti's lawyer, Melvin L. Wulf, said: "It was the Devil's work we did that day."[62] The CIA and government attorneys, of course, viewed the matter differently.

U.S. v. Morison[63]

Whether the decision in the Morison case was a not-so-subtle attempt to throttle leaking from government sources or a legitimate prosecution of a civilian naval intelligence expert who violated the public trust and security rules is in the eye of the beholder. Samuel Eliot Morison was a former naval officer and a grandson of a respected naval historian, a Harvard University faculty member. He began writing for overseas defense publications and clearly broke the secrecy agreement he had signed when cleared for intelligence work. It included provisions prohibiting disclosure of classified material to those not authorized to receive it. In Morison's case, he took home classified documents and satellite photographs, selling the latter to a British publication and using the former to develop stories about Soviet shipbuilding. He was arrested at a Washington airport with his girlfriend, about to use their one-way tickets to England.

One view is that the case represents a legitimate application of the Espionage Act, not for spying, but for selling information to unauthorized individuals. The law from this standpoint is not overly broad or vague. Although recognizing the difficulty of defining "national security" information and the distinct possibility that the Reagan administration might be making an example of a mid-level government employee who leaked information to the news media, the law was fairly applied in this case.[64] It is hard to imagine that a government employee cleared for classified information would not know that "a newspaper is not a government employee and has no legal right to receive government classified information. . . . Therefore, there is no chilling effect on protected rights."[65]

The alternate view is that the "First Amendment should be given greater weight when it is balanced against national security claims of secrecy."[66] The arguments are the democratic necessity for debate of public policy issues and the notion that to understand important defense and foreign affairs issues, the public sometimes needs to be privy to classified material. This line of reasoning leans heavily on certain realities in the nation's capital, where leaking is a way of life. Leaking is a means used to push opinion in one direction or another, a case-by-case flaunting of security restrictions that must be tolerated in our society.[67]

Although the news media supported Morison in his losing appeals on First Amendment grounds, there is little evidence that convicting and jailing Morison shut down the selective leaking of classified information to the news media, or chilled the willingness of the media to chance a prosecution under the Espionage Act.[68] In fact, the act has rarely been used in peace or war to punish offenders in the media community.

Snepp v. United States[69]

Frank Snepp, like Marchetti, was a CIA employee who had signed a nondisclosure agreement with the agency when he accepted employment. His case represents a different legal outcome—not censorship of a book he wrote, as in Marchetti and Marks' case, but an order that he turn over the profits. Unlike Marchetti, Snepp was not accused of using classified information in his book, *Decent Interval*.[70] He described his experiences as a CIA intelligence agent, particularly the civilian side of the American withdrawal from Vietnam in the final years and days of the war. Although the government never asserted any substantial claim that classified information or intelligence methods and sources had been revealed, government attorneys were adamant that Snepp had violated his nondisclosure agreement requiring him to submit any manuscript related to his CIA experiences for pre-publication review. The Supreme Court's brief per curium opinion, by a 6-3 vote, upheld that contract. The decision said, in part: "Undisputed evidence in this case shows that a CIA agent's violation of his obligation to submit writings about the agency for prepublication review impairs the CIA's ability to perform its statutory duties. Admiral Turner, director of the CIA, testified without contradiction that Snepp's book and others like it have seriously impaired the effectiveness of American intelligence operations."[71] Fairness, the Court said, required him to give up his earnings—estimated to be at least $125,000—and place them in a government trust.[72]

First Amendment absolutists by now are squirming in their chairs, upset by the notion that government employees must submit work for pre-publication vetting, or, in the case of Morison, forgo any right to make choices about information they use in freelance work while on the government payroll. The government would argue that some system of control and even punishment—either jail, as in the case of Morison, or forfeiting profits, as in the case of Snepp—is necessary to keep the legal classification system intact. Without these rules and agreements, classified information would be leaked and used even more widely than at present. The possible damage to national security by revelation of plans, sources in foreign powers, technological superiority or other related information is real, from the government standpoint. Those who take on the responsibility of government work, it should be pointed out, are made clearly aware of what is expected of them with respect to classified information, during and after federal employment.

The Media and Government in Wartime or Times That Look Like War

The conflict between the news media and government is more than two centuries old. It is most strained in times of war, or times that look like war. This distinction must be recognized because the United States has not been involved in a declared war since World War II. Military personnel who have carried out foreign policy in Korea or Vietnam might find the distinction a fine point too absurd to warrant worry. But the fact that there hasn't been the equivalent of the War Powers Act of World War II to confer awesome powers on the president is important.

President Franklin Roosevelt had near absolute power to control and censor communications in and out of the continental United States and overseas. Subsequent presidents, however, have had to deal with news censorship on an ad hoc basis, balancing the public need for information about armed forces committed to battle overseas with the need for operational security to protect those fighting the battle. And even during World War II, home-front censorship was "voluntary." This meant asking publishers and broadcasters to comply with sometimes stringent restrictions on news content, without imposing full censorship. This system worked reasonably well, if not perfectly, though there is ample evidence the news media were growing restive and uneasy under the system by war's end.[73]

The clash between the news media and government in wartime is both cultural and legal. And the conflict may not be capable of a perfect solution. Union General William Tecumseh Sherman, hardly a friend of the war correspondents who followed him during the Civil War, said this about those journalists and the problem of war reporting: "Yet so greedy are the people at large for war news, that it is doubtful whether any army commander can exclude all reporters, without bringing down on himself a clamor that may imperil his own safety. Time and moderation must bring a just solution to this modern difficulty."[74]

On one side is the journalistic culture, fiercely independent and protective of what journalists perceive as universal rights of access and unencumbered freedom to report as they see fit. One commentator, Peter Braestrup, sums up the press corps this way:

1. Reporters are not doers, they are observers.
2. Reporters have no rank.
3. They have little or no responsibility for other people.
4. They are not team players.
5. They are competitive within their own organizations.
6. They are determined to keep up with, or beat, other news organizations.
7. They are aggressive.[75]

The military culture, on the other hand, was described as follows by Lieutenant General Jay Garner, assistant vice chief of staff: "The military as an organization really is governed by pretty tight rules and regulations. It's a disciplined organization. It's hierarchical, and it's homogenous. And it's a closed culture—for the most part, it's closed to outsiders."[76] And, we might add, those in uniform are bound by an oath of office, taken upon enlistment or commissioning.

The two critical issues illustrated above are (1) access to places in wartime and (2) censorship of dispatches from a war zone. The two are still in dispute by journalists and scholars, and may ever be, given the competing interests of several groups:

1. Journalists write news, and war is among the greatest of news stories.
2. Government wants to promote its foreign policy goals, which may mean spinning and controlling news flow.
3. The military must fight the battle, if it comes to that, and has a real interest in controlling information about troop dispositions, capabilities, readiness and plans.

The American public is the source of the people who fight the war and the funds to finance it. Execution of foreign policy ultimately means men and women may be asked to risk their lives in the name of national interests and goals. The public has an interest in following the progress of war, if it is to understand it and decide to support it—or not to support it.

Access to Places in Wartime

News media access to battlefields has often been a contentious issue, and seems to have grown more so in the wake of the Persian Gulf War in 1990–91.[77] Predictably, there are commentators who mount arguments on either side of the issue.

Whether arguing for or against a legal right of access to battlefields, authors start with a line of cases beginning with *Branzburg v. Hayes,* which held the news media have no right to information beyond that of the general public. But later cases—*Richmond Newspapers Inc. v. Virginia* and *Press-Enterprise Co. v. Superior Ct.,* for example—began to expand and delineate the *Branzburg* holding, acknowledging the connection between free news media and the right of access to public events such as trials if they are to be adequately reported. In *Globe Newspaper Co. v. Superior Ct.,* the Court recognized that the First Amendment is "broad enough to encompass those rights that, while not unambiguously enumerated in the very terms of the Amendment, are nonetheless necessary to the enjoyment of other First Amendment rights." Put another way, there is a constitutional right of access, "at least under certain circumstances."[78]

Those who argue that the right of access extends to battlefields lean heavily on two unsettled cases. In *Flynt v. Weinberger,* Hustler publisher Larry Flynt challenged the government's decision to bar reporters from the island of Grenada until the brief war was, for all intent and purposes, over.[79] The case was dismissed, but the judge acknowledged there was an important issue of constitutional law involved. Access to a news scene—particularly one as important to the public as a battlefield where Americans are engaged in combat—was vital for the effective functioning of the news media.[80] During the Gulf War, *Nation* magazine, joined by 11 other media organizations and individual journalists, filed a complaint based on their denial of access,[81] particularly in light of the fact that other news organizations had been given access, at a minimum, to media pools operated and controlled by the military in prewar Saudi Arabia. Among the arguments presented by *Nation's* attorneys were the fact that less stringent access requirements had worked effectively in the Vietnam War and no proof had been presented that greater restrictions were needed in the (pending at the time the complaint was filed) Gulf War. They argued that historically those arrangements—based on clearly understood security restrictions that allowed maximum freedom for journalists—had eliminated concerns about violation of security. The presiding judge again ruled the case moot, in that the war was over by the time arguments had been heard and his decision delivered on April 16, 1991. But he repeated arguments found in the *Hustler* case that at a minimum keep alive a legal hope for some constitutionally supported right of access to the battlefield.

Supporters of a battlefield right of access have argued that a three-part test for access is embodied in the *Richmond Newspapers* and *Globe Newspaper* cases: "First the claimant must show that the area has historically been open to the press and general public; (2) the right of access must be significant in the functioning of the process in question and the government as a whole; and (3) assuming the first two tests have been satisfied, access may be denied only if the government establishes that the denial is necessitated by a compelling government interest, and is narrowly tailored to serve that interest. Application of this test to battlefields suggests that the news media have a valid right of access under the First Amendment."[82] History supports the first proposition, the author claims, and the press provides the vital role in providing the raw material of democratic decisions. This being true, the issues of national security and access can be resolved and boundaries identified. A "blanket news blackout unjustified by national security interests" would not survive. Thus, "The military must narrowly tailor its news policies to allow the press access to as much of the battlefield as possible."[83]

The opposite view, supporting at least limited government-military restrictions on news media access in wartime, is predictable from some of the arguments advanced above for freer access. Although the press has been generally "taken along" and granted access to American forces and battle zones, it is hardly logical to think that this is the same kind of public access contemplated in the line of cases opening the judicial system and other public forums.[84] And it seems difficult to argue that media access to the front lines is a significant factor in the functioning of the government and its war fighting capability. "The ability of the media to independently report on the conduct of the war does not contribute significantly to the government's ability to wage war."[85] Put another way, armies fight and win (or lose) wars; reporters write about those events, eliminating any legal nexus compelling their admission to the battlefield. "Operational security and the element of surprise are essential to conducting successful warfare and thus required a controlled press."[86]

Censorship of Dispatches

Although denial of access to a news event in war or peace can be viewed as a prior restraint of a kind, in its narrowest sense it is not the same. Constitutionally, it refers to pre-publication or broadcast restraint of content by court order or some form of censorship, and then only in extraordinary circumstances, eloquently discussed in the landmark decision, *Near v. Minnesota.*[87] It is also in *Near* that the constitutional grounds for censorship are found, in Chief Justice Hughes' comments on exceptions for national security: "When a nation is at war, many things that might be said in time of peace are such a hindrance to its effort that their utterance will not be endured so long as men fight and that no court would regard them as protected by any constitutional right. . . . No one would question but that a government might prevent actual obstruction to its recruiting service or the publication of sailing dates of transports or the number and location of troops."[88]

The Supreme Court has been reluctant to invoke this portion of *Near*, as was made clear in the Pentagon Papers case, but it is still a formidable obstacle to be overcome by journalists when the reasons for censorship in wartime are clearly relevant and well articulated by the government. World War II was the last instance when an aggressive censorship system was in operation. That system included everything from soldier's mail home to routine overseas business telegrams to the thousands of words sent to the United States from hundreds of correspondents on hundreds of battlefronts. Censorship was revived during the Korean War, 1950–53, when correspondents were unsure whether their material was endangering the security of operations in that war. The government practiced no overt censorship during the Vietnam War, although the nature of the war made it difficult for journalists to violate censorship, deliberately or accidentally. Most of the fighting was by smaller units in scattered regions of South Vietnam, and correspondents had no way to file a story until their return to a major city or U.S. military base. But in all wars, the government has reserved the right to extract security agreements from correspondents. These agreements cover what might and might not be militarily sensitive information—troop locations, future plans, operational readiness and so forth. Reporters, although not censored, indicated their agreement with government ground rules in general terms as a condition for being permitted access to units and battle areas.

The system of "security review"—translate that as censorship, if you wish—during the Gulf War was never seriously challenged except for complaints about occasional excesses by reviewers/censors who changed select wording of a few dispatches out of more than 1,500 that underwent "security review." Only a handful of stories was withheld, and most of that handful was eventually cleared for stateside use.

To summarize: Prior restraint on news content has seldom been invoked from World War II to the present day within the United States, although the press agreed to observe voluntary codes covering news content during World War II. Only in the Korean War and the Gulf War was censorship instituted for copy flowing from battle areas to the United States. Access to combat zones was customary, but not universal, during the latter two conflicts. The constitutionality of the most recent controls and restraints—press pools that restricted access and numbers of journalists, and "security review" in the Gulf War— has not been successfully challenged.

Prospects for Checking Excessive Secrecy

Some movement—a ray of hope for more openness on national security issues, if you will—to deal with at least one of the major problems discussed above has been visible in recent years, that of the excessive backlog of documents and the tendency to classify too much material.

President Clinton signed an important executive order on classified national security information in April 1995.[89] In his accompanying message, the president said the order would accomplish some reforms in this area. It would:

1. Reduce the costs of secrecy.
2. Require classifiers to justify what they classify and challenge improper classification, while being protected against retribution for doing so.
3. Initiate automatic declassification of documents instead of line-by-line declassification.
4. Authorize department heads to balance public interest in disclosure against the national security interest in declassification decisions.[90]

Although the president's directive was hailed by many as "the most significant step in reducing government secrecy since the Cold War,"[91] later backtracking by the Clinton administration has come to light. His 1995 announcement did not reveal that the FBI had been granted a blanket exemption from the automatic declassification order. One critic of the FBI exemption termed it "preposterous" and said it covered "hundreds of pages that have nothing to do with national security. . . ."[92] Another dispute between the administration and Congress arose when the president withdrew the security clearance of a State Department official, Robert Nuccio, for providing accurate classified information to a member of the Houses Intelligence Committee related to CIA involvement in covering up murders of two American civilians in Guatemala.[93] The Senate responded with a bill requiring the administration to inform executive branch employees of their right to furnished classified information to Congress,[94] thus reviving classic disputes over national security information between the executive and legislative branches of government.

The other major initiative toward a more balanced policy on openness in national security affairs came from the Commission on Protecting and Reducing Government, chaired by Sen. Patrick Moynihan with a committee representing bipartisan interest in the subject. A statement during a hearing on government secrecy before the Senate Committee on Governmental Affairs described the expense, real and political, involved in the current secrecy system:

1. Direct costs of $5.2 billion in 1996 alone.
2. 21,871 new Top Secret designations and 374,244 "derivative" Top Secret designations in 1995, meaning approximately 400,000 new secrets at that level alone.[95]
3. Delays in scientific and technological progress.
4. Construction of a culture of secrecy that fails to balance legitimate national security interests with the public's right to know.[96]

Sen. Moynihan followed up the commission's work by introducing a bill, the Secrecy Act of 1997, that would outline principles on which to base classification, establish some congressional oversight on secrecy, require the president to ensure that information classified secret would be at the minimum needed to protect national security interests, set time limits on most secrets, and mandate a procedure for declassification.[97] Support for the reforms has been positive and nearly universal, but the law had not been advanced out of committee in early 1999.

Conclusion

This chapter has provided only a bare outline of the issues and problems related to access under the general heading of national security. While certain issues—media access and censorship in wartime and restraining individual rights under the guise of national security, for example—receive frequent media and public attention, central, chronic problems remain unresolved and to a large measure undebated. The secrecy versus openness balancing act becomes more urgent in a world that may see more threats to the nation by international terrorism, such as the World Trade Center bombing, than regional wars fought in Eastern Europe or the Persian Gulf. Open discussion of domestic threats will require, as one recent conference report recommended, "an appropriate balance between public awareness [of threats] and avoiding panic or threatening essential sources of information."[98] This kind of public dialogue will require new attitudes and initiatives to end excessive secrecy and promote public dialogue on critical national issues.

Notes

[1]Dennis Hyatt, Review of *Secrecy: Report of the Commission on Protecting and Reducing Government Secrecy,* 15 Government Information Quarterly 142 (1998).

[2]See Rosamond Thomas, *Espionage and Secrecy* (Routledge, 1991) for a readable analysis of the history and application of the Official Secrets Act, and Ann L. Plamondon, *A Comparison of Official Secrets and Access to Information in Great Britain and the United States,* 16 Communications and the Law 51–68 (1994).

[3]Ford Rowan, *The Media and Government Leaks,* Center Magazine 61 (Sept./Oct.1984).

[4]Steven Aftergood, *The Perils of Government Secrecy,* 8 Issues in Science and Technology 81–88 (1992).

[5]Adapted from Donald Baer, *Can an Open Society Protect Its Secrets?* U.S. News & World Report 26 (June 1, 1987).

[6]20 Human Rights Quarterly 1–11(1998).

[7]*Id.* at 7.

[8]John C. Cruden and Calvin M. Lederer, *The First Amendment and Military Installations,* Det. Col. of L. Rev. 845 (1984).

[9]See *U.S. v. Albertini,* 105 S. Ct. 2897 (1985)

[10]*Greer v. Spock,* 424 U.S. 828 (1976).

[11]367 U.S. 886 (1961).

[12]424 U.S. at 837–38.

[13]For an insightful view of the access problem from the military viewpoint, see Porcher L. Taylor III, *The Installation Commander Versus an Aggressive News Media in an On-Post Terrorist Incident: Avoiding the Constitutional Collision,* 5 Army Lawyer 19–29 (1986).

[14]Malcolm Howard, *Environment of Secrecy: A Lawsuit Alleges Environmental Crimes at the Country's Most Secret Military Base,* 19 Amicus Journal 34–36 (1997).

[15]*Id.*

[16]*Id.*

[17]42 U.S.C. § 9601–9675 (1988).

[18]42 U.S.C. § 11001–11050 (1988).

[19]42 U.S.C. § 9620 (j) (1).

20For a discussion of the problems, see Laurent R. Hourclé, *Military Secrecy and Environmental Compliance,* 2 N.Y.U. Environmental L. J. 316–46 (1993).

21*JB Pictures Inc. v. Department of Defense,* 24 Med. L. Rptr. 2017 (1996) (U.S. Ct. App., D.C. Cir.).

22*Id.*

2324 Med. L. Rptr. 2020.

24For a discussion of this issue, see David Fagelson, *The Constitution and National Security: Covert Action in the Age of Intelligence Oversight,* 5 J. of Law and Politics 275–347 (winter 1989).

25Exec. Order No. 8381, 3 C.F.R. 634 (1938–1943).

26Pub.L. No. 418 ch. 2, § 1, 52 Stat. 3, 3 (1938).

27Exec. Order No. 10,290, 3 C.F.R. 789, 798 (1949–1953).

28See *Developments in the Law—The National Security Interest and Civil Liberties,* 85 Harv. L. Rev. 1130, 1196 (1972).

29Exec. Order No. 10,501, 3 C.F.R. 979 (1949–1953).

30See 5 U.S.C. § 552 (1988).

31See *Note, Keeping Secrets: Congress, the Courts and National Security Information,* 103 Harv. L. Rev. 906, 909 (1990).

32See David C. Morrison, *For Whose Eyes Only?* National Journal 472–76 (Feb. 26, 1994), and Debra Gersh Hernandez, *National Security vs. the Public's Right to Know,* Editor & Publisher 12 14 (March 5, 1994).

33George E. Seay III, *Remote Sensing: The Media, the Military and the National Security Establishment—A First Amendment Time Bomb,* 59 Journal of Air and Space Law 239-87 (1993).

34*Id.* at 241.

35*Id.* at244–45.

3615 U.S.C. § 4202 (1) (Supp. 1989)

37*Id.* at § 4241.

38Seay, *Remote Sensing* at 247.

3918 U.S.C. § 793–95 (1988).

40*Id.*

41Richard Davis, *The Foreign Policymaking Role of Congress in the 1990s: Technology and the Future of Congressional Power,* 19 Congress and the Presidency 176 77 (1992).

42*Id.* at 178–79.

43For other views on this topic, see Gary M. Kramer, *The First Amendment Viewed From Space: National Security Versus Freedom of the Press,* 14 Annals of Air and Space Law 339–68 (1989); Don Sneed and Kyu Ho Youm, *First Amendment Rights in Space: An "Emerging" Constitutional Issue,* Communications and the Law 45–50 (1989); Rita A. Reimer, *News Gathering From Space: Land Remote-Sensing and the First Amendment,* 40 Federal Communications L. J. 321–49; and R.P. Mesrges and G.H. Reynolds, *News Media Satellites and the First Amendment: A Case Study in the Treatment of New Technologies,* 3 High Technology L. J. 1–32 (1988).

44William M. Arkin, quoted in *The Military and the Media: Facing the Future* 99–100 (Nancy Ethiel, ed, Robert R. McCormick Tribune Foundation, 1998).

45*Id.* at 98–113.

46*New York Times Co. v. United States,* 403 U.S. 713 (1971).

47403 U.S. at 727, 730.

48John Cary Sims, *Triangulating the Boundaries of Pentagon Papers,* 2 William and Mary Bill of Rights J. 350 (1995).

49Whitney North Seymour Jr., *Press Paranoia—Delusions of Persecution in the Pentagon Papers Case,* New York State Bar J. 10–12 (February 1994).

50*Id.* at 10.

51*New York Times v. United States,* 403 U.S. 713, 731 (1971).

52*Id.* at 12.

5318 U.S.C. § 793 (e) covers prosecution of those who have unauthorized possession of national security material with reason to believe it could be "used to the injury of the United States or to the advantage of any foreign nation" and "willfully communicates . . . the same to any person not entitled to receive it. . . ."

54467 Wis. F. Supp. 990 (W.D.) (mem.), dismissed, 610 F.2d 819 (10th Cir. 1979).

55Erwin Knoll, "*If. . .*" Quill 31 (June 1979).

56*Id.* at 31–32.

57*Id.* at 25.

58*Id.* at 27.

59See Michael M. Mooney, *Right Conduct for a Free Press,* Harper's Magazine 35-44 (March 1980) and Wallace B. Eberhard, *From Balloon Bombs to H-bombs: Mass Media and National Security,* 61 Military Review 2–8 (1981).

60466 F.2d 1309, 1 Med. L. Rptr. 1051 (4th Cir. 1972). See also *Alfred Knopf v. Colby,* 509 F.2d 1362 (4th Cir 1975).

61(Alfred A. Knopf, 1974.)

62*Id.* at xxiv.

63844 F.2d 1057 (4th Cir.), *cert. denied,* 488 U.S. 908 (1988).

64Jereen Trudell, *The Constitutionality of Section 793 of the Espionage Act and Its Application to Press Leaks,* 33 Wayne L. Rev. 205–28 (1986).

65*Id.* at 225.

66David H. Topol, *United States v. Morison: A Threat to the First Amendment Right to Publish National Security Information,* 43 South Carolina L. Rev. 581–615 (1992).

67*Id., passim.*

68*Id.*

69444 U.S. 507, 5 Med .L .Rptr. 2409 (1980).

70(Random House, 1977.)

71444 U.S. at 512.

72*Top Court Rules CIA Has Power to Screen Writings by Past and Current Employees,* The Wall Street Journal, (Feb. 20, 1980).

73See Theodore Koop, *Weapon of Silence* (University of Chicago Press, 1942); Byron Price, *A Report on the Office of Censorship,* (U.S. Government Printing Office, 1945); and Wallace B. Eberhard, *Retraining a*

Free Press in Wartime: Voluntary Censorship at the Grassroots Level, (research paper presented at the American Journalism Historians Association Convention, Lawrence, Kan., Oct. 1, 1992).

[74]Quoted in 30 (2) Columbia Journalism Rev. (July/August 1991).

[75]Quoted in The Washington Post D1 (Feb. 21, 1991).

[76]Ethiel, ed., *The Military and the Media* 16.

[77]408 U.S. 665, 684 (1972).

[78]*Note: The Pentagon v. the Press: Is the Pool System a Solution to the Conflict?* 13 Bridgeport L. Rev. 140 (1992).

[79]762 F.2d 134 (D.C. Cir. 1985).

[80]*Id.* at 358.

[81]*Nation Magazine v. U.S. Department of Defense,* 762 N.Y. F.Supp. 1558 (S.D.1991).

[82]David A. Frenznick, *The First Amendment on the Battlefield,* 23 Pacific L. J. 348 (1992).

[83]*Id.*

[84]Brian W. DelVecchio, *Press Access to American Military Operations and the First Amendment: The Constitutionality of Imposing Restrictions,* 31 Tulsa L. J. 249 (1995).

[85]*Id.,* quoting Karl T. Olson, *The Constitutionality of Department of Defense Press Restrictions on Wartime Correspondents Covering the Persian Gulf War,* 41 Drake L. Rev. 529 (1992).

[86]DelVecchio, *Press Access* 249.

[87]283 U.S. 697 (1931).

[88]*Id.* at 716 (dicta).

[89]Executive Order 12958, Classified National Security Information (April 17, 1995).

[90]*Statement on Signing the Executive Order on Classified National Security Information,* 31 (16) Weekly Complication of Presidential Documents 63B64 (April 24, 1995).

[91]George Lardner Jr., *FBI Won Exception to Presidential Order Declassifying Secrets,* The Washington Post A3 (July 19, 1998).

[92]*Id.*

[93]Duncan Levin, *Muzzling Executive Employees; Clinton Policy: Don't Tell Congress About National Security Matters,* The Baltimore Sun L1 (April 26,1998).

[94]*Id.*

[95]Prepared Testimony of Sen. Patrick Moynihan before the Senate Committee on Governmental Affairs (May 7, 1997), Federal News Service (accessed at Lexis/Nexis website).

[96]For the full report of Sen. Moynihan's commission, see *Secrecy: Report of the Commission on Protecting and Reducing Government Secrecy.*

[97]*Editorial: Trading Secrets for Sunshine,* The Sacramento Bee B6 (May 30, 1997).

[98]*Terrorism, Weapons of Mass Destruction, and U.S. Security,* Executive Summary, Sam Nunn Policy Forum 8 (University of Georgia, 1997).

10

We the People: State and Federal FOI Resources and Activities

—Herb Strentz and Kathleen Richardson

The open government movement in the United States is a tale of battles won and lost, of heroes and villains in the fight for access. The struggle for openness is filled with untold stories of everyday people who find themselves fighting against the very public servants they elect and pay to represent their interests for documents as benign as water bill records and city budgets. Fortunately, citizens have allies: freedom of information groups founded by volunteers determined to fight government secrecy at the local, state and federal level. At the heart of this grassroots movement is the National Freedom of Information Coalition, a consortium of state open government groups that provide advice and assistance to those seeking access to government records and meetings. This chapter highlights just a few of the heroes of the open government wars and provides a listing of a few of the more prominent freedom of information groups fighting for the people's right to know.

Introduction: A Government of the People, by the People, for the People

The Constitution, after all, begins, "We the people . . . " So it should not be surprising that stories about access to public records are not stories only about legislation and litigation. Ultimately, it does not matter whether access is by computer, court order or cajoling. Likewise, the lessons about access to meetings of public agencies are not, at their heart, lessons about meeting notices, agendas and threats of circumventing the law by e-mail or telephone. The stories and the lessons are rather about people. People who, in the provocative words of one access advocate, "fight the bastards in the trenches."

The following profiles highlight just a few of the most valuable players in the fight for freedom of information: people who expend time, energy and resources as they battle in the trenches.

Lizbeth White's Crusade Against Government by Intimidation

Lizbeth White's one-woman crusade against the "good old boys" of Clinton County, Ohio, and what she calls their "government by intimidation" was long and often lonely. It cost her six years, her house and two jobs. It made her a pariah in her community. At one point, she racked up $68,000 in legal fees and faced bankruptcy—just because she wanted to see the minutes of meetings of the Clinton County commissioners. But White eventually won—and the struggle, as much as the victory, changed her life.

White was the environmental health director of Clinton County, a rural area about 35 miles southeast of Dayton, when in 1991 she notified the Ohio Environmental Protection Agency that raw sewage appeared to be seeping from a horse barn owned by Ralph "Larry" Roberts. Roberts was president of a trucking company, the county's largest private employer, and one of its wealthiest residents.

Roberts responded by running full-page ads in the local newspaper denouncing White. He threatened to have her fired and filed a $10 million defamation suit against her. (The lawsuit was later dropped.) Protesters rallied at the courthouse, carrying placards that read: "Liz must go."

White worked for the district health board, which was not under the county commissioners' control. However, she shared office space with and worked closely with the building and zoning inspectors, who *were* county employees. The inspector who had accompanied White on investigations of Roberts' property was ordered by the county commissioners not to work with her again. The inspector was later fired on grounds not directly related to the controversy.

When White asked to see minutes of the meetings at which the commissioners made the decisions affecting her work, she was told that no minutes were kept. Only votes were recorded, not discussion. "Decisions were being made outside the public eye on development issues," said White. "It was so outrageous, what they were doing." She quoted one official as telling a reporter, "We know it's public record, but it's none of Liz White's business."

In 1993, White sued the Clinton County commissioners, charging them with violating the state open records law. "Reporters ask me, 'How could you do this?' " White said. "My response is, 'How could I *not* do this?' [The commissioners] were relieving us of such fundamental rights. . . . I really believe we are going to forfeit true democracy in our country if we don't fight for it."

The commissioners threatened to evict the health department from its offices. They successfully campaigned against renewal of a levy to support the health district's programs.

Meanwhile, White's legal bills mounted by thousands of dollars and she became the victim of a campaign of harassment. In retrospect, she said, it was "a well-organized plan to discredit me. . . . I'd come home night after night and pick up the paper to see stories. . . . Roberts threatening to close his trucking terminal and move 3,000 jobs out of the county, saying, 'It's Liz White's fault!' " Her home and office were both broken into, and records pertaining to the Roberts case and the lawsuit were taken; the sheriff's department declined to investigate. A convoy of trucks drove past her rural home, horns blasting. Phone calls warned her that the sheriff's department was going to plant drugs in her home or car. Co-workers received threats on their answering machines. "We put locks on our doors for the first time in 16 years," White said. "It was scary." She and her husband, Paul, had one daughter at home during the court fight. "She had a rough time in high school," said White.

In 1994, a Clinton County judge sided with White and ordered the commissioners to prepare "complete and accurate minutes" of their meetings. He also ordered them to pay her attorney's fees, which had topped $50,000. The commissioners appealed the decision; the Whites were forced to sell their house to pay mounting legal bills.

Community reaction was mixed, said White, with most of her support coming from retired people who could afford to be independent. "It was a small county and people were afraid," she said.

Her initial victory was overturned in 1995 by an appeals court, which ruled that the Clinton County commissioners had maintained all the records that the law required.

"What was hardest for me was the impact the court fight had on how I was doing my job," White recalled. She ended up quitting because "as long as I worked there, the department would suffer; it would be a target." Her co-workers were threatened with layoffs. "What right had I to jeopardize [these families]?" White said.

At that stage, the Whites had spent $68,000 on the legal battle. They were facing bankruptcy and could no longer continue the fight. White remembers this as "the lowest point for me." She suffered "serious depression during this time. . . . I wondered if anyone cared, wondered whether I made a difference."

The day after she quit, Logan County, Ohio, offered White a job. Still, she had to use her retirement funds to buy a house there and her husband had to commute on weekends because he couldn't afford to change companies.

Meanwhile, "different groups started helping out . . . really came up to the plate," White said. The Ohio Coalition for Open Government, formed by several Ohio newspapers, the Ohio Newspaper Foundation and Common Cause, a government watchdog group, financed White's appeal to the State Supreme Court. David Marburger, an attorney with the law firm of Baker & Hostetler, provided *pro bono* support, with *amicus* support from the League of Women Voters, Investigative Reporters and Editors and the ACLU.

Clinton County was backed by the County Commissioners Association of Ohio, which argued that requiring detailed transcripts of meetings would be an expensive burden for rural counties.

In August 1996, the Ohio Supreme Court unanimously ruled that Clinton County commissioners violated the law by reporting only roll-call votes and no discussions. County commissioners must keep "complete and accurate" records of their meetings, including discussions, the court ruled. "One of the strengths of American government is the right of the public to know and understand the actions of their elected representatives," wrote Justice Evelyn Stratton. "This includes not merely the right to know a government body's final decision on a matter, but the ways and means by which those decisions were reached. There is great historical significance to this basic foundation of popular government, and our founding fathers keenly understood this principle."

The court also ordered the county to pay White's legal expenses. In February 1997, the court awarded White nearly $58,000. While thousands of dollars short of the $100,000 she had estimated, the award meant that White emerged with no legal debts, thanks in part to attorneys donating their services or forgiving some of their bills.

But the real price that White paid for demanding open government in Clinton County, she said, was that she was eventually forced to leave her profession. "My notoriety followed me to Logan County. . . . "It wasn't far enough away. Some people saw me as a threat."

When her husband was transferred to Louisville, Ky., White decided that she "couldn't separate my activism from my work." She became a full-time citizen activist, working as a volunteer with the League of Women Voters: organizing campaign finance reform rallies, speaking out about her experience, trying to educate residents on open government laws and "how to be effective citizens."

"Because of my own experience, I know how important this is. . . . The public doesn't understand that by not participating in government, we are losing democracy by default. . . . I spend all my time now trying to re-engage the public in government." Her biggest frustration continues to be "the arrogance of government . . . the audacity of government officials," she said. "They always assume that the public is not smart enough, not interested enough to be taken seriously."

Connie and Howard Clery, in Memory of Jeanne Clery (1966–1986)

Howard and Connie Clery became access crusaders when grief over the murder of their daughter, Jeanne, at Lehigh University in Pennsylvania was compounded by learning that the university had kept secret—even from the Lehigh board of trustees—the extent of violent crimes on campus.

The Clerys became the catalysts for other parents coming forward with horror stories of campus violence and secrecy about the violence. Their major foes during these years were the U.S. Department of Education and the higher-education establishment—institutions usually held in high regard. But universities and colleges, Connie Clery said, "treated parents of campus crime victims like lepers." From the time colleges recruit students to the time they have to deal with grieving parents of students assaulted or murdered on campus, the Clerys say, higher education tries to keep information about campus violence secret and to downplay causes of campus violence—alcohol and drug abuse, for example.

Higher education is able to do this partly because of the so-called "Buckley Amendment," the Family Educational Right to Privacy Act (FERPA), which Connie Clery calls "a fraud on the American people because of the cover-ups it allows" and the double standard it creates for criminal activity on the nation's campuses. The Buckley Amendment can serve as a bad example of privacy legislation. It is not enforced because of its draconian nature. The only stated FERPA penalty for violating a student's privacy is loss of all federal funding, presumably forever—a fine of millions or billions of dollars.

But the Buckley Amendment serves as a first resort of higher-education administrators who want to keep information secret. Much of the FOI battle against the education establishment in the 1980s and 1990s has been to try to make it clear that information regarding murders, rapes and assaults on campus are not "educational records" under FERPA. Amazingly, that was not a simple task.

But that is what Howard Clery took on when he sold his interest in a business-forms company and founded Security on Campus Inc., in 1987. ("Howard's retired and I'm over-tired," Connie joked.) Their efforts helped lead to passage of the Federal Campus Security Act of 1990, and to significant amendments to that act in 1998.

The amendments increased the responsibilities of colleges and universities when it comes to keeping and providing access to information about crimes and disciplinary proceedings on campus. The amendments also set a maximum fine of $25,000 for each violation, and renamed the measure the "Jeanne Clery Disclosure of Campus Security Policy and Campus Crime Statistics Act."

The work continues to have its frustrations. Connie Clery said, "It took us six years to find out how to file a complaint" under the 1990 act, partly because of the recalcitrance of the education establishment. Indeed, when the mother of a Clemson University student sought information about the rape of her daughter, an Atlanta, Ga., official of the Department of Education dismissed the 1990 measure as "a useless Act . . . passed by Congress to pacify the parents of a murdered student."

On the other hand, as they and other parents sought access to information about crimes on campus, the Clerys spoke highly of the "teamwork" and support they found among access advocates such as the Student Press Law Center and the Society of Professional Journalists.

Judith Krug: "Freedoms Can Die Very Fast"

Judith Krug has been heralded as a defender of intellectual freedom and champion of the First Amendment—and vilified as an enemy of "family values." As director of the American Library Association's

Office for Intellectual Freedom in Chicago since 1967, she has devoted almost all of her professional life—and a great deal of her emotional energy—to leading the fight against censorship.

When Krug was named the 1998 recipient of the Joseph W. Lippincott Award, the highest honor in librarianship, the chairman of the award jury noted that "over the past 30 years, Judy has personified the profession's commitment to intellectual freedom, articulated its principles; educated, inspired and supported librarians and trustees; [and] built coalitions to defend the First Amendment. . . ." "I can't change the world, but I'm doing my part to make it a better place for my children and grandchildren," said Krug, "a world where information is available and accessible, and where they can use it without having somebody tell them how they can use it."

According to Krug, the library association's intellectual freedom program "is in large measure responsible for the freedoms of speech and press we enjoy today. . . . Our allies grew over the years, as the issues grew more complex and serious, but somebody has to be in the lead. . . ."

Krug said she was "somewhat frustrated that journalists aren't more supportive of concerns about freedom of information. "It bothers me because without a press willing to take risks . . . these freedoms can die very fast." She sees a conservative bias in the press, and said newspapers justify not covering freedom of information issues by claiming that readers aren't interested. "It is a very detrimental attitude. . . . We aren't getting the full story."

She said that it also worries her when people seek to subordinate First Amendment freedoms to a litany of what they see as overriding interests, such as protecting children from pornography. "I tell them, 'Without the First Amendment, you couldn't stand up and say what you just did, you couldn't undertake the actions you did to get the things you want.' "

Electronic issues increasingly dominate Krug's time. She does not waver in her belief that the Internet should be readily available in libraries—"in fact, I've become more adamant"—despite protests from parents fearful that their children will have access to sexually oriented material. "[Computer] filters in the home environment are OK, but not in public institutions, in libraries," Krug said. "Filters eliminate so much material that kids need." Censorship is inappropriate for libraries because they "deal with all the children of all the people in a community," and family values vary widely, said Krug. In addition, computer censorship can give parents and others "a false sense of security." "We can turn off the Internet . . . and kids will find out about sex the way you and I did," she said dryly.

Despite the costs of her devotion to access issues ("My kids' teen-age years are sort of a blur"), she said, "It really has been an exciting and fulfilling career . . . working for people I admire immensely. Most people have strong affection for their community libraries, but those who are outside this profession can't understand how dedicated and concerned the local librarians are. My admiration for my col-leagues grows daily. . . . They put themselves on the line to do what is right, what no one else is going to do if they don't. . . . We cer-tainly haven't changed the world, but we've led the way on issues that are absolutely vital for the furtherance, the growth, of this society."

Jim Warren, a Gadfly of Some Substance

"In 1997 I hit a burnout wall." That confession from Jim Warren came as a surprise to someone whose sole exposure to him had been through his newsletter, his columns and his omnipresence in Inter-net commentary on privacy and access issues. The question occurred, "If this is what this guy does when he said he was burned out, what . . .?"

Well, what he did, not necessarily in order, was use public records to rally a homeowner fight against officials in San Mateo County, just south of San Francisco; mediate differences between Secret Service agents concerned about wire fraud and computer users who feared the onset of the fascist state; use public records to rally another fight against county officials, this time about abuse of condemnation pow-ers; earn graduate degrees in mathematics and statistics (Texas), med-ical information science (University of California Medical Center), and computer engineering (Stanford); start publications and write columns (for *MicroTimes* and *Government Technology*); organize conferences and teach about computer-related issues years, almost decades, before the Web and the Internet were on the access/privacy agenda. He also was a named plaintiff in the successful effort to over-turn as unconstitutional the Internet censorship provisions of the Communications Decency Act that was part of the Telecommunica-tions Act of 1996.

"I've been sort of a rebel by inclination since I was a kid," he said. "In the '60s, I was very active in the anti-war and alternative lifestyles of that era. In the early 1980s, I was president of the local community association and we got in a tangle with our county gov-ernment . . . over our preferred rural lifestyle. . . . I simply used the California Public Records Act . . . to access . . . records of the county agencies and then published the records and compared them to other counties and it turned out that San Mateo County was way, way out of line in charging fees, using code infractions against property owners . . . greater than adjacent counties and collecting huge penalty fees."

In 1993, Warren worked with California Assemblywoman Deborah Bowen to make California the first state to put legislative information on the Internet for public access without cost, a model, he said, that has been used in 15 to 30 other states. He used his Internet savvy to alert citizens to when the measure would be considered by various legislative committees and to counter arguments that such access would be too costly or of little interest to the public. "With the Net you can report on things in time for the general public to respond," he said.

Informed by Bowen and her aide when a committee meeting on Assembly Bill 1623 was scheduled, Warren would put the word out on the Internet, and "committee members and assistants would get this barrage of phone calls and faxes about a know-nothing bill, a weird little bill. It ended up being a bill that no one dared oppose; we had four committee and three floor votes without a single dissenting vote"—an accomplishment all the more significant because some state government administrators opposed the measure.

For that and other accomplishments, Warren was a first-year recipient of the Electronic Frontier Foundation's Pioneer Award, received the James Madison Freedom-of-Information Award from the Northern California Society of Professional Journalists, and—still among others—the Hugh M. Hefner First Amendment Award from the Playboy Foundation.

Taking stock of access in the late 1990s, Warren said, "If anything, we have had a government that has been much more cloistered and closed in its activities than we have today. We did not really get the heavy push for open records until essentially the 1960s and even the 1970s. . . . Government is the leading advocate of privacy for anything it does."

"Access to federal legislation is a mixed bag," he said. "The ringer is they make the pretense of putting records on-line, but some of the most crucial information, like a bill markup and the chairs' markups, is not available, and that is the stuff we really need access to if we are to be active participants."

As evidence that activism pays, Warren still enjoys the rural life in Woodside, San Mateo County—a way of life protected through the use of public records.

Theresa Amato: Nurturing Citizenship in Suburbia

Theresa Amato strikes you as the sort of woman who could do anything she wanted, anywhere she wanted. What she wants to do is practice community law from a storefront across from a city hall in the western suburbs of Chicago.

Amato's resume earned her *The American Lawyer*'s ranking as one of the top young public-service lawyers in the nation: Harvard undergraduate (cum laude); New York University law school class of 1989; FOI expert with Ralph Nader's Public Citizens Litigation Group; international speaker on freedom of information issues.

In 1994, after spending several years in Washington, D.C. writing "very pointy-headed appellate briefs," Amato decided she could do more good at home. And "home" was in suburbia. "I grew up in the suburbs," she said. "I knew there was very little public-interest law being practiced in the suburbs," despite the rapid development, population growth and accumulation of wealth occurring on the outskirts of the nation's cities.

Looking for a place close to where she grew up, Amato settled in Elmhurst, a conservative, ethnically diverse bedroom community of 42,000 in DuPage County, Ill. Her mission? To encourage area residents to get involved in local government and to give them the tools to take control of their civic lives.

Funded by individual donations and foundations, powered largely by legal interns and volunteers, Amato's nonpartisan, not-for-profit Citizen Advocacy Center "builds democracy for the 21st century" by going into the schools, holding workshops in the community, monitoring local government and, when necessary, going to court on behalf of citizen causes.

The center has helped Hispanic residents displaced by a city project, has fought to turn the state tollways into freeways and has protested excessive fees charged by local governments for photocopying public documents. Amato and her crew produced an array of brochures on everything from "know your local government" and consumer rights to electronic democracy, open meetings law, solid waste, home rule and corporate charters. "It's been a tremendous experiment . . . and a tremendous success," said Amato. Her biggest frustration is that constant headache of the public-service sector: limited resources: never enough time, never enough people, never enough money.

Her next step? Evangelism. As word of her work spread, Amato fielded calls from other communities eager to launch their own citizen advocacy centers. The seeds planted in Elmhurst were beginning to bear fruit throughout the country.

However, the accomplishment Amato is most proud of is also one of the more modest—and one of the most difficult to measure. It is seeing one citizen "develop the personal capacity to participate in public affairs": the high school student who registers to vote, and does; the little old lady who has won one battle against city hall, and becomes a community activist—"Somebody who has made a difference, and wants to continue to make a difference," said Amato.

Kyle Niederpruem: Making Democracy Percolate

Kyle Niederpruem enlisted in the freedom of information battle the first time a government official denied her information she knew she was entitled to. "It just gets your blood to boiling," said the veteran reporter and one-time FOI chair for the Society of Professional Journalists, the nation's largest journalism organization, of which she now serves as president. For Niederpruem, citizens' right to open government is what "makes democracy percolate."

In recent years, she has seen the circle of people devoted to FOI issues spread beyond journalism to embrace average citizens who are angered when they are denied information about things that touch their lives—their schools, their environment, their neighborhoods. "You can see people get mad," said Niederpruem, environmental reporter for *The Indianapolis Star* and *The Indianapolis News*. "That motivates them to become more and more involved." And that's good, because journalists can't win the access battle by themselves, she said. Many political skirmishes are won by the side with the most bodies and the loudest voices—and the new citizen-activists are not squeamish about speaking out.

In fact, journalists' reluctance to lead the charge on FOI issues is one of Niederpruem's biggest frustrations. Journalists, fearful of jeopardizing their objectivity and hobbled by ethical concerns, often fail to embrace issues that they should be championing, she said. Motivated citizens, on the other hand, are "very bulldoggish, more so than journalists," said Niederpruem. "They are bright people, passionate," and, unencumbered by either ethical fears or deadlines, "they don't give up. . . . I find that very inspiring."

Niederpruem is also frustrated by "the way we [journalists] talk to the public. We fail to explain ourselves on access issues." For example, when Indiana newspapers went to court to force the release of a coroner's report on the slaying of a female college student, readers reacted in outrage at what they perceived as ghoulishness. Niederpruem said the papers could have headed off the ill will by explaining why it was so important—for the victim's family, for the university community, for public safety—for the information to be released.

In 1998, Niederpruem helped organize and report a massive landmark project that investigated the accessibility of government records throughout the state of Indiana. Seven newspapers sent personnel to government offices around the state and requested documents clearly defined as public records. "There were red lights and flags all across the state," Niederpruem said. "You would have thought the Martians had landed." The results "stunned even us," she said. Many requests for information were denied; some of those who requested documents were lied to and harassed.

Reaction to the project was immediate and dramatic: legislative hearings produced even worse stories of denial of citizens' rights. The governor appointed a public access counselor, issued a memo to government agencies directing them to release information, and committed to forming a task force to examine the problem. "In all the years I have been a reporter, it is the only thing I've been involved in that has gotten such an immediate response," said Niederpruem. "Things are changing. . . . It is a chance for democracy to work again."

John Kuglin and Robert Johnson: Not Exactly Separated at Birth, but . . .

Discussing John Kuglin and Bob Johnson in tandem makes sense for at least two reasons. Each performs FOI labors in a large but sparsely populated state—Montana and New Mexico, respectively—and each is linked with the Associated Press. Kuglin and Johnson typify the FOI leadership that AP bureau chiefs have provided in several other states around the nation, including Alaska, Iowa, Minnesota, Mississippi, New York, New Jersey, North Dakota, South Dakota and Washington.

Kuglin, AP bureau chief in Montana, observed, "Despite all the lawsuits [and] . . . legislation . . ., state and local officials spend more time hiding things that do not need to be hidden. They forget who they work for. . . . It's this 'us against them' mentality. They think they are working for their agency, not for the public. What they do for the [governmental] agency becomes an end in itself."

Kuglin had to be pressed to talk about the frustrations because he would much rather talk about significant access victories won in Montana—thanks, in part, to what he characterizes as the "strongest constitutional provision of any state for open government. Everything is open unless the demand for individual privacy clearly exceeds the public's right to know."

So one recent court victory said the legislature must open its party caucuses to public scrutiny, an important step since the caucuses are where legislative decisions are made. In another case, the Montana Supreme Court said the state's corrections departments could not keep secret the process for deciding who would build and operate Montana's first private prison. At first, Kuglin said, government would not even disclose who was on the committee to make the privatization decision.

Kuglin has been chairman of the Montana FOI Hotline Corporation since it was founded in 1988. The operation, funded at about $7,000 a year by the state's news media and others, provides information for persons facing problems regarding access to governmental meetings, court proceedings and public records.

The work is not without its lighter, even absurd moments. For example, in retaliation for the suit against closed caucuses, the Montana legislature struck from state law a provision that there should be a press room in the capitol. Kuglin said legislators decided "a higher purpose could be served by converting the third floor press room into a men's rest room." (Legislators may be having second thoughts about that—not because of any desire for openness, but because of the inconvenience caused when legislators or their aides have to seek out a reporter.)

Then there's the episode in Fromberg, Mont., where the city council granted the city clerk censorship powers over an area newspaper and also told the editor that while she could print stories about their meetings she could not use direct quotes. And among the government information still kept confidential in Montana, despite the constitutional mandate are pet adoption records.

As for Johnson, if you make a list of the top news stories of the last 30 or 40 years, you'll be paging through his scrapbook. As the AP bureau chief in Dallas, he wrote the first bulletin and directed news coverage of the assassination of President Kennedy; he supervised coverage of the nation's space flights from the Houston Space Center from Gemini 4 through Apollo 11. As general sports editor of the AP, he directed coverage of the massacre of Israeli athletes at the Munich Olympics in 1972. Three years later, as AP managing editor, he oversaw coverage of the last days of Watergate and President Nixon's resignation.

Nowadays he expresses outrage when the Clayton, N.M. school board selects a new superintendent without having that item on its agenda, and he responds when McKinley County officials refuse to say whether a deputy sheriff was temporarily suspended because he was a suspect in the theft of drug money.

Johnson deals with these and hundreds of other access issues each year—hotline calls now top 700 a year—as executive director of the New Mexico Foundation for Open Government (FOG). As AP bureau chief in Albuquerque, Johnson helped found FOG and then became its executive director in 1989 after serving 42 years with AP. He had arranged a final tour of AP duty in his native Southwest as a retirement move.

"After 42 years of journalism and encountering government secrecy at all kinds of levels . . . it just seemed like a really worthwhile cause. It is something that needs to be done," Johnson said. "Before we began this state organization, the general public and reporters had little recourse. I think government agencies got away with a lot more. . . . People who felt frustrated before, now that they have a place to turn for advice or help, are more aware of things that government is doing, and government bodies are more aware. . . . At least now they know that someone is watching, and someone will call them on it."

Each issue of *FOG Light,* the foundation's newsletter, testifies to the "watching" by chronicling openness problems and solutions across the state. With a 25-member board of directors in every section of the state, "we're alert to almost everything going on." About a third of the FOG directors are from the news media, about a third are lawyers and a third are from the general public. FOG's annual budget is about $32,000. Drawing upon a modest litigation fund of $12,000 and services from 14 *pro bono* lawyers, Johnson and FOG have the resources to do more than just complain about violations of the law. FOG won a protracted battle against the University of New Mexico, when the state legislature—in a special session—passed a law to force the university to provide more openness in its search for a president.

But it is not all conflict with government. Organizational members of FOG include the state association of counties and the Hobbs, N.M. police department—testifying to a measure of teamwork between governmental agencies and FOI advocates that is found in many states.

A former Marine officer in World War II and Korea, Johnson likened his New Mexico work to the mud-slogging infantry in combat. Sure, there are national organizations, "but we're the foot soldiers," he said. "When I started this job, I agreed to work for the Social Security earnings cap, which was then, in 1989, about $7,000. . . . FOG's income is limited . . . and we can't afford to pay more than the cap. So I continue to work for the cap, which this year is $14,500. That's not much for a 40 to 60 hour week, and of course if I didn't have an AP pension and Social Security I couldn't do it. On the other hand, I'm working for a cause and it keeps me from becoming a grumpy old man in a rocking chair, keeps me in touch with young journalists and lawyers—the kind of people I get along with best—and keeps my brain engaged. Those are advantages that go beyond money for a 75-year-old. Besides, because of this job, I have been a member of the New Mexico Historical Records Advisory Board—one of my interests is Southwestern history—since 1993, have served on two joint state Supreme Court-Bar Association committees on access and improving the public image of the court system and am a member of the University of New Mexico Student Publications Board. Far as I'm concerned all this beats the hell out of feeling obligated to become a gardener or spend my time muddling around a golf course."

Rhode Island Secretary of State James Langevin: Giving Something Back

James Langevin has said he is driven by the desire "to give something back" to the people of Rhode Island for the kindness shown him when he was paralyzed as a teenager. "It was a humbling experience. Here were all these people who came out of the woodwork, strangers, to help me and my family. I wanted to give something back. I didn't know that was going to be through running for public office."

As Rhode Island secretary of state, Langevin dedicated himself to eliminating the secrecy that had prevailed in many government quarters. A letter nominating him for a 1998 Society of Professional Journalists Sunshine Award said that prior to Langevin's campaign, "citizen complaints of an inaccessible government, closed-door deals and favoritism were largely ignored and nearly impossible to document."

In 1997, Langevin's office joined forces with the Alfred Taubman Center for Public Policy at Brown University to conduct a six-month study of the General Assembly's committees to determine compliance with the state's Open Meetings Law. The study concluded that legislative committees violated either the spirit or the letter of the law more than half the times they met. Committees acted on 236 bills without public notice.

As a result of the study, the Rhode Island Senate formed a commission to investigate how that body does business and how it can improve public access. The number of open-meetings violations dropped and legislative committee members began posting meeting notices. As the Sunshine Award nomination noted, "In releasing the report, Langevin, a Democrat and a former state legislator, took on not only his former colleagues, but some of the most powerful players in his party."

These stories, selected from countless tales of government secrecy at every level, forcefully demonstrate that for proponents of open government, the work is never done and the price is often steep.

Some Resources: Freedom of Information as a Self-Evident Truth

The birthday for the FOI movement in the United States is difficult to determine. Take your pick.

1. In 1955, Rep. John E. Moss of California began focusing attention on government secrecy, an effort that resulted in passage of the Federal FOIA in 1966 and subsequent amendments in 1974, 1986 and 1996.
2. FOI laws in the states preceded the federal legislation on access. So there are start-up dates from those perspectives, too.
3. Jean Otto, as head of the First Amendment Congress, worked to establish the birthday of James Madison, March 16, as National FOI Day because of Madison's role in drafting the First Amendment and his eloquence on behalf of an informed citizenry.

For obvious reasons, it also would be useful to link the FOI movement to July 4, 1776—the traditional birthday of the nation. Certainly access to information is inseparable from thoughts of self-government. Happily, Thomas Jefferson, Benjamin Franklin, John Adams and the others who had a hand in the Declaration were not without FOI and access concerns. Their "decent Respect to the Opinions of Mankind" compelled them to point out that among the grievances against King George III was that "He has called together Legislative Bodies at Places unusual, uncomfortable, and distant from the Depository of their public Records, for the sole Purpose of fatiguing them into Compliance with his Measures."

That reference has remarkable poignancy more than 200 years later, as we marvel at how latter-day King Georges at the federal, state and local levels persist in having their meetings and conversations in ways hidden from public view, and how the modern would-be monarchs make it difficult to gain access to records—hoping that such efforts will fatigue citizens or prove too costly to combat.

Nevertheless, the argument that such governments derive "their just Powers from the Consent of the Governed"—that the individual citizen counts for something—continues to be an exciting idea. Given such inspiration, one can argue that the FOI/access movement has never been stronger than it is at the close of the 20th century and likely will be even stronger into the 21st century. It is an open question, however, as to whether pressures for secrecy are greater than ever, too, or whether the secrecy is more evident today because of the efforts of the FOI/access movement.

Either way, the resources listed below are heartening evidence of the potential impact of the FOI movement, especially since the listing constitutes only the proverbial tip of the iceberg. And that is the case, too, with this roundup of some of the "usual suspects," who can be called upon in the battle for access to government information.

The Reporters Committee for Freedom of the Press

The Reporters Committee is widely recognized as one of the most important allies in protecting the First Amendment rights of the working journalist. The committee is involved in virtually every free expression issue that comes before the United States Supreme Court and also provides advice and assistance to reporters at the local level.

Its website offers practical access hints—free to everyone, not just journalists—and its publications include periodic surveys of trends and issues on the FOI front, on such topics as privacy, access to news sites, access to police records and state laws on taping conversations.

The Reporters Committee has benefited from the longevity and dedication of its two executive directors—Jack Landau, who served from July 1976 to April 15, 1985, and Jane Kirtley, the executive director since then. Another benefit is the involvement of marquee journalists on the committee's board, including television network anchors and others of national and international stature.

An estimated 2,000 working journalists are served every year and, since the committee's founding in 1970, no reporter has ever paid for the committee's help in defending First Amendment rights.

Address and telephone number:
1101 Wilson Blvd., Suite 1910
Arlington, VA 22209
(703) 807-2100 or (800) 336-4243
Website: www.rcfp.org

What it can do for you: The Reporters Committee publishes a quarterly magazine, *The News Media and the Law*, and a biweekly newsletter, *News Media Update*. The group's website includes references to publications available on-line (for example, The *First Amendment Handbook* and *Can We Tape?* on the legality of tape-recording phone calls). There is freedom of information assistance, including a fully automated, fill-in-the-blanks FOI letter generator, and a 24-hour hotline. The committee's *Tapping Officials' Secrets*, a guide to open meetings and open records statutes in all 50 states and the District of Columbia, is available both in print and on-line.

The Freedom Forum

With an endowment of about $1 billion, The Freedom Forum supports a wide range of First Amendment programs. Its innovative approaches and services are limited only by its imagination—and The Freedom Forum has proved to be imaginative.

The forum was established in 1991 under the direction of Allen H. Neuharth as a successor to the Gannett Foundation. It serves a wide range of constituencies—from working journalists and journalism critics to the general public. It is not a resource for grants and support. The forum funds its own programs and does not accept unsolicited funding requests. The range of programs and offices hinted at below is supplemented by offices in Buenos Aires, Hong Kong, Johannesburg and London.

Paul McMasters serves as the Forum's "First Amendment ombudsman," monitoring free-expression issues in Washington, D.C., facilitating dialogue on those issues and writing and speaking extensively on First Amendment concerns. He has assumed responsibility, too, for the "Education for Freedom" program of the First Amendment Congress, an umbrella organization that ceased operation in 1997.

The "Education for Freedom" program provides First Amendment instructional material, lesson plans, etc., for grades kindergarten through 12, and organizes workshops to train teachers in the use of the program. Several hundred teachers completed the program under First Amendment Congress auspices. Chief among those conducting the workshops around the nation were Sue Hale of FOI Oklahoma and Nancy Monson of the FOI Foundation of Texas. (Hale also is a past president of the National FOI Coalition and on-line manager for the *Daily Oklahoman* in Oklahoma City.)

McMasters said those efforts will be continued under the Freedom Forum. Persons interested in "Education for Freedom" should contact him at the Forum offices in Arlington, Va.

Address and telephone number:
World Center
1101 Wilson Blvd.
Arlington, VA 22209
(703) 528-0800
Website: www.freedomforum.org

What it can do for you: The Freedom Forum fosters understanding and exercise of First Amendment freedoms through workshops, reports and booklets. It has published a variety of periodicals, including *The Freedom Forum* and *Newseum News, Media Studies Journal, First Amendment News* and *Legal Watch*. It also sponsors an on-line forum for discussing media issues, and provides commentary on news coverage of current events and issues.

The Freedom Forum's website serves as an entry point to information about its other offices in the United States, including the Pacific Coast Center in San Francisco, the First Amendment Center at Vanderbilt University in Nashville, Tenn., and the Media Studies Center in New York City.

The National Freedom of Information Coalition

The National FOI Coalition is a confederation of a score of nonprofit state FOI organizations. It was incorporated in January 1992, thanks in large part to leadership from the Texas FOI Foundation, whose executive director, Nancy Monson, also became the executive director of the NFOIC. The NFOIC serves at least three major purposes: providing exchange of information and ideas among existing state organizations; encouraging and nurturing the creation of new state organizations; and seeking grants and other financial support for access work at the state and local levels. Perhaps the NFOIC's most tangible accomplishment was securing a three-year, $300,000 grant from the John S. and James L. Knight Foundation to support FOI activities by individual state organizations.

The individual state groups are not of the cookie-cutter variety; each has developed in the context of its state's resources. The nature of state activities and memberships varies considerably. Some states have primarily, if not exclusively, news media membership in their FOI organizations. Others, like Virginia, Oklahoma and New Mexico, have a broad-based membership that includes governmental associations, appointed and elected public officials and any citizen who recognizes the stake that people have in access issues. A listing of the programs, publications and services of the state organizations is found in *The State Media Law Sourcebook*, published by The Brechner Center for Freedom of Information at the University of Florida.

Information about NFOIC members and other state organizations also is available at the NFOIC website. The operations range in size from those with annual operating budgets of about $150,000—such as the California First Amendment Coalition, the Florida First Amendment Foundation and the Freedom of Information Foundation of Texas—to those with resources well under $10,000—such as the Minnesota Joint Media Committee, FOI Oklahoma Inc. and the Utah Foundation for Open Government. Among the younger and more vigorous state organizations are the Georgia First Amendment Foundation, started in 1994, and the Virginia Coalition for Open Government, started in 1996, which now have annual operating budgets of about $42,000 and $60,000 respectively.

Representatives of organizations interested in joining the NFOIC or in starting state FOI organizations should contact NFOIC President Joel Campbell at the Salt Lake City Deseret News or Executive Director Monson at the Texas FOI Foundation. Campbell, associate business editor at the Desert News, is also president of the Utah Foundation for Open Government.

Addresses and telephone numbers:
Joel Campbell
300 East 100 South
Salt Lake City, UT 84110
e-mail: joelc@desnews.com
(801) 237-2181

Nancy Monson
Texas FOI Foundation/NFOIC
400 S. Record, Suite 240
Dallas, TX 75202
e-mail: FOIFT@airmail.net
(214) 977-6658
Website: www.reporters.net/nfoic

Academic Centers

Universities and colleges across the nation have faculty deeply involved in issues relating to the First Amendment and freedom of information in areas of research, public service and teaching. They provide access services to the citizens and news media of their regions.
Two of the flagship institutions in this regard have been the University
of Missouri and the University of Florida—Missouri for its FOI
Center, founded in 1958, and Florida for its Brechner Center.

Journalism Professor Paul L. Fisher served as director of the
Missouri FOI Center from its founding until his retirement in 1989.
The University Libraries had assumed administrative responsibilities
for the center in 1986, and current manager Kathleen Edwards began
her involvement with the center at that time. At the heart of the center's operation is a collection of more than one million articles and
clippings about FOI issues, kept up to date on a daily basis by
Edwards, assistant librarian Robert Anderson and student assistants.
The center receives as many as 3,000 inquiries a year from around
the world. The center's web page averages about 1,000 visits a
month.

An ambitious publications program begun by Fisher in 1958
helped establish the center's reputation by providing reports, digests,
opinion and position papers, and research articles on FOI issues and
concerns. That publications program, however, was discontinued in
1985.

Address and telephone number:
127 Neff Annex
University of Missouri
Columbia, MO 65211
(573) 882-4856
Website: www.missouri.edu/~foiwww

At the University of Florida, the Brechner Center is the successor
to the Florida Freedom of Information Clearing House, established in

1977 by then-dean Ralph Lowenstein of the College of Journalism and Communications and supported with funds from the Florida news media. Joseph L. Brechner, an Orlando broadcaster, provided more than $1 million for an eminent-scholar endowment, for a suite of offices and for increasing the Clearing House operational endowment. In 1986, the Clearing House was renamed to reflect Brechner's support for the FOI program.

Bill F. Chamberlin, the center's director and the Brechner Eminent Scholar, was a leader in the creation of the National FOI Coalition. The assistant director is Sandra Chance of the Florida Department of Journalism.

Because of its links with the College of Journalism and Communications and the Florida College of Law, the center has helped produce media lawyers and university professors involved in research on such access issues as prosecutions under FOI laws, laws affecting computerized records, gag orders on trial participants and subpoenas received by news media.

The center publishes *The Brechner Report,* a monthly newsletter summarizing developments in Florida's open meetings and records laws, and has compiled *The State Media Law Sourcebook,* a state-by-state list of newsletters, hotlines and organizations devoted to increasing access to government information. (The book can be ordered through the center and is also available on-line.)

In addition to workshops and conferences, the Brechner Center sponsors an annual $3,000 cash award recognizing excellence in news reporting about access or First Amendment issues.

Address and telephone number:
3208 Weimer Hall
College of Journalism and Communications
University of Florida
Gainesville, FL 32611-8400
(352) 392-2273
Website: www.jou.ulf.edu/brechner/brochure.htm

While operating on smaller scales, other academic institutions and faculty serve the public and work with the media in their states on access issues. Listed below is a sampling.

1. The Ohio Center for Privacy and the First Amendment at Kent State University is directed by Journalism Professor Tim Smith, who is a lawyer and chair of the Media Law Committee of the Ohio Bar. He edits the center's newsletter, which circulates to about 4,000 public officials and journalists in Ohio.

2. The Iowa Freedom of Information Council has had its office in the School of Journalism and Mass Communication at Drake University since its founding in 1977. Since 1979 the council has published seven editions of a widely used handbook on the state open meetings and open records laws and since 1980 it has served as the Iowa Supreme Court's coordinator for access of broadcast and photo journalists to Iowa courts.

3. Barbara Croll Frought of Syracuse University manages an Internet discussion group on FOI and access issues for the National FOI Coalition. She teaches broadcast journalism and communications at the S.I. Newhouse School of Public Communication. To subscribe to the FOI List, send an e-mail message to: listserve@listserv.syr.edu. In the body of your message type: sub foi-l yourfirstname yourlastname.

Government Agencies

A common lament in FOI circles is that attorneys who are public employees or retained by school boards, city councils and other public agencies define their clients as the agencies who pay them. Citizens who think a public agency has violated an access law, or citizens with concerns about public access to meetings and records, often say they are rebuffed by county attorneys, attorneys general and other "public" lawyers.

Yet, several states have created public agencies or provided time for "public" lawyers to respond to citizen concerns, or even to take action on their own—thus helping citizens get access to records and meetings without time-consuming and costly litigation. Here is a sampling of such approaches:

Massachusetts Public Records Division

The Public Records Division of the Massachusetts secretary of the commonwealth office is charged with making government records accessible and enforcing disclosure laws. If a citizen has difficulty obtaining a public record, he or she can appeal in writing to the Supervisor of Public Records. An administrative appeal will be opened. If the complaint is judged to be valid, the supervisor can then order the custodian of the record to provide it.

Address and telephone number:
Office of the Secretary of the Commonwealth
1 Ashburton Place, Room 1719
Boston, MA 02108
(617) 727-2832
Website: www.magnet.state.ma.us/sec/

What it can do for you: The Public Records site includes commonly asked questions about public records, bulletins from the Supervisor of Public Records and *A Guide to Massachusetts Public Records Law.*

New York State Department of State Committee on Open Government

New York's Committee on Open Government is responsible for overseeing the state's Open Meetings, Freedom of Information and Personal Privacy Protection laws. It provides written and oral advice to both government agencies and citizens, issues regulations and mediates in FOI controversies. The 11-member commission is composed of five government officials and six members of the public (including two current or former journalists).

Executive Director Robert J. Freeman said the committee operates more in "an ombudsman role, as opposed to Connecticut's quasi-judicial function." He said the organization provides "instant response" to questions and complaints—and sometimes that is enough.

Freeman said one of the committee's biggest roles is to function as "an educational resource"; he does a lot of public speaking on FOI issues, mainly to government groups.

Address and telephone number:
Robert J. Freeman, Executive Director
41 State Street
Albany NY 12231
(518) 474-2518
Website: www.dos.state.ny.us/coog/coogwww.html

What it can do for you: The site provides information on the Open Meetings, Privacy and FOI laws (i.e., how to obtain records, including legislative and court records; sample request and appeal letters), publications and committee reports.

State of Connecticut Freedom of Information Commission

Connecticut has one of the strongest government FOI programs in the nation—primarily because the commission has the authority to impose fines on violators of the state's open meetings and open records laws.

Complaints first go through an ombudsman program; those that aren't settled at that stage go to an administrative hearing. A hearing officer writes a report that is passed on to a five-member commission, which meets every two weeks. The commission can authorize disclosure of the records, levy civil penalties and nullify action taken in illegally closed meetings.

Address and telephone number:
18-20 Trinity
Hartford, CT 06106
(860) 566-5682
Website:www.state.ct.us/foi/

What it can do for you: The website contains *A Citizen's Guide to the Freedom of Information Act* and the decisions of the commission.

Similar state forums are available in other states, too. In Maryland, it is an open-meetings compliance board, created by statute, that offers advisory opinions on complaints about violation of the law. In Indiana, in response to the state-wide public records project conducted by seven newspapers, the governor appointed an access counselor to work with citizens and a legislative committee on state government recommended several amendments to the state public records law.

Unfortunately, in most states, citizens seeking public information must do battle not only with public agencies but with the agency attorneys who—too often—see a client's desire for secrecy as having priority over a citizen's need for access.

Additional Freedom of Information Resources

Even a novice user of the Internet knows that there is an increasing wealth of information available on-line—either free or for a price—about freedom of information issues: organizations, newsletters, legal advice, government documents. Some time spent diligently in front of a computer screen will yield everything from crime statistics and security policies on campuses around the nation, to automated fill-in-the-blank FOI request forms. Following are representative resources, both traditional and on-line, that will prove useful in information access efforts. It is certainly not a definitive list of all the organizations involved in the FOI battle, but merely some launching points. Most of the websites provide not only information compiled by the host, but also directories of and links to related groups.

ACCESS Reports

Address and telephone number:
1624 Dogwood Lane
Lynchburg, VA 24503
e-mail: 75111.743@compuserve.com
(804) 384-8272

What it does: *ACCESS Reports* is a biweekly newsletter that provides readable and timely updates on FOI and privacy issues at the federal, state and international levels. The publication, usually 12 to 16 pages, monitors information-policy developments at the legislative, executive and judicial branches. Editor/Publisher Harry A. Hammitt is a frequent speaker and consultant on access issues.

What it can do for you: Although the subscription price of $325 a year is prohibitive for most individuals, a community is well-served if local public libraries or college libraries subscribe. Also, the publication provides timely information for government attorneys and public agencies.

American Library Association Office for Intellectual Freedom

Address and telephone number:
50 East Huron St.
Chicago, IL 60611
(800) 545-2433 ext. 4223
Website: www.ala.org/oif.html

What it does: The American Library Association bills itself as "committed to protecting public access to information in all forms" through a program of "legislative advocacy, public awareness and professional education." The Office for Intellectual Freedom implements the ALA's intellectual freedom policies by educating librarians and the public, and by providing support (including direct intervention) in local censorship cases.

What it can do for you: The office publishes the *Intellectual Freedom Manual* (5th ed.), which offers advice in anticipating and fighting censorship, and the *Intellectual Freedom Action News* newsletter. Library associations on the local, state and national levels can be powerful allies in the fight for access to information.

American Society of Newspaper Editors (ASNE)

Address and telephone number: 11690B Sunrise Valley Dr.
Reston, VA 20191
(703) 453-1122
Website: www.asne.org

What it does: For more than four decades the ASNE has been at the forefront of the access wars. Its pantheon of FOI heroes includes such past ASNE presidents as J. Russell Wiggins of *The Washington Post,* J. Edward Murray of *The Detroit Free Press,* James Pope of *The Louisville Times* and *The Courier Journal,* and ASNE legal counsels Harold Cross and Richard M. Schmidt Jr.

What it can do for you: ASNE publications and position papers on First Amendment and access issues provide both perspective on trends and timely commentary on current events and congressional issues.

BRB Publications Inc.

Home of the Public Record Research Library

> **Address and telephone number:**
> 4653 S. Lakeshore No. 3
> Tempe, AZ 85282
> (800) 929-3811
> **Website:** www.brbpub.com

What it does: The Public Record Research Library provides an in-depth look at public records, public agencies and record-retrieval firms.

What it can do for you: The PRRL sells a host of books and electronic products with such titles as *Public Records Online, Find Public Records Fast* and *Get the Facts on Anyone.* The BRB website also has free links to related sites—Social Security Number Verification and Commercial Airline Schedules, for example—and access to free public records from various state agencies throughout the nation at www.brbpub.com/pubrecsites.htm

Electronic Privacy Information Center

> **Address and telephone number:**
> 666 Pennsylvania Ave. Southeast, Suite 301
> Washington, D.C. 20003
> (202) 544-9240
> **Website:** www.epic.org

What it does: EPIC is a public interest research center that focuses on civil liberty, First Amendment and privacy issues.

What it can do for you: The center publishes *The Epic Alert,* a newsletter on civil liberties in the Information Age. The EPIC website includes current and back issues of the newsletter, "the Internet's only bookstore devoted to online freedom," copies of previously classified government documents, a guide to legislation on privacy and cyber-space issues and a guide to privacy resources—sites, newsletters, conferences and organizations.

Federal Web Locator

Website: www.law.vill.edu/Fed-Agency/fedwebloc.html

What it does: The Federal Web Locator is a service of the Villanova Center for Information Law and Policy, a "one-stop shopping point for federal government information on the World Wide Web."

What it can do for you: The website has links to everything from the Library of Congress and the U.S. Sentencing Commission to the Commodity Futures Trading Commission and the Export-Import Bank.

Federation of American Scientists Project on Government Secrecy

Address and telephone number:
307 Massachusetts Ave. Northeast
Washington, D.C. 20002
(202) 546-3300
Website: www.fas.org/sgp

What it does: The Federation of American Scientists is a privately funded organization that lobbies on such issues as nuclear weapons, arms sales, biological hazards, secrecy and space policy. The federation's Project on Government Secrecy challenges excessive secrecy, supports journalists and promotes public oversight.

What it can do for you: The federation publishes a *Secrecy and Government Bulletin*. Its website has links to other secrecy-related sites, including worldwide news archives, congressional news, military periodicals and defense contractor news. The site contains government documents and information on intelligence, military and space programs, budgets, agencies and contractors.

FOI Services, Inc.

Address and telephone number:
11 Firstfield Road
Gaithersburg, MD 20878-1703
(301) 975-9400
Website: www.foiservices.com

What it does: FOI Services provides custom document retrieval for a price. Using the Freedom of Information Act, the business has collected over 150,000 internal documents from U.S. agencies, focusing especially on the Food and Drug Administration.

What it can do for you: You can shop for documents regarding the approval and regulation of such things as food, cosmetics, medical devices, pharmaceuticals and veterinary products. FOI Services can also request a document, if it isn't on file in its library. The FOI Services website provides access to DIOGENES and 21CFR on-line databases of FDA and Drug Enforcement Administration information.

GPO Access

Website: www.access.gpo.gov

What it does: GPO Access, a service of the U.S. Government Printing Office, is billed as "virtually the only government website that provides access to information from all three branches of the federal government."

What it can do for you: GPO Access provides free on-line use of many federal databases, including the Congressional Record, the Federal Register and the full text of all published versions of bills introduced in Congress. Individual agency files are available for downloading. The site provides assistance in finding government information through the Catalog of U.S. Government Publications, the Government Information Locator Service and 24-hour on-line access to government information from participating federal depository libraries, which were established more than 130 years ago to ensure that Americans have access to government information.

Investigative Reporters and Editors

Address and telephone number:
138 Neff Annex
Missouri School of Journalism
Columbia, MO 65211
(573) 882-2042
Website: www.ire.org

What it does: IRE provides training for investigative reporters and editors, including computer-assisted reporting through its National Institute for Computer-Assisted Reporting (NICAR).

What it can do for you: The IRE website offers information on conferences and seminars, a directory of investigative journalists and job postings. The IRE Resource Center is a "rich reserve of stories, handouts and guides that can help you start and complete the best work of your career." NICAR's collection of government databases includes records on everything from campaign contributions, aviation safety and hazardous chemical spills to NASA and the FBI Uniform Crime Reports.

National Coalition Against Censorship

Address and telephone number:
275 Seventh Ave.
New York, NY 10001
(212) 807-6222
Website: www.ncac.org

What it does: The National Coalition Against Censorship is an alliance of "over 40 national non-profit organizations, including literary, artistic, religious, education, professional, labor and civil rights groups," that strives to educate the public about the dangers of censorship.

What it can do for you: The coalition's website includes government e-mail addresses (including the White House and Congress), and primers on finding court decisions and federal legislation. There is a guide to government databases and Internet anti-censorship organizations.

National Security Archive

Address and telephone number:
The Gelman Library, George Washington University
2130 H St. Northwest, Suite 701
Washington, D.C. 20037
(202) 994-7000
Website: www.seas.gwu.edu/nsarchive

What it does: The archive is an independent research institute that collects and publishes declassified documents acquired through the Freedom of Information Act.

What it can do for you: The archive's collection of documents covers everything from current news events to the Cuban Missile Crisis and the Richard Nixon-Elvis Presley papers.

The Poynter Institute for Media Studies

Address and telephone number:
801 Third St. South
St. Petersburg, FL 33701
(813) 821-9494
Website: www.poynter.org

What it does: The institute, best known for its seminars, also provides a research and resource center.

What it can do for you: The research center on-line includes everything from the texts of media-related speeches to a compilation of calculator reference tools. There is a host of directories with such titles as *Internet Resources for Journalism, A Journalist's Guide to the Internet, Journalistic Resources Page* and *Journalism, Mass Communications and New Media Websites.*

Public Citizen Litigation Group and the Freedom of Information Clearinghouse

Address and telephone number:
1600 20th St. Northwest
Washington, D.C. 20009-1001
(202) 588-1000
Website: www.citizen.org/litigation/foic/foic.html

What it does: Public Citizen Litigation Group is a Ralph Nader-founded public-interest law firm. The Freedom of Information Clearinghouse is a closely related project housed in the same offices. Both groups fight government secrecy and seek to enhance public access to government-held information.

What it can do for you: The clearinghouse provides technical and legal assistance to individuals, public-interest groups and the media seeking access to information held by government agencies. Its website walks you through use of the federal Freedom of Information Act, and includes sample request, appeal and complaint letters. The site also has links to some FOIA resources on the Internet and lists FOIA administrative and legal contacts at federal agencies.

Security on Campus Inc.

Address and telephone number:
215 W. Church Road, Suite 200
King of Prussia, PA 19406-3207
(610) 768-9330
Website: www.soconline.org

What it does: Security on Campus is "geared exclusively to the prevention of campus violence." It helps campus victims obtain their legal rights and works to improve freedom of information laws and disclosure of campus crime statistics and security policies.

What it can do for you: Security on Campus publishes a newsletter. Its website provides nationwide campus crime statistics and information on legislation. It has lists of on- and off-campus victim-assistance resources, crime-prevention tips and links to related resources.

Society of Professional Journalists

Address and telephone number:
16 South Jackson St.
Greencastle, IN 46135-1514
(765) 653-3333
Website: www.spj.org

What it does: The Society of Professional Journalists—founded in 1909 as Sigma Delta Chi—is the nation's largest and most diverse journalism organization, with 13,500 members at the professional and collegiate levels. SPJ encourages "the free practice of journalism, stimulating high standards of ethical behavior and perpetuating a free press."

What it can do for you: SPJ's on-line FOI Resource Center includes information from all 50 states, contacts for federal agencies and how-to help on filing freedom of information requests. The website includes information on FOI advocacy groups, organizations and resource centers, hotlines, periodicals, books and booklets, Internet mailing lists and newsletters. The SPJ Legal Defense Fund assists news media with legal expenses, particularly in FOIA cases. SPJ's FOI Committee coordinates a nationwide Project Sunshine network with "Sunshine" chairs in each state. An annual SPJ Freedom of Information conference includes seminars, lectures and discussions designed to teach journalists how to be better access advocates. *Quill,* the organization's magazine, publishes an excellent annual FOI Special Report, a status report on the battle for access to government information. The Special Report typically covers such topics as cameras in the courtroom, access to public records, Internet services and freedom of the student press. Articles are accompanied by state-by-state legal updates. The Special Report also includes extensive resource lists on federal agency contacts, state contacts and advocacy groups, perhaps the best such compilation available in print.

Student Press Law Center

Address and telephone number:
1101 Wilson Blvd., Suite 1910
Arlington, VA 22209
(703) 807-1904
Website: www.splc.org

What it does: For scholastic journalists, their teachers and advisers, the SPLC should be a first resort in times of access and First Amendment issues. The center provides legal help and information to high school and college journalists and journalism educators.

What it can do for you: The center produces a newsletter and its on-line legal clinic provides information on censorship, libel, copyright laws, freedom of information and other media topics.

ISBN 0-8138-2567-9